T0301317

Non-market Entrepreneurship

Non-market Entrepreneurship

Interdisciplinary Approaches

Edited by

Gordon E. Shockley

Arizona State University, USA

Peter M. Frank

Wingate University, USA

and

Roger R. Stough

George Mason University, USA

Edward Elgar

Cheltenham, UK • Northampton, MA, USA

Published by
Edward Elgar Publishing Limited
The Lypiatts
15 Lansdown Road
Cheltenham
Glos GL50 2JA
UK

Edward Elgar Publishing, Inc.
William Pratt House
9 Dewey Court
Northampton
Massachusetts 01060
USA

A catalogue record for this book
is available from the British Library

Library of Congress Control Number: 2008932863

Mixed Sources
Product group from well-managed
forests and other controlled sources
www.fsc.org Cert no. SA-COC-1565
© 1996 Forest Stewardship Council

ISBN 978 1 84720 006 8

Printed and bound in Great Britain by MPG Books Ltd, Bodmin, Cornwall

Contents

PART 4   ONLY A SEMANTIC DIFFERENCE? SOCIAL
         ENTREPRENEURSHIP, NONPROFIT
         ENTREPRENEURSHIP AND SOCIAL
         ENTERPRISE

Figures and boxes

FIGURES

BOXES

Contributors

Zoltan J. Acs is University Professor at the School of Public Policy and Director of the Center for Entrepreneurship and Public Policy at George Mason University, Fairfax, VA, USA. He is also a Research Scholar at the Max Planck Institute for Economics in Jena, Germany, and Scholar-in-Residence at the Kauffman Foundation. He is coeditor and founder of *Small Business Economics*, the leading entrepreneurship and small business publication in the world. Acs is a leading advocate of the importance of entrepreneurship for economic development. He received the 2001 International Award for Entrepreneurship and Small Business Research on behalf of The Swedish National Board for Industrial and Technical Development. He has published more than 100 articles and 20 books, including articles in the *American Economic Review, Review of Economics and Statistics, Kyklos, Journal of Urban Economics, Economica, Research Policy* and *Science Policy*. His most recent publication is *Entrepreneurship, Geography and American Economic Growth*, Cambridge University Press.

Robert B. Anderson is a Professor with the Faculty of Business Administration of the University of Regina in Regina, SK, Canada. Prior to joining the faculty, Anderson spent ten years with the First Nations University of Canada. He has a PhD in regional economic development (geography). Anderson also has an MBA and is a Certified Management Accountant. He has authored numerous peer-reviewed papers and made many conference presentations on economic development and entrepreneurship. He is the author of two books on the subject, co-author of a third and co-editor of a handbook research on indigenous entrepreneurship. More recent work has expanded to include corporate social responsibility and sustainable development. Anderson is the editor of the *Journal of Small Business and Entrepreneurship*, the regional editor for Canada for the *International Journal of Entrepreneurship and Small Business*, an associate editor of the *Journal of Aboriginal Economic Development,* an associate editor of the *Journal of Asia Entrepreneurship and Sustainability* and a founding editor of the *Journal of Enterprising Communities*. He is the past President of the Canadian Council for Small Business and Entrepreneurship and a past Director of the International Council for Small Business. He is also a member of the Small Business Research Advisory Committee of the Department of Industry and Commerce Canada.

Robert F. Ashcraft is Founding Director of the Lodestar Center for Philanthropy and Nonprofit Innovation at Arizona State University, Phoenix, AZ, USA, and Associate Professor of Nonprofit Studies in the School of Community Resources and Development at ASU. Ashcraft teaches courses in nonprofit management, fundraising/philanthropy and graduate seminars in critical issues of the nonprofit sector. His research interests have resulted in publications on subjects dealing with nonprofit organization leadership and management, youth development, philanthropy and volunteerism. He serves in a number of leadership roles including his current role as President of the Nonprofit Academic Centers Council. Ashcraft earned his baccalaureate degree from the University of Arizona, an MA in education from Northern Arizona University, and his PhD from Arizona State University.

David B. Audretsch is Director of the Max Planck Institute of Economics in Jena, Germany. He also serves as a Scholar-in-Residence at the Ewing Marion Kauffman Foundation. In addition, he is an Honorary Professor at the Friedrich Schiller University of Jena, Research Professor at Durham University, a Distinguished Professor and the Ameritech Chair of Economic Development and Director of the Institute for Development Strategies at Indiana University, an External Director of Research at the Kiel Institute for the World Economics, and is a Research Fellow of the Centre for Economic Policy Research (London). Audretsch's research has focused on the links between entrepreneurship, government policy, innovation, economic development and global competitiveness. Audretsch is ranked as the 21st most-cited scholar in economics and business, 1996–2006. His research has been published in over 100 scholarly articles in the leading academic journals. His books include *Entrepreneurship and Economic Growth*, with Oxford University Press in 2006 and *The Entrepreneurial Society*, also with Oxford University Press in 2007. He is co-founder and co-editor of *Small Business Economics: An Entrepreneurship Journal*. He was awarded the 2001 International Award for Entrepreneurship and Small Business Research by the Swedish Foundation for Small Business Research.

Peter J. Boettke is University Professor of Economics at George Mason University, Fairfax, VA, USA. He is the author of several books on the history, collapse and transition from socialism in the former Soviet Union: *The Political Economy of Soviet Socialism: The Formative Years, 1918–1928* (Kluwer, 1990); *Why Perestroika Failed: The Economics and Politics of Socialism Transformation* (Routledge, 1993); and *Calculation and Coordination: Essays on Socialism and Transitional Political Economy* (Routledge, 2001). He is also co-author, along with David Prychitko, of the classic principles of economics texts of Paul Heyne's *The Economic Way of*

Thinking (10th edn, Prentice Hall, 2002). Boettke has edited: *Socialism and the Market: The Socialist Calculation Debate Revisited*, 9 vols (Routledge, 2000); *The Legacy of F.A. Hayek: Politics, Philosophy, Economics*, 3 vols (Edward Elgar, 1999); *The Market Process*, 2 vols (Edward Elgar, 1998); *Market Process: Essays in Contemporary Austrian Economics* (Edward Elgar, 1994); *The Collapse of Development Planning* (New York University Press, 1994); and *The Elgar Companion to Austrian Economics* (Edward Elgar, 1994).

Christopher J. Coyne is Assistant Professor in the Department of Economics at West Virginia University, Morgantown, WV, USA, a Research Fellow at the Mercatus Center, and an Associate Editor for the *Review of Austrian Economics*. He has published articles in numerous scholarly journals and is the author of *After War: the Political Economy of Exporting Democracy* (Stanford University Press, 2007).

Sameeksha Desai is Assistant Professor of Entrepreneurship and Innovation at the Henry W. Bloch School of Business and Public Administration, University of Missouri, Columbia, MO. She is also a Visiting Research Fellow at the Max Planck Institute of Economics. She is a multi-year grantee of a joint fellowship from the Kauffman Foundation and Max Planck Institute of Economics. Her research interests are entrepreneurship, political instability and conflict, and social innovation.

Peter M. Frank is Assistant Professor of Economics at The School of Business, Wingate University, Wingate, NC, USA. His recent research focuses on the application of entrepreneurship theory in non-market contexts, namely the role of entrepreneurs in the nonprofit sector and their contribution to regional economic development. He holds a BA in economics from Grove City College, Grove City, PA, an MS in economics from the University of North Carolina at Charlotte, and a PhD from The School of Public Policy, George Mason University, Fairfax, VA.

Kingsley E. Haynes is the Ruth D. and John T. Hazel MD Professor of Public Policy and Dean of the School of Public Policy at George Mason University, Fairfax, VA, USA. He holds his PhD in Geography and Environmental Engineering from The Johns Hopkins University. Haynes was the director of McGill's Urban Studies Center, Texas' Joint Center for West Texas Environmental Studies and Indiana University's Regional Economic Development Institute. He worked overseas on air transport projects, regional development programming, water resource and environmental management projects, and investment evaluation programs. In North America he has worked on coastal zone management projects, environment and energy projects, and transportation projects. Haynes is also an active researcher in the field of regional economic development policy with over 200 articles, 150 professional reports and ten books and has received numerous awards, fellowships, and recognition for his research. From 1995 to 1997 he was President of the 40-nation Regional Science Association International.

Kevin G. Hindle is Professor of Entrepreneurship at the Australian Graduate School of Entrepreneurship, Swinburne University of Technology, Melbourne, VIC, Australia. He is a researcher, educator, management consultant and private equity investor. His variety of expertise and interests embrace many aspects of managing in conditions of uncertainty. His research, teaching, managerial and consulting work focuses on entrepreneurial business planning but also include investment evaluation (especially in the field of venture capital), market and financial modeling, change management, organizational design, corporate strategy and management training. Applying leading-edge research to practical problems, he has initiated and developed new ventures and worked for organizations large and small, public and private, Australian and international. As a researcher, Hindle has authored over 80 publications including more than 50 peer-reviewed papers in a range of respected international journals and conference proceedings. He is Australian Project Director of the *Global Entrepreneurship Monitor* (GEM), the world's largest entrepreneurship research initiative. He is a ministerially appointed foundation member of Australia's National Innovation Awareness Council and on the advisory board of the International Danish Entrepreneurship Academy (IDEA).

Bob Kayseas is a member of the Fishing Lake First Nation, a Saulteaux community in east central Saskatchewan, Canada. Kayseas obtained a degree in Business Administration and a Master of Business Administration from the University of Regina. He is presently enrolled in a PhD (Enterprise and Innovation) program at the Australian Graduate School of Entrepreneurship, Swinburne University of Technology in Melbourne, Australia. He has been employed, first as a Lecturer and currently as an Assistant Professor, at the First Nations University of Canada, School of Business and Public Administration since the fall of 2000 and was appointed Department Head in April 2007. His primary areas of research are in the economic development and entrepreneurship of Indigenous Canadians with a particular focus on the reserve 'status' populations. He also teaches economic development, entrepreneurship, and small business management courses.

Roger Koppl is the Director of the Institute for Forensic Science Administration of Fairleigh Dickinson University, Madison, NJ, USA, where he is also a Professor of Economics and Finance. He has served on the faculty of the Copenhagen Business School, Auburn University, and Auburn University at Montgomery. He has held visiting positions at George Mason University, New York University, and the Max Planck Institute of Economics. He is the editor of *Advances in Austrian Economics* and the book review editor of *Journal of Economic Behavior and Organization*. Koppl conducts research in forensic science administration, which studies how error rates in forensic science are affected by institutional and organizational structures.

Miri Lerner is Associate Professor at the Academic College of Tel-Aviv-Yaffo, Tel-Aviv, Israel, The School of Management and Economy and the head of its entrepreneurship unit. Her current research interests include corporate entrepreneurship, R&D transfer, social entrepreneurship, and immigrants and women entrepreneurship. She was the team leader of GEM (*Global Entrepreneurship Monitor*) in Israel from 1999 to 2006, and currently serves as a team member. She is the author of many scholarly articles and has published in journals such as *Research Policy, Journal of Business Venturing, Small Business Economics, Journal of World Business, Journal of Small Business Management, Journal of Social Policy*, and *Work and Occupations*.

Scott W. MacAulay earned his PhD from the University of Leeds, West Yorkshire, England, where he also completed his Master's degree. His research interests include political economy, community economic development, and the sociology of disability. MacAulay has played a central role in many activities of Cape Breton University's Community Economic Development Institute, including the MBA program in Community Economic Development.

Maria Minniti is Professor and Bobby B. Lyle Chair in Entrepreneurship at the Cox School of Business at Southern Methodist University, Dallas, TX, USA. Minniti holds a PhD in Economics from New York University, a Master of Science in Economics from Auburn University, and an undergraduate degree in Political Science from the University of Rome, Italy. Minniti has also been a visiting professor in several universities, including London Business School, Humboldt University, Copenhagen Business School and the Max Planck Institute of Economics. She has published numerous articles on entrepreneurship, economic growth and complexity theory, as well as book chapters and research monographs. She is associate editor of *Small Business Economics Journal* and a member of the *Global Entrepreneurship Monitor* (GEM) project, the world's largest ongoing cross-country study of entrepreneurial dynamics.

Simon C. Parker is a Professor at Durham University in Durham, England and Head of the Department of Economics and Finance at Durham Business School in the United Kingdom. He is a Research Professor at the Max Planck Institute of Economics and a Fellow of IZA, both in Germany. Parker publishes widely in the economics of entrepreneurship.

Ronnie J. Phillips received his BA in Urban Studies from the University of Oklahoma, Norman, OK, USA, in 1973 and his PhD in Economics from The University of Texas at Austin in 1980. He is a Senior Fellow at Networks Financial Institute in Indianapolis, IN, and Professor of Economics at Colorado State University, where he has taught since 1983. From 2001–2006, he was Chairman of the Economics Department. He was the recipient of the Oliver Pennock Distinguished Service Award from CSU in 2000. He has published widely on banking issues, entrepreneurship, and public policy in books, academic journals, newspapers, magazines, and public policy briefs. His current research interests are payday lending and entrepreneurship in the music industry. He also has been a visiting scholar in many educational and government institutions and is a past president of the Association for Evolutionary Economics.

Moshe Sharir is Acting Director of the Institute for Immigration and Social Integration at Ruppin Academic Center, Emek Hefer, Israel, focusing especially on the center policy and activities in civic engagement. He lectures also on social entrepreneurship at Ashkelon Academic College, coming to the field after a long career in managing educational and welfare organizations. A reserve colonel, Sharir served in the Israel Defense Forces for nearly 25 years and in his last assignment was responsible for the pre-military training of Israeli youth. He was the division head of the American joint distribution committee in Israel and the director general of Ben Gurion College at Sde Boker. He was also the founder and chairperson of the first incubator for social entrepreneurs in Israel. He holds a PhD from Ben-Gurion University of the Negev.

Gordon E. Shockley is Assistant Professor of Social Entrepreneurship and a Faculty Associate of the Lodestar Center for Philanthropy and Nonprofit Innovation at Arizona State University, Phoenix, AZ, USA. His research interests span non-market entrepreneurship, public policy analysis, and the politics, economics, and sociology of the arts and humanities. He earned a PhD in public policy from George Mason University, an MM from the J.L. Kellogg Graduate School of Management, Northwestern University, and a BA in Ancient Greek and English Languages and Literature from the University of California, Los Angeles. He also has several years of public service at all levels of US government.

Roger R. Stough is the NOVA Endowed Chair, Eminent Scholar and Professor of Public Policy, Associate Dean for Research, Director of Mason Enterprise Center, and Director of the National (USDOT UTC) Transport and Regional Economic Development Research Center, all at George Mason University, Fairfax, VA, USA. Stough's education includes a BS in International Trade from Ohio State University; an MA in Economic Geography from the University of South Carolina; and a PhD in Geography and Environmental Engineering from the Johns Hopkins University. He also holds a *Honoris Causa* Doctoral degree from Jonkoping University in Jonkoping, Sweden. His research specializations include leadership and entrepreneurship in regional economic development, regional economic modeling and transport analysis and planning. During the past 10 years Stough has been heavily involved in development related research in China and India and in the development of entrepreneurship training and education programs including advising enterprise development and incubation centers there. He currently serves as President of the Regional Science Association International (RSAI) (2007–2008) and is the joint editor of the *Annals of Regional Science*. He is also the President of the Technopolicy Network, a global membership organization that promotes the use of science and technology in the development process.

Ronit Yitshaki is Assistant Professor in the department of sociology at Bar Ilan University, Ramat-Gan, Israel. Her dissertation 'Relations between venture capitalists and entrepreneurs: managerial interventions in high technology companies in Israel' examined the determinants of the level of venture capitalists' involvement in high technology start-ups. Her dissertation was accorded a writing scholarship from the Israel Foundation Trustees (Ford Foundation) and also received the Schnitzer Foundation Award for Research on the Israeli Economy and Society for its contributions to the Israeli economy. Her research interests include venture capital investments, high technology firms' failure, and social entrepreneurship.

Dennis R. Young is the Bernard B. and Eugenia A. Ramsey Professor of Private Enterprise in the Andrew Young School of Policy Studies at Georgia State University, Atlanta, GA, USA, where he directs the school's nonprofit studies program. He is also President and Founding CEO of the National Center on Nonprofit Enterprise. His interests focus on the management and economics of nonprofit organizations. He is the founding editor of the journal *Nonprofit Management and Leadership* and past president of the Association for Research on Nonprofit Organizations and Voluntary Action (ARNOVA). He is the author of many scholarly articles, and author or editor of several books on nonprofit organizations including *If Not for Profit for What?* (Lexington Books), *A Casebook of Management for*

Nonprofit Organizations (Haworth Books), *Governing, Leading and Managing the Nonprofit Organization* (with Robert Hollister and Virginia Hodgkinson, Jossey-Bass), *Nonprofit Organizations in a Market Economy* (with David Hammack, Jossey-Bass), *Economics for Nonprofit Managers* (with Richard Steinberg, The Foundation Center), and *Effective Economic Decisionmaking for Nonprofit Organizations* (The Foundation Center). Young has received a number of honors, including ARNOVA's 2004 Award for Distinguished Achievement and Leadership in Nonprofit and Voluntary Action Research, and the Award for Innovation in Nonprofit Research from the Israeli Center for Third Sector Research at Ben Gurion University in 2005. He was named to the *Nonprofit Times* Power and Influence Top 50 List in 2004.

PART 1

Foundations of non-market entrepreneurship

1. Introduction: the emerging field of non-market entrepreneurship

Gordon E. Shockley, Peter M. Frank and Roger R. Stough

PART 1. FOUNDATIONS OF NON-MARKET ENTREPRENEURSHIP

Non-market Entrepreneurship: Interdisciplinary Approaches represents an initial contribution to building a theoretical edifice within the field of entrepreneurship research to encompass the myriad forms of *non-market entrepreneurship*, which we define as activity that still partakes of entrepreneurial activity (for example opportunity recognition, proactive action, and so on) but not undertaken solely for the purpose of profit maximization or commercialization. As it matures from borrowed to its own terminology and methods (Cornelius, Landstrom and Persson, 2006, p. 376), general entrepreneurship research is one of the most exciting social scientific fields of inquiry with which to be associated nowadays because of its scope, promise and interdisciplinary demands. Non-market entrepreneurship indeed magnifies the excitement of general entrepreneurship research. Certain forms of non-market entrepreneurship have received more attention in the recent past, such as public sector and policy entrepreneurship. Other fields are presently in vogue, such as social entrepreneurship and (depending on the definition) social enterprise. And still others are just being recognized, many of which appear in these pages. Yet, while some attention has been given to the different forms of non-market entrepreneurship, there has been no attempt to look at them synoptically as theoretically related and possibly comprising a coherent field of research, that is to say, the field of non-market entrepreneurship. And there has been no single academic discipline able to satisfactorily contain even the idea of non-market entrepreneurship. Identifying the tentative boundaries for this emerging field is one of the main objectives of *Non-market Entrepreneurship: Interdisciplinary Approaches* (*NME*).

Identifying the boundaries of the emerging field of non-market entrepreneurship is only one component of the triad of research, theory and teaching that might be called the 'Foundations of non-market entrepreneurship', the title of this volume's first part. The two other chapters in Part 1 complete the triad. Koppl and Minniti's 'Entrepreneurship and human action' provides a philosophical justification for the categorical existence of non-market entrepreneurship. 'A unified and comprehensive theory of entrepreneurship', they argue, 'is possible if and only if we see entrepreneurship as a universal form of human action'. Indeed, the very idea of non-market entrepreneurship as partaking of entrepreneurial activity but not done solely for the purpose of profit maximization or commercialization must depend on entrepreneurship being a universal form of behavior. While Koppl and Minniti find entrepreneurial behavior in the psychology of learning, the innovation and imitation of the great Renaissance artist Raphael, and the sociology and philosophy of Max Weber and Alfred Schutz, this volume further stretches their insight by looking at entrepreneurial activity outside of the commercial sector in the non-market settings of the public and social sectors.

Ashcraft's chapter 'Teaching entrepreneurship outside of business schools' also reaches beyond the commercial sector as it addresses how theories as well as practice of non-market entrepreneurship might be taught in academic units other than business schools, where it is incorrectly assumed entrepreneurship education naturally and exclusively resides. He takes up this vital topic by examining the case of Arizona State University developing a social entrepreneurship offering outside of the business school. 'Business schools', Ashcraft asserts, 'are not the only drivers of social entrepreneurship education in colleges and universities as the field emerges in multi-disciplinary, inter-disciplinary and transdisciplinary ways'. This chapter is particularly timely in that it is to the author's knowledge the first academic paper to incorporate the Nonprofit Academic Centers Council's (NACC) curricular guidelines for both undergraduate and graduate nonprofit education.

PART 2. NON-MARKET ENTREPRENEURSHIP: SOCIETY AND ECONOMY

Non-market entrepreneurship has implications for the larger society and market economy. This is the theme linking the three chapters of Part 2. In 'Non-market sources of American entrepreneurial capitalism', Acs, Phillips, Audretsch, and Desai discuss the effects of non-market entrepreneurship in relation to the historical phenomenon of American capitalism. The key lies in what they call the 'entrepreneurship-philanthropy nexus'. Their argument is that philanthropy drives a positive feedback loop underlying American capitalism as 'American philanthropists – especially those who have made their own fortunes – create foundations that, in turn, contribute to greater and more widespread economic prosperity through opportunity, knowledge creation and entrepreneurship'. The ultimate effect of this non-market entrepreneurship is that it supports the process of economic development and the United States' continued economic dominance.

Boettke and Coyne's 'The political economy of the philanthropic enterprise' is the converse of Acs, Phillips, Audretsch, and Desai's chapter. Instead of looking at the causal effects of philanthropic effects of the economy, they turn the relationship around and look at 'the contributions of for-profit activities to the betterment of society' through the non-market vehicle of philanthropic enterprise. 'We wish to highlight that while charitable donations are one means of giving to society, so is the provision of jobs as well as new products and services available at decreasing costs'. They make the intriguing point that the traditional separation of civil society from the market economy is a false dichotomy and offer as a substitute the distinction between civil society as 'self-governance' and the state as 'enforced order'. Boettke and Coyne conclude that 'philanthropic enterprise is really a function of betting on people, not on projects'.

Anderson, MacAulay, Kayseas, and Hindle's 'On their own terms: indigenous communities, entrepreneurship, and economic development in the New Economy' completes Part 2. In introducing to many readers the concept of 'Indigenous entrepreneurship', Anderson, MacAulay, Kayseas and Hindle take up several themes raised in *NME*. Like the two preceding chapters in this part, they examine the effects of a form of non-market entrepreneurship (that is, Indigenous entrepreneurship) on society and economy (that is, Indigenous economic development). Like most of the chapters in this volume, it articulates another form of non-market entrepreneurship, which is one of the primary objectives of *NME*. Like Koppl and Minniti's chapter in Part 1, Anderson, MacAulay, Kayseas, and Hindle's definition of indigenous entrepreneurship exclusively in terms of general entrepreneurship underscores the universality of entrepreneurial activity, thus invoking the first and last chapters and bringing the reader full-circle. And, together with all of the chapters in this book, 'On their own terms: Indigenous communities, entrepreneurship, and economic development in the New Economy' begins to sketch the boundaries of the emerging field of non-market entrepreneurship, which, again, is one of the main objectives of *NME*.

PART 3. ENTREPRENEURSHIP IN PUBLIC AFFAIRS

NME is a Popperian exercise in theory-building for entrepreneurship research. The eminent philosopher of science Karl Popper writes in

Objective Knowledge (1989): '. . . while we cannot ever have sufficiently good arguments in the empirical sciences for claiming that we have actually reached the truth, we can have strong and reasonably good arguments for claiming that we may have made progress towards the truth . . .' (pp. 57–8). Without sound theories to account for all of the entrepreneurial phenomena now being observed within and across the for-profit, nonprofit, and governmental sectors all around the world, the progress of entrepreneurship research will be impeded and our understanding of the diversity, ubiquity, and essence of entrepreneurial activity will be incomplete. Bygrave and Hofer (1991) wrote early in the 1990s that 'a major challenge facing entrepreneurship in the 1990s is to develop models and theories built on solid foundations from the social sciences' (p. 13). While significant progress was indeed made in the 1990s theorizing on commercial forms of entrepreneurship, the theory-building on entrepreneurship was far from being finished. A decade after Bygrave and Hofer, Shane and Venkataraman (2000) write, 'Perhaps the largest obstacle in creating a conceptual framework for the entrepreneurship field has been its definition' (p. 218). To develop theory for entrepreneurship research by thoroughly if not exhaustively articulating the various forms of non-market entrepreneurship is another of *NME*'s main objectives.

One way to distinguish the two chapters of 'Entrepreneurship in public affairs' (Part 3) is entrepreneurial activity inside government organizations (Stough and Haynes' chapter) on the one hand and entrepreneurial activity outside in the political environment (Shockley's chapter) on the other. In 'Intrapreneurship in the public sector', Stough and Haynes examine entrepreneurial activity inside public sector organizations by utilizing and stylizing the notion of 'intrapreneurship' for the public sector. In so doing, they accomplish a multi-dimensional comparison piece by contrasting both *intra*preneurship from *entre*preneurship and intrapreneurship in the public sector from intrapreneurship in the commercial sector, where the notion is popular and relatively well-developed. They then develop the idea of public sector intrapreneurship by applying it to the public-works cases of Robert Moses, William Mulholland and Franklin Delano Roosevelt in the earlier half of the twentieth century. The novelty of their case analyses is not in bringing to light new details of these fairly well-known cases but rather in interpreting already established case information with the theoretical lens of public sector intrapreneurship. Although Stough and Haynes' focus is intrapreneurship within the public sector, this form of non-market entrepreneurship has considerable policy implications for the political environment.

Shockley's 'Policy entrepreneurship: reconceptualizing entrepreneurship in public affairs' reworks the idea of policy entrepreneurship previously offered by distinguished political scientists over the last few decades by adapting to policy studies the insights of the classical entrepreneurship theorists Joseph Schumpeter and Israel Kirzner. Based on what he calls the first classical insight (the ubiquity of entrepreneurship in all human endeavors), he reclassifies entrepreneurship in public affairs as policy entrepreneurship emphasizes not the descriptive power of identifying individual policy entrepreneurs as has been preferred in prior research but rather the explanatory power of entrepreneurship in public policy.

PART 4. ONLY A SEMANTIC DIFFERENCE? SOCIAL ENTREPRENEURSHIP, NONPROFIT ENTREPRENEURSHIP, AND SOCIAL ENTERPRISE

While the theory-building chapters develop and assess different forms of non-market entrepreneurship, there is no single, general theory of entrepreneurship espoused or endorsed in these pages. All of the contributors to this volume were invited to discuss a particular form of 'non-market entrepreneurship' (as defined above) from a theoretical, mostly qualitative perspective without any particular commitment to what constitutes 'entrepreneurship' itself. The four chapters of Part 4 suggest that this open invitation to the contributors has become one of the volume's strengths. Four chapters on entrepreneurship in the social sector are juxtaposed: social enterprise (Young), nonprofit entrepreneurship (Frank), social entrepreneurship (Parker), and social ventures (Yitshaki, Lerner, and Sharir). As the reader engages these chapters, he or she is invited to consider whether the differences between them are real, thus comprising distinct forms of non-market entrepreneurship in the social sector, or whether the differences between the forms are only semantic.

Frank's 'A model of nonprofit and socially motivated entrepreneurial behavior' provides 'a conceptual model to explain the various forms of entrepreneurship that result from socially motivated discovery and creativity'. He develops a typology of entrepreneurial behavior and divides nonprofit entrepreneurship into first nonprofit enterprise, which he defines as 'the entrepreneurial act of discovering or creating innovative approaches to non-market solutions to social problems by establishing a nonprofit organization', and then social enterprise, which he defines as 'the entrepreneurial act of discovering or creating an earned income strategy by a nonprofit or the creation of separate income generating entity by a nonprofit'. Franks' model transcends the for-profit/nonprofit distinction by examining entrepreneurial behavior 'occurring in both the nonprofit and market sectors that is considered, at least in part, to be socially motivated'.

Instead of distinguishing different forms of non-market entrepreneurship in the social sector, Young in 'A unified theory of social enterprise' brings them all together into a unified theory of demand and supply that accounts for all types of social enterprise. Similar to Frank, Young finds 'cross-sector' social enterprise. Social enterprise can arise from the demand side as consumers might prefer social instead of commercial enterprise, corporations might seek strategic partnerships with nonprofits, and governments seeing efficient or effective provision. Social enterprise can also arise from the supply side in competition for entrepreneurial talent, giving and volunteering behavior, and labor priced below-market cost. Young's unified theory is premised on the idea of nonprofits as multi-product organizations.

Parker takes more of a behavioral approach to entrepreneurship in the social sector. Assuming that the reader already is comfortable with the distinctions between for-profit and social entrepreneurship as well as paid employment and volunteering, Parker wants to the know the 'why' and 'when' of an individual's decision to engage in voluntary social entrepreneurship. 'A key insight from this work', he expresses in the argot of the neoclassical economics, 'is that individuals only become entrepreneurs if they obtain greater than expected utility from entrepreneurship than from paid employment; otherwise, they become employees'. One instantly wants to know if these decisions will vary with different forms of non-market entrepreneurship. 'More generally', Parker observes, 'the field of non-market entrepreneurship needs to develop a strong body of empirical work focused on social entrepreneurs', as he has done in his chapter.

Yitshaki, Lerner, and Sharir also have an empirical focus in their chapter on entrepreneurship in the social sector. In 'What are social ventures? Toward a theoretical framework and empirical examination of successful social ventures', they look at social ventures, which (fitting squarely within *NME*'s general definition of non-market entrepreneurship) are 'social enterprises that are initiated by individual entrepreneurs not for the purposes of profit maximization or commercialization, but for attaining and implementing various social goals'. Social ventures survive, they find, 'if they have the ability to raise financial resources for ongoing operations, gain legitimacy and draw in followers, and develop personal networks and internal capabilities'. They also identify the scale of operation as an additional factor contributing to the success of a social venture 'a national mode of operation' increased the chances of survival than 'a local or self-help mode of operation'. Theory-building is incomplete without at least recognizing the empirical application of the theories being built. Yitshaki, Lerner, and Sharir's chapter together with Parker's provide that for *NME*.

ACKNOWLEDGMENTS

We gratefully acknowledge many people in the production of *Non-market Entrepreneurship: Interdisciplinary Approaches*. We first thank Alan Sturmer, Tara Gorvine and Bob Pickens of Edward Elgar, Inc. for their patience and support as we put together what we hope is a top-notch edited volume for scholars of entrepreneurship research. We also heartily appreciate the contributors, most of whom are well-established scholars, for lending their credibility to this volume and treating us with respect and seriousness. No doubt the editorial presence of Dr Roger Stough, whose kind mentorship continues to support us, helped us in this regard. We also very much appreciate the initial financial support from Alan Carsrud and Eugenio Pino and Family Global Entrepreneurship Center at Florida International University, and the E.M. Kauffman Foundation, as well as the financial support from Arizona State University's School of Community Resources and Development (Directors Kathleen Andereck, PhD; Rhonda Phillips, PhD; and Randy Virden, PhD) and College of Public Programs (Dean Debra Friedman, PhD) to finish up the volume.

REFERENCES

Bygrave, W.D. and Hofer, C.W. (1991), 'Theorizing about entrepreneurship', *Entrepreneurship Theory and Practice*, **16**(2), 13–22.

Cornelius, B., Landstrom, H. and Persson, O. (2006), 'Entrepreneurial studies: the dynamic research front of a developing social science', *Entrepreneurship Theory and Practice* **30**(3), 375–98.

Popper, K. (1989), *Objective Knowledge: An Evolutionary Approach*, Oxford: Oxford University Press.

Shane, S. and Venkataraman, S. (2000), 'The promise of entrepreneurship as a field of research', *Academy of Management Review*, **25**(1), 217–26.

2. Entrepreneurship and human action

Roger Koppl and Maria Minniti

INTRODUCTION[1]

The central figure in entrepreneurship research is the entrepreneur. Without the entrepreneur our object of inquiry disappears. One might expect, then, that all our efforts would be based on a clear, scientific understanding of the entrepreneur and his function. This is not the case, however. We do not know who the entrepreneur is, and we do not know what makes him an entrepreneur. The purpose of this chapter is to clarify who the entrepreneur is and what makes him an entrepreneur. Confusion over the identity of the entrepreneur does not reflect any neglect of the question by entrepreneurship scholars. On the contrary, the problem has received considerable attention in the entrepreneurship literature. It is a difficult scientific problem, however, to decide precisely who is an entrepreneur and what entrepreneurial behavior is. Different answers have been proposed without a consensus view emerging (Gartner, 2001). A unified and comprehensive theory of entrepreneurship, we argue, is possible if and only if we see entrepreneurship as a universal form of human action.

Overall, a large amount of research on entrepreneurs and entrepreneurship has been conducted in recent years.[2] Yet, no consensus has emerged on who is an entrepreneur. This fact reflects a difficulty with entrepreneurship research that might be attributed to its relative youth as a separate discipline.[3] Entrepreneurship research today is rich in facts, but poor in theory. Entrepreneurship scholars have produced many important empirical results. No broad theoretical framework has yet emerged, however, that might give them coherence and order. But there is no progress without theory. Without a broad theoretical framework for scholarly work in entrepreneurship it is hard to decide which empirical results are complementary and which are contradictory, which are more important and which less. It is hard to know what general inferences to draw and which puzzles and questions are most worth examining. 'We are getting more pieces of the puzzle, but no picture is emerging' (Koppl and Minniti, 2003: 81).

We have said that there are many empirical works in entrepreneurial studies, but no unifying theory. This claim should not be taken to imply that these empirical works are, somehow, theory free. They often have quite strong theoretical grounding. But there is little or no theoretical consistency from one scholar to the next, one study to the next. We believe the root cause of this unproductive form of theoretical diversity is the lack of generally agreed upon criteria for what counts as entrepreneurial behavior. Along similar lines, Shane and Venkataraman argue that 'Perhaps the largest obstacle in creating a conceptual framework for the entrepreneurship field has been its definition' (Shane and Venkataraman, 2000: 218).

Within entrepreneurial studies, two competing notions of entrepreneurship dominate. On the one hand, entrepreneurship may refer to what entrepreneurs are like. On the other hand, it may refer to what the entrepreneur does. This basic division was already in place in 1990 when Gartner published a study showing that the professionals he surveyed fell into two groups, each with a different basic concept of entrepreneurship. 'The first group thought of the characteristics of entrepreneurship; the second group thought of the outcomes of entrepreneurship such as creating value or owning an ongoing business' (Gartner, 1990: 27).

Gartner's first definition, concerning the 'characteristics of entrepreneurship', is most commonly identified today as opportunity recognition. Entrepreneurs are distinguished by their propensity to recognize opportunity.[4] Advocates of this definition of entrepreneurship include Shane and Venkataraman (2000). Gartner's second definition, concerning the 'outcomes of entrepreneurship', is most commonly identified today as innovation and firm formation. Entrepreneurs launch innovations and found enterprises. Advocates of this definition of entrepreneurship include Low and MacMillan (1988).

Many scholars in entrepreneurship believe that opportunity recognition is the characteristic feature of entrepreneurial behavior. Other scholars, instead, believe that innovation is the characteristic feature of entrepreneurial behavior. Both concepts are quite reasonable and a good case can be made for either. We are not aware of any compelling argument to abandon one of the two in favor of the other. And because each definition excludes the other, neither one enables us to enjoy the full benefits of the diversity of disciplinary perspectives relevant to entrepreneurship (Gartner, 2001).

We need a broad theory of entrepreneurship that will bring order, coherence, and unity to the growing body of empirical research in entrepreneurship. In this sense, we need a unifying theory. In this chapter we will not pretend to provide all details of such a theory. We will, however, attempt to explain the most important and fundamental elements of such a theory. The unified view of entrepreneurial behavior as a human universal was put forward by Israel Kirzner (1973, 1982, 1997). Kirzner's theory has been misconstrued as static and narrowly economic, as the example of Scott Shane (2000) illustrates. A proper understanding of Kirzner's theory, however, shows that it is a vital and dynamic element of a general social theory comprising insights from a variety of social and behavioral sciences such as economics, sociology and psychology. Indeed, Kirzner's theory emerged from and is a part of the modern Austrian tradition of social theory.[5]

Following Kirzner, as we argue below, entrepreneurs are not a class of people distinct from other persons and entrepreneurial behavior is not a class of actions distinct from other actions. Entrepreneurship is an aspect of all human action. Entrepreneurship is a human universal. If so, then entrepreneurship theory must be a part of a broader social theory that encompasses areas of inquiry typical of all social sciences but provides questions and applications for the humanities as well.

If entrepreneurs were, say, especially dynamic business owners, then entrepreneurship theory would be a business discipline. It would not have the broad scope we claim for it. But if entrepreneurship is an aspect of action, then any scholarly discussion of human action must take due account of entrepreneurship. The need to recognize the entrepreneurial dimension of action applies to the humanities as well as the social sciences. In the history of art, for example, we recognize Picasso as more entrepreneurial than, say, Miro because of the greater number of new forms and styles he created. We recognize innovators and imitators. We see that the science of perspective represented an opportunity for Renaissance artists, who seized it eagerly. And so on.

ENTREPRENEURSHIP AS A HUMAN UNIVERSAL

The theory of entrepreneurial behavior we propose in this chapter might be divided into three main parts. First there are the most fundamental elements identifying what entrepreneurs do and what entrepreneurs are like. As we shall see, the key concepts are alertness, discovery, and innovation. Thus, the first subsection below discusses the elements of our theory. Second, we may ask in what context these elements apply. Thus, the second subsection discusses what we call the groundhog principle, with which we show that every context for action is in some degree novel. Third, we may ask what sort of a world permits alert entrepreneurs to discover opportunities for innovations. Thus, the third and final subsection below argues that such innovations are possible only in the context of 'uncertainty' and explains the theory of uncertainty in entrepreneurship.

Fundamental Elements of Entrepreneurship Theory

The key concepts of entrepreneurship theory are Israel Kirzner's twin notions of 'alertness' and 'innovation' and his notion of 'discovery' as a bridge linking alertness to innovation. As we will explain presently, alertness leads necessarily to discovery and discovery leads necessarily to innovation.

Alertness is the leading concept in entrepreneurship theory. Alertness is alertness to opportunities. We are alert to opportunities to revise our plans and habits, to do something new. Thus, we are alert to desirable ways of changing the ends-means framework with which we have been operating (Kirzner, 1982, in particular see pp.143–5). When a farmer tries a new type of fertilizer, he is employing a new means to the end of growing wheat. When he experiments with new crops he is seeking a new end. Of course that new end is but the means to the larger end of, say, providing for his family. Every end is the means to some higher end in a series culminating in some absolute value or in the generalized goal of 'increasing utility'. One ends-means framework tells us to rub a lucky rabbit's foot before crossing the street. Another tells us to look both ways. An alert pedestrian may notice that looking both ways works better than rubbing a rabbit's foot. He will act on this discovery and move, thereby, to a better ends-means framework.

If the prospective change is desirable, it is because it seems to offer a gain, that is, an improvement, no matter how small, in one's condition. Discovery is finding such an opportunity. As the term is used in entrepreneurship theory, an entrepreneur may 'discover' the results of his or her own creative imagination. Sometimes the entrepreneur discovers what is 'out there'; sometimes the entrepreneur 'discovers' his or her own creation. Finally, when a discovery is made, the entrepreneur acts on it by taking the innovative action standing newly before him. The concept, though not the word, innovation is prominent in Kirzner's work. As we note again, for Kirzner, the 'element' in decision making that 'cannot . . . be explained by [standard economic] rationality', is 'the selection of the ends-means framework' within which action occurs. The move to a new ends-means framework is necessarily an innovation for the person undertaking it. Kirzner notes that the selection of an interpretive framework is 'essentially creative' (Kirzner, 1982, in particular see pp.143–4). This 'creative' act is necessarily an innovation for the person undertaking it. Thus, the concept of innovation is essential to Kirzner's theory even though he tended to use a different vocabulary.

Kirzner recognized the creative element in entrepreneurship in his seminal article of 1982. There he notes that 'Alertness must, importantly, embrace the awareness of the ways in which the human agent can, by imagination, bold leaps of faith, and determination, in fact create the future for which his present acts are designed' (Kirzner, 1982: 150). He cites favorably Lawrence White's remark that 'Entrepreneurial projects are not waiting to be sought out so much as thought up' and Ludwig Lachmann's dictum that 'The future is unknowable, though not unimaginable' (Kirzner, 1982: 156–7).

This brief sketch of the theory of entrepreneurship applies quite widely. At the highest level of abstraction, entrepreneurship is an aspect of action (Kirzner, 1982, in particular see p.139). Thus, we may use a simple and homey example to illustrate the leading ideas of the theory of entrepreneurial behavior. Among other things, this provides one more example of a new ends-means framework.

A professor walks the same route to class every day.[6] His path is optimal given his knowledge; it gets him there in the least time. One day he discovers that a slightly roundabout route allows him to avoid his dean, who usually pesters him along his accustomed path. He takes the new route and avoids the dean. Our professor has found a new ends–means framework. He had been minimizing travel time; he now minimizes the bother of getting to class, considering both travel-time and obnoxious deans. Thus, his ends have changed. The means have changed too; he takes a different route. Our professor could have made this change only by being 'alert' to the opportunity to improve his situation by changing his route. The new, roundabout route was an opportunity; he could benefit from by switching to the new route. When he discovered it, his actions changed. His actions had to change if the new route was truly an opportunity. For him this is an innovation. If he had considered the new route but found it to be too long, then it would not have been a true opportunity and he would not have taken it. Of course, the dean may find the professor along the new route too and the new plan may fail.

The Groundhog Principle

As we have noted already, entrepreneurship is an aspect of action. In Kirzner's words, 'the entrepreneurial element cannot be abstracted from the notion of individual human action' (Kirzner, 1982: 139). This fact follows from what we will call the groundhog principle. The groundhog principle says that every context for action is in some degree novel, if only because the actor has lived through all his previous experiences before the current situation arose. This point was made by the philosopher Henri Bergson and, perhaps, by others before him.[7] More recently, it was used as a plot device in the Hollywood movie *Groundhog Day*.[8] The protagonist rises each day to find that it is precisely the same as the previous day.

Everyday is 2 February; everyday is Groundhog Day. The townspeople are unaware of this and behave identically on each repeated day. But the protagonist is aware of the past Groundhog Days and behaves differently from repeated day to repeated day. Even in the fantasy setting of this Hollywood movie, every context for action is in some degree novel, if only because the individual has lived through all his previous experiences before the current situation arose. This insight is the groundhog principle.

The protagonist of *Groundhog Day* varied his actions over time, sometimes slightly, sometimes radically. By the groundhog principle, he was always facing something at least a little bit new and unprecedented. Thus, he had to improvize even if only slightly. The groundhog principle tells us, then, that all action must be in some degree an improvization. To improvize is to do something new and different. It is to innovate. Thus, all action is innovation. But an innovation implies a previous discovery of an opportunity. And such a discovery can be made only if the actor is alert.

It is only by viewing entrepreneurship as an aspect of all human actions that we can hope for theoretical unity in entrepreneurship studies. Any other approach to identifying entrepreneurial behavior would have us divide observable behaviors into those we will classify as 'entrepreneurial' and those officially labeled 'non-entrepreneurial'. But any such division is more or less arbitrary and open to objection. For example, if 'opening a business' is the dividing line, some will object that intrapreneurs and social entrepreneurs are wrongly excluded.

Of course, although entrepreneurship as an aspect of all human actions, most studies in entrepreneurship will, presumably, be conducted at a somewhat lower level of abstraction. For example, the operational meaning of 'entrepreneurship' will often be 'starting a new business'. Almost by definition, however, any theory capable of integrating the many diverse strands of entrepreneurship research will have to be relatively abstract and general. At the highest level of abstraction, all persons are entrepreneurs, entrepreneurial behavior is a human universal, and the theory of entrepreneurship is a way of looking at all human action. Thus, entrepreneurship theory is the social science that views social processes from the perspective of the element of change and improvization in all human action. For this reason it is sensible to have theories of 'non-market entrepreneurship', 'new-venture creation', and so on. As mentioned earlier, the field is not defined by its object of inquiry, but by its point of view (Kirzner, 1976).

Understanding Entrepreneurial Uncertainty

As we have seen in the context of the groundhog principle, every context for action is in some degree novel and every action is in some degree an improvization. Thus, entrepreneurs live in an uncertain world. Indeed, what sense would it make to imagine innovative entrepreneurs in a mechanical world without uncertainty? Uncertainty is an important and, we shall argue, necessary element of the world in which entrepreneurs act. It is important, therefore, to have as much clarity as we can about the nature of uncertainty and its influence on action.

Israel Kirzner's teacher, Ludwig von Mises defined the 'entrepreneur' as an 'acting man exclusively seen from the aspect of the uncertainty inherent in every action' (Mises, 1949: 254). As the word is used here, uncertainty is distinguished from risk. When numerical probabilities (a) exist, (b) are known, and (c) cover all possibilities, the situation is one of risk. When one or more of these three conditions fails the situation is one of 'uncertainty', not 'risk'. In situations of risk, one may apply the probability calculus and the logic of Bayesian decision making. In situations of uncertainty this is generally not possible.[9]

Discussions of risk and uncertainty can grow complicated. For example, in the last paragraph we spoke of situations of risk and situations of uncertainty without specifying whose perceptions of risk and uncertainty matter. If we observe someone rolling dice who cannot calculate the probabilities involved, we might say this is a 'situation of risk' because we, the observers, know the probability of each outcome. We might, however, say that this is a 'situation of uncertainty' because the person rolling the dice does not know the relevant probabilities. Some writers rank situations of uncertainty according to how fundamental, in some sense, the uncertainty is (Dequech, 2006). From such a perspective, it may seem a mild form of uncertainty when probabilities are merely hard to calculate, whereas a more fundamental uncertainty exists when different outcomes do not exist ahead of time. 'Fundamental uncertainty', Dequech says, 'is characterized by the possibility of creativity and non-predetermined structural change. The list of possible events is not predetermined or knowable ex ante, as the future is yet to be created' (Dequech 2006: 112).

Kirzner's concept of uncertainty is close to Dequech's 'fundamental uncertainty'. In the 'open-ended' world Kirzner imagines, entrepreneurial behavior is linked to 'the unpredictable, the creative, the imaginative expressions of the human mind' (Kirzner, 1982: 147). Kirzner links uncertainty to 'an element' in decision making that 'cannot . . . be explained by [standard economic] rationality', namely, 'the selection of the ends–means framework' within which action occurs (Kirzner 1982, p.143). The selection of an interpretive framework is 'essentially creative' (Kirzner, 1982: 144). Kirzner emphasizes that uncertainty in his sense is not just the difficulty of forecasting. For Kirzner, it 'is not a matter of two unfolding tapestries, one the realized future, the second a fantasized' picture of 'what the first might look like'. Instead, the entrepreneur is 'motivated *to bring about* correspondence' between his vision and reality (Kirzner, 1982: 149).

Kirzner's last point may deserve some elaboration. Consider a theater patron after the second act. He does not know what will happen in the third act. He might guess, but his guesses won't influence what the actors do on stage. Social scientists often think of uncertainty in such theater-going terms. It is an error to do so. Entrepreneurship theory recognizes that entrepreneurs are not like theater patrons. They can act, and their actions are aimed precisely at changing the future. As Butos and Koppl have put it, 'our knowledge of future events is in the form of a kind of architecture of the situation. The future is not a sequence of specific events, but a field of action. Indeed, if the future were not uncertain for the passive observer, it could not be the object of action for the active participant. We act in the world precisely to change the course of events. Uncertainty does not prohibit action; it makes action possible' (Butos and Koppl, 2001: 84).

In this section we have outlined the elements of entrepreneurship theory. The most fundamental elements of the theory are the concepts of alertness, discovery, and innovation. By the groundhog principle, we know that alertness, discovery, and innovation are possible only in a world of time and uncertainty. We thus examined the theory of uncertainty. We believe these elements will prove to be indispensable foundations for a unified theory of entrepreneurial behavior. If that claim is correct, however, it must be consistent with the long-established fact that the field of entrepreneurial studies draws on the results of several disciplines and is, in this sense, transdisciplinary, as we will explain later in the chapter.

THE ENTREPRENEUR AS A CATALYST OF CHANGE

As described in the previous sections, the entrepreneur is someone who has the ability to perceive and exploit an opportunity in an uncertain situation. But we also believe that 'entrepreneurship creates more entrepreneurship' (Holcombe, 1998). This happens in two ways. First, each act of entrepreneurship creates new opportunities for other entrepreneurs. Second, each act of entrepreneurship is a favorable example for others to follow. Every time an entrepreneur seizes a new opportunity, the possibility for new action and change is created. Thus, we argue, the entrepreneur is a catalyst of activity for the community as a whole.

Like any human decision, the choice to develop or exploit an opportunity is formed and revised given the knowledge available to the individual. Different people have different knowledge, thus different perceptions about the uncertainty and cost associated with a perceived opportunity. These perceptions are all aspects of one's knowledge of 'where to obtain information (or other resources) and how to obtain it' (Kirzner, 1979: 8). They are thus aspects of Kirznerian alertness. Thus, the individual's social environment influences the quality and the quantity of alertness loose in the community.

The observation of much entrepreneurial activity in one's proximity tends to make one more alert and, therefore, more likely to discover an entrepreneurial opportunity. Thus, entrepreneurship, whether consisting of starting a new business, reforming institutions, or developing an opportunity in the non-market sector, creates a network externality and has implications at the aggregate level. If the entrepreneur is a catalyst of further action then entrepreneurship breeds entrepreneurship, and the aggregate level of entrepreneurial activity within a community is determined by a path-dependent process (Minniti, 2005). Such results provide a clear example of Hayekian spontaneous order in the sense that, as in many complex phenomena, the aggregate outcome 'cannot be reduced to the regularities of the parts' (Hayek, 1967: 74). The following thought experiment helps us see the point.

Assume each individual faces an opportunity and has only two options, that is, whether or not to act on a perceived opportunity. And let the amount of entrepreneurial activity in a person's vicinity be an indicator of the individual's perception of the general possibilities for action. Some individuals will recognize the opportunity facing them, others will not. Individuals who seize the opportunity become entrepreneurs; all others do not.[10]

After taking into account the costs and benefits associated with becoming an entrepreneur, and analogously to the professor deciding which route to take walking to class, each individual chooses the one activity whose utility is higher. Each individual is endowed with an initial set of characteristics, both biological and sociological. Those characteristics, as well as social circumstances such as employment, education, etc., determine the individual's position with respect to any opportunity. And since these characteristics differ across individuals, the population is heterogeneous with different individuals facing different opportunity costs when acting to exploit the opportunity they recognized.

If individuals' decisions about entrepreneurship are independent of each other, the levels of entrepreneurial activities across similar regions should represent averages of large numbers of independent decisions. These averages should be free from the effects of random idiosyncratic error terms and close to the expected population means. This, of course, cannot explain the concentration of entrepreneurship in certain times, places and fields of endeavor. For example, the Italian Renaissance produced a disproportionate share of innovations, and of these innovations a disproportionate share was in the field of art. That example suggests that, as in our thought experiment, entrepreneurship decisions are not independent. Social interaction creates enough interdependence across individual decisions to explain high variance of entrepreneurship levels in spite of otherwise similar characteristics.

For each individual, the relative return to entrepreneurship depends on a set of personal characteristics, the individual's initial endowment, and on level entrepreneurship itself. Since entrepreneurship creates more entrepreneurship, the higher the amount of entrepreneurial activity, the stronger is the incentive to exploit perceived opportunities, independently of initial personal characteristics. Among other things, this point highlights the importance of institutions and of non-market entrepreneurial activities. As Boettke and Coyne (2006) point out

> Institutions refer to the formal and informal rules governing human behavior and vary across time and space. In contrast to other schools of economic thought, the Austrians have not only realized the importance of institutions, but have attempted to provide a connection between . . . institutions, the market process and entrepreneurship. This is an important connection because institutions create the 'rules of the game' that influence the behaviors of private actors including entrepreneurs.

While some researchers have recognized the aggregate importance of entrepreneurship, the amount of research on the macro-implications of entrepreneurship is still relatively small, and primarily confined to economic arguments dealing with increased competition and productivity.[11] Although these studies are important, they only cover a very small portion of the role played by entrepreneurship in society as they ignore the important role played by entrepreneurial behavior in activities that are not immediately associated with monetary profits. And yet, entrepreneurship is present in many aspects of daily life that are not immediately associated to monetary rewards.

Our approach to the contribution of entrepreneurship to non-market activities is based on the interdisciplinary insights offered by studies of social interdependence. As with many social phenomena, we argue that perceptions about the desirability of being entrepreneurial are formed and revised given the knowledge available to each agent. A large part of such knowledge is collected locally, within the social circle of the individual. Different agents know different things and have, therefore, different perceptions about the uncertainty and cost associated with behaving entrepreneurially. Thus, different sequences of choice, that is different institutions and local histories, may cause significant differences among the levels of entrepreneurial activity of different groups, in spite of relatively modest differences among their economic characteristics.

In one time, place, or field of endeavor chance produces few initial innovations and only relatively modest levels of entrepreneurship. This slow beginning may lead to persistently low levels of entrepreneurship. In another time, place, or field of endeavor chance produces more initial innovations and relatively large levels of entrepreneurship. This active beginning may lead to persistently high levels of entrepreneurship. In this way the fact that entrepreneurship tends to produce more entrepreneurship leads to the clustering of entrepreneurship in certain times, places, and fields and suggests that certain institutional settings are more conducive to entrepreneurial behavior than others.

Entrepreneurship is a complex phenomenon in Hayek's sense. This supports the claim that entrepreneurship itself matters in determining the growth and development of a society in both its economic and non-economic aspects since, depending on the nature and strength of certain social traits, a community may or may not develop a high level of entrepreneurial activity. Randomly, a particular sequence of choices causes history to bend toward a specific outcome among all the possible ones and let certain social norms emerge. A different past history, however, would have put that community on an alternative track and the level of entrepreneurial activity would be different.[12]

DISCIPLINARY AND TRANSDISCIPLINARY PERSPECTIVES ON ENTREPRENEURIAL BEHAVIOR

The theory of entrepreneurship outlined in the previous sections and its implications for society let us examine the entrepreneur from several diverse perspectives, including those of complexity theory, economics, sociology, psychology and other social sciences and the humanities. Unfortunately, Kirzner's work has sometimes been misconstrued as somehow prohibiting researchers from taking a transdisciplinary approach. Scott Shane provides a rather flamboyant example of this error.

Shane (2000) contrasts psychological approaches to entrepreneurship with the supposed approach of the Austrian school. From our perspective, this is a puzzle. While Kirzner largely eschewed psychological inquiries, especially in *Competition and Entrepreneurship* (1973), he explicitly recognized that psychological factors influence the different degrees of alertness characterizing different people. 'To be a successful entrepreneur', Kirzner explains, 'requires vision, boldness, determination, and creativity'. Kirzner continues, 'There can be no doubt that in the concrete fulfillment of the entrepreneurial function these psychological and personal qualities are of paramount importance. It is in this sense that so many writers are undoubtedly correct in linking entrepreneurship with the courage and vision necessary to *create* the future in an uncertain world' (Kirzner 1982: 155). Under Kirzner's direction, Benny Gilad (1981) wrote a dissertation on entrepreneurship that relied on a psychological concept that was explicitly dismissed by Shane as, somehow, inconsistent with the Austrian school, namely, 'locus of control'.[13] Citing Gilad, David Harper (1996) makes use of this same psychological concept of 'locus of control', to explain both why some individuals are more entrepreneurial than others and why different social and legal institutions tend to produce different levels of entrepreneurship in the populations subject to them.

Shane's notion that the psychological dimension of entrepreneurship is somehow denied by the Austrian school becomes even more puzzling when we consider that learning is, after all, a psychological phenomenon. It was the great Austrian economist F.A. Hayek who first argued that any statement about the process of equilibration is necessarily a statement about entrepreneurial learning. The 'assertion that a tendency toward equilibrium exists', Hayek explained, 'can hardly mean anything but that, under certain conditions, the knowledge and intentions of the different members of society are supposed to come more and more into agreement or, to put the same thing in less general and less exact but more concrete terms, that the expectations of the people and particularly of the entrepreneurs will become more and more correct' (Hayek, 1937: 44). Kirzner's theory was always a theory about learning. And learning, as we have noted, is a psychological process. Far from being inconsistent with the Austrian school, as Shane claims, the psychological understanding of entrepreneurship is central to it.

As discussed in the previous section, entrepreneurs are social actors. Therefore, social psychology should not be neglected by scholars of entrepreneurship. Evolutionary psychology is an important recent development which has not yet had as great an influence on entrepreneurial studies as it probably deserves.[14] The recent revolution in cognitive science may also prove useful to entrepreneurship researchers (for example, see McCabe *et al.*, 2001). Like psychology, sociology is also an important perspective on the entrepreneur.

Entrepreneurship theory builds on the foundations of sociology of Max Weber and Alfred Schutz.[15] Thus, it is not imperialistic toward sociology or, indeed, any other social science or business discipline. The Weberian tradition is only one of many valuable sociological traditions on which scholars of entrepreneurship should build. Among them, for example, Mark Granovetter's network analysis has provided important tools of analysis as illustrated by Aldrich and Ruef (2006).

Psychology, sociology, and economics are but three of the many disciplines upon which scholars of entrepreneurship should draw. Complexity theory, for example, helps us to understand how the actions of individual entrepreneurs influence the overall behavior of the system. Minniti (2005) provides an important example of how to link individual action and overall outcome in the context of a complexity model.

Between economics and sociology is the important field of economic sociology as developed by Richard Swedberg and others.[16] Unfortunately, entrepreneurship scholars do not seem to have made much use of this literature, in spite of several works from this tradition that directly address issues in entrepreneurship.[17] This fact may represent an opportunity for an academic entrepreneur to bring the literature on economic sociology into greater contact with the literature in entrepreneurial studies.

There are important opportunities for exchange between entrepreneurship theory and the humanities as well. On the one hand, entrepreneurship theory applies to the humanities. Kirzner's description of the 'ways in which the human agent can, by imagination, bold leaps of faith, and determination, in fact *create* the future' is a perfect description of the sort of creativity often examined in the humanities (Kirzner, 1982: 150). On the other hand, the humanities should inform the development of entrepreneurship theory. An episode from the life of Raphael provides an example of how entrepreneurship theory and the humanities may illuminate one another.

According to Giorgio Vasari (1568 [1996]), Raphael moved from his native Perugia to Florence in order to study the new style of painting created by Leonardo da Vinci. Raphael was a fast learner and his reputation grew so quickly that he was soon called to the Vatican to paint what are now known as 'Raphael rooms'. At about the same time, Michelangelo was forced to flee from Rome while painting the ceiling of the Sistine Chapel. An important friend and relation (Bramante) secretly arranged to let Raphael see the great work while it was still in progress. That unauthorized visit allowed Raphael to copy Michelangelo's trade secrets for making painted figures appear grand and monumental. Armed with this somewhat ill-gotten knowledge, Raphael repainted the figure of Isaiah that he had earlier completed in the Roman church of Sant'Agostino.

This story shows how entrepreneurship theory applies to the humanities. It reveals Raphael as both innovator and imitator, and both Michelangelo and Raphael as discovering and taking advantage of an opportunity to gain from a new ends-means framework, namely a new way to paint monumental figures. While Raphael's discovery of the new methods of Michelangelo and Leonardo was not planned, he would not have recognized the opportunity at all if he were not alert to the possibility of learning new techniques of painting.

CONCLUSION

The entrepreneur is the central individual in entrepreneurial studies. We have not had, however, a clear and well developed theory of the entrepreneur. In this chapter we have tried to show that Austrian social theory gives us a useful and, indeed, necessary theory of the entrepreneur by allowing us to view entrepreneurship as a universal characteristic of human action. The key to doing so is Kirzner's insight that what the entrepreneur is like (alert) necessarily determines what he does (innovate). We have also argued that, by influencing formal and informal institutions, entrepreneurship breeds entrepreneurship and that, as a result, the entrepreneur is a catalyst of innovation and social change.

Martinelli argues that, 'future research on entrepreneurship' should adopt 'a multidisciplinary comparative approach, capable of integrating the analysis of the context (market, social structure, culture) with a theory of the actor (both individual or collective) with his or her motives, values, attitudes, cognitive processes, and perceived interests' (Martinelli, 2001: 4551). The Austrian school provides the theoretical framework which allows us to integrate the many different disciplinary perspectives Martinelli rightly calls for. Without such a framework, no integration is possible and the different disciplinary perspectives on entrepreneurial behavior will remain so many separate pieces sitting side by side.

The conceptual clarity about what, precisely, we mean by 'the entrepreneur' requires us to recognize that entrepreneurship is an aspect of action. In this sense, everyone is an entrepreneur. We believe that we cannot hope for theoretical clarity in entrepreneurial studies without this broad understanding of who the entrepreneur is. For this reason, we have argued for the view that entrepreneurship theory is the social science that views social processes from the perspective of the element of change and improvisation in all human action.

To summarize, in this chapter, entrepreneurial behavior is described as a universal aspect of human action related to individuals' ability to perceive opportunities for potential changes that may improve their lives and the lives of those in their communities. Entrepreneurs are individuals motivated by incentives, but also by personal aspirations and social considerations and constraints. Incentives, in fact, come in a variety of forms and entrepreneurial behavior, being a form of human action, finds applications in all aspects of life.

Finally, and perhaps most importantly, the chapter introduces readers to the opportunities presented by a truly scientific approach to the study of entrepreneurial behavior. Although contributions to our understanding of entrepreneurial behavior must be grounded in disciplinary foundations such as those provided by both social sciences and the humanities, only by viewing the study of entrepreneurial behavior as a universal aspect of human actions we can hope for theoretical unity in entrepreneurship studies. Any other attempt to understand entrepreneurship would have to divide observable behaviors between the entrepreneurial and the non-entrepreneurial. But any such division would necessarily be arbitrary and, therefore, scientifically unsatisfactory. For this reason, we define entrepreneurship theory as the social science that views social processes from the perspective of the element of change and improvization in all human action.

NOTES

1. This chapter relays significantly on Koppl (2006).
2. For an overview of the literature see Minniti (2003).
3. Scholarly work on entrepreneurship goes back at least as far as Richard Cantillon who noted in 1755 that 'the Beggars even and the Robbers are Undertakers', that is, entrepreneurs, who 'may be regarded as living at uncertainty'. See Higgs (1964: 55). But a separate discipline of 'entrepreneurial studies' did not exist until, perhaps, shortly before the opening of the Center for Entrepreneurial Studies of Babson College in 1978. The center is now called The Arthur M. Blank Center for Entrepreneurship.
4. Gartner (1989) rightly criticizes the view, which has since lost currency, that entrepreneurship can be defined by some special psychological characteristics such as a 'need for achievement'.
5. The volume *Austrian Economics and Entrepreneurial Studies, volume 6 of Advances in Austrian Economics*, edited by R. Koppl in 2003 (Koppl, 2003) brings Austrian economics and entrepreneurial studies together. In that volume, see especially the essay by Minniti and the introduction to the volume by Koppl.
6. The illustration is borrowed from Koppl and Minniti (2003).
7. Bergson's point was explained and emphasized by O'Driscoll and Rizzo (1985), who note that 'the swelling of memory alone changes the perspective from which the world is seen', (p. 62). They explicitly follow Bergson in developing their concept of 'real time'. When Bergson described the flow of consciousness as 'a river without bottom and without banks', he alluded to Heraclitus' remark, 'One cannot step twice into the same river, for the water into which you first stepped has flowed on' (Bergson, 1961).
8. Sony Pictures, 1993.
9. A Bayesian might object, arguing that one simply assigns prior probabilities and that Bayesian logic identifies the uniquely rational way to update probabilities. This response might have some force when we can list all possible contingencies, although we will point to some limits to Bayesianism even in such cases. The Bayesian response we have imagined has less force, however, when we cannot list all the possible outcomes in a situation. The best one might do is to create a residual category containing 'everything else'. It is not clear, however, how one might assign a reliable or meaningful subjective probability value to such a contingency. Even when this 'listing problem' does not arise, real people may not be able to calculate probabilities. Even values that are not 'hard' to compute in any formal mathematical sense may be too much for real people. The notion that Bayesian logic somehow 'saves' probabilistic reasoning seems to be an expression of faith and not a legitimate conclusion of analysis. On 'hard' problems, see Axtell (2005).
10. Whether or not the individual will be successful in his entrepreneurial endeavor is not an issue at this point.

11. For a statement of the problem see Baumol (1968).
12. See for example, the famous discussion of productive, unproductive and destructive entrepreneurship in Baumol (1990). Also, for a detailed analysis of the importance of the institutional environment see Boettke (1993) and Chamlee-Wright (1997).
13. Shane claims that in the Austrian theory, entrepreneurial action 'depends on factors other than people's ability and willingness to take action' (Shane 2000: 450).
14. The central statement of the theory of evolutionary psychology is Barkow *et al.* (1992). A primer by L. Cosmides and J. Tooby can be found at http://www.psych.ucsb.edu/research/cep/primer.html. The work of David Sloan Wilson represents another tradition that might also be considered 'evolutionary psychology'. For example, see Sober and Wilson (1998). The Austrian tradition also values Hayek's psychological work, *The Sensory Order* (1952), which is an example of evolutionary psychology in the broad sense. For a potentially useful resource on how to apply evolutionary psychology to issues in social science, see Koppl (2004).
15. This is the tradition of 'interpretive' sociology. See Koppl (2002), Boettke and Koppl (2001), Oakley (1997), and Prendergast (1986).
16. For example, see Smelser and Swedberg (2005).
17. A good start is Swedberg (2000). Swedberg's introductory chapter includes a valuable review of the social science literature on entrepreneurship.

REFERENCES

Aldrich, H. and M. Ruef (2006), *Organizations Evolving*, revised edn, Thousand Oaks, CA: Sage Publications.

Axtell, R. (2005), 'The complexity of exchange', *The Economic Journal* **115**(504), F193–F210.

Barkow, J., Cosmides, L. and J. Tooby (eds) (1992), *The Adapted Mind: Evolutionary Psychology and the Generation of Culture*, Oxford, UK: Oxford University Press.

Baumol, W.J. (1968), 'Entrepreneurship in economic theory', *American Economic Review*, **58**(2), 64–71.

Baumol, W.J. (1990), 'Entrepreneurship: productive, unproductive and destructive', *The Journal of Political Economy*, **98**, 893–921.

Bergson, H. (1961), *Introduction to Metaphysics*, New York: Wisdom Library, reprinted in G. Davenport (1979), *Herakleitos & Diogenes*, San Francisco, CA: Grey Fox Press.

Boettke, P. (1993), *Why Perestroika Failed: The Politics and Economics of Socialist Transformation*, New York: Routledge.

Boettke, P.J. and C. Coyne (2006), 'Entrepreneurial behavior and institutions', in Maria Minniti (ed.), *Entrepreneurship: The Engine of Growth – Volume 1: People*, Westport, CT: Greenwood Publishing: Perspective Series.

Boettke, P. and R. Koppl (2001), 'Introduction', *Review of Austrian Economics, Special Issue on Alfred Schütz Centennial*, **14**(2/3), 111–17.

Butos, W and R. Koppl (2001), 'Confidence in Keynes and Hayek: reply to Burczak', *Review of Political Economy* **13**(1), 81–6.

Cantillon, R. (1755) [1964], *Essai sur la Nature du Commerce en Général* (H. Higgs, trans. and ed.), New York: Augustus M. Kelley.

Chamlee-Wright, E. (1997), *The Cultural Foundations of Economic Development*, London and New York, Routledge.

Dequech, D. (2006), 'The new institutional economics and the theory of behavior under uncertainty', *Journal of Economic Behavior & Organization* **59**(1), 109–31.

Gartner, W. (1989), '"Who is an entrepreneur?" is the wrong question', *Entrepreneurship Theory and Practice* **13**(4), 47–68.

Gartner, W. (1990), 'What are we talking about when we talk about entrepreneurship?' *Journal of Business Venturing* **5**(1), 15–28.

Gartner, W.B. (2001), 'Is there an elephant in entrepreneurship? Blind assumptions in theory development', *Entrepreneurship Theory and Practice* **25**(4), 27–39.

Gilad, B. (1981), 'An interdisciplinary approach to entrepreneurship: locus of control and alertness', Ph.D. Dissertation, New York University, USA.

Harper, D. (1996), *Entrepreneurship and the Market Process: An Inquiry into the Growth of Knowledge*, London: Routledge.

Hayek, F.A. (1937), 'Economics and knowledge', *Economica*, **4**(13), 33–54.

Hayek, F.A. (1952), *The Sensory Order*, Chicago, IL: University of Chicago Press.

Hayek, F.A. (1967), *Studies in Philosophy, Politics and Economics*, Chicago, IL: University of Chicago Press.

Holcombe, R.G. (1998), 'Entrepreneurship and economic growth', *Quarterly Journal of Austrian Economics*, **1**, 45–62.

Kirzner, I.M. (1979), Perception, Opportunity and Profit: Studies in the Theory of Entrepreneurship, Chicago, IL: University of Chicago Press.

Kirzner, I. (1973), *Competition and Entrepreneurship*, Chicago, IL: University of Chicago Press.

Kirzner, I. (1976), *The Economic Point of View*, Kansas City, MO: Sheed and Ward, Inc.

Kirzner, I. (1982), 'Uncertainty, discovery, and human action: A study of the entrepreneurial profile in the Misesian system', in Israel Kirzner (ed.), *Method, Process, and Austrian Economics: Essays in Honor of Ludwig von Mises*, Lexington, MA and Toronto, Lexington Books.

Kirzner, I. (1997), 'Entrepreneurial discovery and the competitive market process: An Austrian approach', *Journal of Economic Literature* **35**, 60–85.

Koppl, R. (2006), 'Entrepreneurial Behavior as a Human Universal', in Maria Minniti (ed.), *Entrepreneurship: The Engine of Growth – Volume 1: People*, Westport, CT: Greenwood Publishing: Perspective Series.

Koppl, R. (2002), *Big Players and the Economic Theory of Expectations*, London and New York, Palgrave Macmillan.

Koppl, R. (ed.) (2003), *Austrian Economics and Entrepreneurial Studies*, volume 6 of *Advances in Austrian Economics*, Amsterdam: JAI, an imprint of Elsevier Science.

Koppl, R. and M. Minniti, (2003), 'Market processes and entrepreneurial studies', in Acs, Zoltan J. and David B. Audretsch (eds), *Handbook of Entrepreneurial Research*, Boston, MA: Kluwer.

Koppl, R. (2004), 'Economics evolving: An introduction to the volume', in Roger Koppl (ed.), *Evolutionary Psychology and Economic Theory*, volume 7 of *Advances in Austrian Economics*, Amsterdam: JAI, an imprint of Elsevier Science.

Low, M.B. and I.C. MacMillan, (1988), 'Entrepreneurship: past research and future challenges', *Journal of Management* **35**, 139–161.

Martinelli, A. (2001), 'Entrepreneurship', in N.J. Smelser and P.B. Baltes (eds), *International Encyclopedia of the Social & Behavioral Sciences*, Amsterdam: Pergamon, an imprint of Elsevier Science.

McCabe, K., D. Houser, L. Ryan, V. Smith and T. Trouard (2001), 'A functional imaging study of cooperation in two-person reciprocal exchange', *Proceedings of the National Academy of Sciences* **98**, 11832–5.

Minniti, M. (2003), 'Entrepreneurship studies: A stocktaking', in Roger Koppl (ed.), *Austrian Economics and Entrepreneurial Studies*, in volume 6 of *Advances in Austrian Economics*, Amsterdam: JAI, an imprint of Elsevier Science.

Minniti, M. (2005), 'Entrepreneurship and network externalities', *Journal of Economic Behavior and Organization* **57**(1), 1–27.

Mises, L. (1949), *Human Action: A Treatise on Economics*, New Haven, CN: Yale University Press.

Oakley, A. (1997), *The Foundations of Austrian Economics from Menger to Mises: A Critico-Historical Retrospective of Subjectivism*, Cheltenham, UK and Lyme, USA: Edward Elgar.

O'Driscoll, J and M. Rizzo (1985), *The Economics of Time and Ignorance*, Oxford: Basil Blackwell.

Prendergast, C. (1986), 'Alfred Schütz and the Austrian School of Economics', *American Journal of Sociology*, **92**(1), 1–26.

Shane, S. (2000), 'Prior knowledge and the discovery of entrepreneurial opportunities', *Organization Science*, **11**(4), 448–69.

Shane, S. and S. Venkataraman (2000), 'The promise of entrepreneurship as a field of research', *Academy of Management Review*, **25**(1), 217–26.

Smelser, N.J. and R. Swedberg (2005), *The Handbook of Economic Sociology*, 2nd edn, Princeton, NJ: Princeton University Press.

Sober, E. and D.S. Wilson (1998), *Unto Others: The Evolution and Psychology of Unselfish Behavior*, Cambridge, MA: Harvard University Press.

Swedberg, R. (2000), *Entrepreneurship: The Social Science View*, Oxford: Oxford University Press.

Vasari, G. (1568 [1996]), *Lives of the Painters, Sculptors and Architects*, London: Everyman's Library.

3. Teaching entrepreneurship outside of business schools

Robert F. Ashcraft

INTRODUCTION

When the question of which academic unit stakes a claim to teaching entrepreneurship is posed, it is expected that schools of business within most universities will rise above all others. However, when the question is asked about teaching social entrepreneurship, it is apparent that many disciplines and organizing units of universities stake a claim. Therefore, to appreciate the teaching of entrepreneurship in all of its variations requires an analysis that extends well beyond schools of business if a complete understanding of the topic is to be achieved.

According to the University Network for Social Entrepreneurship (UNSE), the top ten business schools in the United States (Harvard, Stanford, Wharton, Sloan, Kellogg, Tuck, Haas, Chicago, Columbia and Ross) have developed at least one or more courses in social entrepreneurship. Moreover, the American Association of Colleges of Schools of Business reports 31 member schools of business that have social entrepreneurship programs. Clearly, approaches to teaching social entrepreneurship are found in business schools across the United States and in selected locations internationally. UNSE notes several trends driving interest in the field including: (a) increased market demands from students, practitioners and educators desiring more educational opportunities; (b) heightened media attention drawing attention to the subject; (c) significant philanthropic investments to colleges and universities for expansion of curricular and extracurricular offerings; and (d) increased numbers of national and international competitions and awards to social entrepreneurship exemplars. The case for developing and teaching social entrepreneurships courses within business schools is largely self-evident. However, business schools are not the only drivers of social entrepreneurship education in colleges and universities as the field emerges in multi-disciplinary, inter-disciplinary and transdisciplinary ways. The purpose of this chapter is to consider the teaching of social entrepreneurship outside business schools. The framework considers multiple perspectives and is within the context of a new and emerging field of nonprofit and philanthropic studies.

WHAT IS KNOWN ABOUT SOCIAL ENTREPRENEURSHIP OFFERINGS OUTSIDE OF BUSINESS SCHOOLS?

A multi-year study of nonprofit management education by researchers at Seton Hall University, funded initially by the W.K. Kellogg Foundation, reveals at least 25 universities that offer one or more courses in social entrepreneurship (Table 3.1). These data are self-reported and may not fully represent offerings found throughout US higher education. They represent universities that have specifically identified social entrepreneurship in course titles. It is acknowledged that given the growth of nonprofit management education curricula nationwide (more than 250 universities offering some level of curricular programming nonprofit management education), social entrepreneurship is included as a topic within a course differently titled. Nonetheless, it is generally acknowledged that the leading universities that teach social entrepreneurship are catalogued on Seton Hall's web-based repository of nonprofit management education offerings. The data show that 60 percent of the social entrepreneurship courses are organized outside the respective university's business school. In fact the organizing academic unit varies and includes colleges of arts and sciences, schools of social work, schools of public affairs, a school of community resources and development and even a department of community, agriculture, recreation and resource studies. In some cases the teaching is accomplished through an interdisciplinary institute or a partnership between schools and colleges. In other cases, social entrepreneurship and social enterprise courses are found in multiple locations at one university. For example, Harvard University's School of Business offers a graduate course titled, 'Effective Leadership of Social Enterprise' whereas its Kennedy School of Government offers a graduate course titled, 'Entrepreneurship for Social Value Creation'.

Clearly, social entrepreneurship courses and leading programs are found within business schools. It is often the courses and programs emanating from such schools that garner the greatest public and media attention. However, it also clear that a review of educational courses and programs in the social entrepreneurship field is incomplete without a study of those models emerging elsewhere in the academy outside of the business school domain.

An analysis of academic unit(s) that houses one or more courses in social entrepreneurship is one helpful way to think about teaching in the

Table 3.1 Selected universities that offer one or more courses in social entrepreneurship by organizing academic unit and level of student/participant

Name of university	Organizing unit	Type of offering
Arizona State University	School of Community Resources and Development	• undergraduate • graduate • professional development/noncredit
Portland State University	School of Social Work	• graduate
University of Michigan	School of Social Work	• graduate
Indiana University	School of Public and Environmental Affairs	• graduate
Michigan State University	Department of Community, Agriculture, Recreation and Resource Studies	• noncredit/continuing education
University of Texas at San Antonio	Department of Public Administration	• noncredit/continuing education
Harvard University	• School of Business • School of Government	• graduate
State University of New York at Buffalo	School of Social Work	• graduate
Boston College	School of Social Work	• graduate
University of Colorado at Denver	School of Public Affairs	• graduate
School for International Training	Graduate and Professional Programs	• graduate
Brandeis University	School for Social Policy and Management	• graduate
Georgetown University	Public Policy Institute	• noncredit/continuing education
University of Wisconsin–Milwaukee	Interdisciplinary Institute	• noncredit/continuing education
Seattle University	College of Arts and Sciences	• undergraduate

Source: Seton Hall University, 2007.

field. Another analysis considers the type of offerings based upon student/participant levels in and market demand for such instruction. As noted in Table 3.1, among universities operating social entrepreneurship courses outside a business school, such offerings are found across the full range of undergraduate, graduate, continuing and professional education student markets. Some courses are offered for academic credit while others are offered as short-course, non-credit workshops. In addition to considering the academic organizing unit, it is also helpful to consider approaches to teaching social entrepreneurship, beyond disciplinary perspectives, based upon student market demand. Table 3.1 also reveals that selected programs have been designed at all levels including undergraduate, graduate, executive education, and non-credit professional development offerings.

FRAMING THE TEACHING OF SOCIAL ENTREPRENEURSHIP – A CASE STUDY

Arizona State University (ASU) is an example of one university where social entrepreneurship curricula has been developed outside of the school of business. Organized by ASU's Lodestar Center for Philanthropy and Nonprofit Innovation (hereafter, the Center) – a nonprofit academic center – and developed in concert with a multi-disciplinary School of Community Resources and Development (SCRD), the evolution of ASU's social entrepreneurship curriculum provides a case study worth noting.

The Center was created in 1999 within ASU's College of Public Programs to 'help build the capacity of the social sector by enhancing the effectiveness of those who lead, manage, and support nonprofit organizations'. As such, the Center was developed through a partnership of academics, nonprofit practitioners, funders and community leaders coming together to provide knowledge and tools to build the capacity of nonprofit organizations, professionals, board members and volunteers by offering research, technical assistance, workshops, conferences, classes, and capacity building programs. The Center grew from a successful undergraduate nonprofit leadership and management program initiated at ASU in 1980. The undergraduate program is affiliated with American Humanics, Inc., a Kansas City, MO-based national nonprofit education organization founded in 1948, now operating on more than 70 campuses, to prepare and certify students for the nonprofit career field. The Center also grew from a commitment to professional development education resulting in the founding of the university's Nonprofit Management Institute (NMI) in 1992. NMI grew from a partnership between the Phoenix area's United Way and ASU's extended education college. It was moved into the Center for Nonprofit Leadership and Management (now the Lodestar Center) in 2003 as the Center's professional development education enterprise. As conceived, the Center serves as the university's organizing unit 'umbrella' for developing and supporting the range of nonprofit education programs at the undergraduate, graduate and professional development education levels.

Student Marketing and Motivations

Because the Center is organized as a comprehensive nonprofit academic center designed to be responsive to stakeholder needs, market demand for social entrepreneurship curricula could not be ignored. In general, three distinct student markets emerged as desiring the subject matter with each exhibiting various motivations as follows:

1. Undergraduate students
   (a) students already working as an entry-level nonprofit professional within an existing nonprofit and captivated by the notion of entrepreneurship;
   (b) students with social concerns and some notions about creating a nonprofit to help with that social concern;
   (c) students exploring various subject areas but lacking specific goal clarification about applying knowledge learned in any real way.
2. Graduate students
   (a) current nonprofit professionals yearning for new skills to move up in their current organization or elsewhere at greater levels of responsibility and salary;
   (b) a re-careerist desiring to move into the nonprofit sector for the first time from the business or government sectors;
   (c) a self-identified social entrepreneur desiring some assistance to take an idea and go to some scale; and
   (d) a student with exploratory interest in subject area within their larger nonprofit studies degree program.
3. Professional development education students
   (a) nonprofit practitioners, often with advanced degrees, desiring immediately useable knowledge to hone skills for developing and implementing earned-income strategies;
   (b) a re-careerist desiring to move into the nonprofit sector for the first time from the business or government sectors; and
   (c) an individual motivated around some cause or concern and desiring to create a nonprofit organization and the notion of social entrepreneurship seems to fit their motivation.

Table 3.2   Case study student markets and primary student/participant motivations for taking social entrepreneurship course(s)

Program	Primary student / participant market	Primary student / participant motivations
Undergraduate	Bachelor's degree-Seeking Students	• Entry level nonprofit job seekers • Desire to create new nonprofits • Exploratory interest in subject
Graduate	Masters degree-seeking Students; non-degree seeking students desiring post-baccalaureate education	• Existing nonprofit professional seeking upward job mobility • Re-careerist from other industry seeking nonprofit knowledge for career move • Non-degree seeking student interested in subject matter to take social idea to some scale by forming new nonprofit • Exploratory interest in subject area within a larger nonprofit studies degree program
Professional development education	Knowledge-seeking professionals	• Desiring immediately useable knowledge, especially earned income strategies, to apply directly in the workplace • Re-careerist from other industry seeking nonprofit knowledge for career move • Seeking subject matter to take social idea by forming new nonprofit

Table 3.2 provides a summary of the student/participant market and primary motivations observed within these markets. As such, the summary offers a new conceptual way to frame the student marketing and motivations that might inform the programmatic design of social entrepreneurship educational programs.

Conceptual and Content Considerations for Social Entrepreneurship Course Offerings

To meet these market demands the Center developed curricular offerings for both degree-seeking students (undergraduate and graduate) and for professional development education participants. At each level, instruction considers two convergent streams of conceptual thought, activity and impact associated with the field of social entrepreneurship. First is the role of social entrepreneurs, defined as, 'society's change agents: pioneers of innovations that benefit humanity' (Skoll Foundation, 2007). This understanding of leadership characteristics of such entrepreneurs reveals the application of selected business principles to social issues. The nonprofit organization form is examined as both an independent entity and one that is interdependent on government and commerce for long-term viability and sustainability. This understanding of individual and organizational dynamics leads to an examination of social enterprise, the second major stream of content for the curriculum that is defined as, 'any earned-income business or strategy undertaken by a nonprofit to generate revenue in support of its charitable mission. "Earned income" consists of payments received in direct exchange for a product, service or privilege' (Social Enterprise Alliance, 2007). To guide the overall framework for these courses is the definition of social entrepreneurship as promulgated by faculty and staff of the Center, which is, 'the creation of social value through the innovative application of the best of for-profit and nonprofit practices, including the diversification of income sources with earned income strategies'.

Considering this overarching definition therefore places social entrepreneurship within a broader context that includes effective nonprofit practice and embeds the topic inside a larger and more comprehensive curricular program. While a student or participant may enroll in a single course or workshop only to obtain the content related to social entrepreneurship, the course(s) are contextualized within a broader and more comprehensive emerging field of study known as nonprofit leadership and management education, philanthropic studies, or more generally, nonprofit studies. Social entrepreneurship and social enterprise, therefore is not considered as a course topic in isolation to the broader field of study concerned with civil society, the role of philanthropy (voluntary action for the common good), the intersection of the nonprofit sector with government and business forms, and other considerations.

Curricular Framework in Building the Field of Nonprofit Studies

As posited in this chapter, social entrepreneurship education at ASU teaches students about how social value is created through innovative and effective practice and includes an examination of earned income strategies. The courses are taught within the context of a larger set of political, economic and social considerations found within communities both nationwide and worldwide. The courses are not mutually exclusive to subject matter taught within a broader curriculum of nonprofit leadership and management (undergraduate) and nonprofit studies (graduate). Participants in noncredit offerings (professional development education) receive similar content with a greater premium placed on immediately useable knowledge that can be directly applied to practice upon completion of the course content. Given this learning scaffolding, what guides the curricular framework for such a program if not within a business school structure?

For programs like those at ASU, the guiding framework is provided by the Nonprofit Academic Centers Council (NACC). NACC was established in 1991 as an association comprised of member academic centers or programs at colleges and universities that focus on the study of nonprofit organizations, voluntarism and/or philanthropy. NACC is the first group entirely dedicated to the promotion and networking of academic centers that provide research and education in philanthropy and the nonprofit sector. It is within NACC institutions that the field of nonprofit management and philanthropic studies education is being advanced through curricular guidelines at both the undergraduate and graduate levels. In many ways NACC has emerged as the primary intellectual content driver of the field and it is within their guidelines that the content for social entrepreneurship/ social enterprise curricula is also being advanced. NACC does not accredit programs and the guidelines are offered to suggest content areas for universities serious about offering high quality academic programs in the field. NACC does not suggest that each major heading be an individual class, nor do they suggest the guidelines be treated in sequence as if one heading is a prerequisite for another.

Whereas social entrepreneurship may be taught as a single course within or outside a university's business school, NACC's approach is to develop comprehensive guidelines that represent fully developed content for degree programs in the field as opposed to guidelines for a specific course. Of the nearly 50 university members of NACC, the majority of members are from academic centers whose core disciplines reside outside business to include public affairs, social work and interdisciplinary units. Business schools represent less than 10 percent of NACC membership. NACC's approach to curricular guidelines is interdisciplinary in that members contribute expertise form their disciplines in creating the guidelines and the membership adopts them through both a vetting and voting process.

Undergraduate Curriculum Considerations

The NACC curricular guidelines for undergraduate degree programs include content for what students should know about the nonprofit sector and the role of philanthropy in society. They also include a focus on careers in the nonprofit sector for students desiring an applied approach to their education. The guidelines are updated annually and NACC should be consulted directly for the latest iterations. However, if social entrepreneurship is also about innovative and effective practice, then the subject is appropriate to any number of content areas including sections such as 'foundations of philanthropy and the nonprofit sector', 'ethics and values', and 'leading and managing nonprofits'. The following framework provides categories and summations of core content within each major heading of the *NACC Curricular Guidelines for Undergraduate Study in Nonprofit Leadership, the Nonprofit Sector and Philanthropy* (NACC, 2007) (social entrepreneurship and social enterprise are embedded within the nonprofit economics content section; therefore that section below is expanded. The other categories representing the guidelines are noted only by their major headings. Addendum 1 contains all categories and sub-categories):

- Foundations of philanthropy and the nonprofit sector
- Global and comparative perspectives on voluntary action
- Ethics and values
- Nonprofit economics

Economic theory as it applies to the nonprofit sector and as understood in multi-sector economies; the impact of market dynamics on the sector as a whole, within nonprofit sub-sectors and between and among the public, for-profit and nonprofit sectors; Recent and emerging trends such as social enterprise, micro-enterprise and entrepreneurship, and their implications for nonprofit performance and for mission achievement:

- Advocacy, public policy and the law
- Nonprofit governance and leadership
- Leading and managing organizations
- Nonprofit finance and resource development
- Financial management
- Managing staff and volunteers
- Nonprofit marketing
- Professional and career development

Graduate Curriculum Considerations

The NACC curricular guidelines for graduate programs consider the range of content areas appropriate to full degree programs. As with the undergraduate guidelines, if innovative and effective practice is considered an expression of social entrepreneurship, then several content areas pertain included under the headings of 'History and theories of philanthropy, voluntarism and the nonprofit sector', 'Ethics and values', and 'Leadership, organization and management'. Also as with the undergraduate guidelines, updates are made annually to the graduate program content and NACC should be consulted directly for the latest iterations. The following framework provides categories and summations of core content within each major heading of the *NACC Curricular Guidelines for Graduate Study in Nonprofit Leadership, the Nonprofit Sector and Philanthropy* (social entrepreneurship and social enterprise are found within the 'Nonprofit finance, resource development and fund-raising management' section specifically and is expanded below. The other categories representing the guidelines are noted only by their major headings. Addendum 2 contains all categories and sub-categories):

- Scope and significance of philanthropy and voluntarism in a global context
- History and theories of philanthropy, voluntarism and the nonprofit sector
- Global and comparative perspectives on voluntary action
- Ethics and values
- Nonprofit governance and leadership
- Advocacy and public policy
- Nonprofit law
- Nonprofit economics
- Nonprofit finance, resource development and fund-raising management

Theory of nonprofit finance, including knowledge of the various types of revenues pursued by nonprofit organizations, the strategic choices and issues associated with each type of revenue, and the methods used to generate these revenues; the relationship between and among earned income, government funding and philanthropic gifts and grants, and how they influence fulfillment of an organization's mission; the history and function of philanthropic gifts and grants as distinctive dimensions of the nonprofit sector as well as the various strategies and techniques that are part of a comprehensive fund development process; the emergence, growth and implications of government funding as a significant source of sector revenue; the history, expansion and implications of earned income as a significant source of nonprofit sector revenue; recent and emerging trends in sources of sector revenue (e.g., micro-enterprise, social enterprise and entrepreneurship) and a critical examination of their use as a means of and for mission achievement

- Financial management and accountability
- Leadership, organization and management
- Human resource management
- Nonprofit marketing
- Information technology and management
- Assessment, evaluation and decision-making methods

Continuing and Professional Education Considerations

NACC does not provide curricular guidelines for continuing and professional education offerings in the field of Nonprofit Leadership, the Nonprofit Sector and Philanthropy and therefore there is none related to social entrepreneurship and social enterprise. Generally, professional development education is fee-based, cost-recovered and based upon market demand for content. At times costs are underwritten by funders who have a particular interest in capacity building around a certain content theme. Guiding an offering to this student market, therefore, is about honing a curriculum to that is often immediately useable by practitioners. A premium is placed on short courses and workshops that provide applicable knowledge and tools. Such training responds to frequently asked questions by stakeholders desiring such training that allows them to recognize and pursue opportunities to create social value by crafting innovative approaches to addressing social needs in a community.

Four general headings with corresponding questions frame the demand and response to professional development education in social entrepreneurship:

- *Sustainability issues:* How can I sustain my nonprofit through earned income strategies? How do social entrepreneurs fund their enterprises?
- *Impact and performance issues:* What is the impact of the enterprise under question? What tools exist to measure the impact and effectiveness of social enterprises and how do I use them?
- *Leadership issues:* How do I lead others to think and act in entrepreneurial ways? How do I engage volunteers, staff, board leaders and others in ways that are culturally competent, values based and congruent with our mission?
- *Innovation issues:* what new and innovative approaches are there that I can learn from in either creating a new nonprofit or taking an existing nonprofit with which I'm affiliated to new levels of mission attainment?

CONCLUSION

The teaching of entrepreneurship, especially social entrepreneurship, often occurs outside business schools. A growing field of study at all levels (undergraduate, graduate, professional development) is evident as noted by the plethora of university programs now offered in nonprofit leadership and management, the nonprofit sector, philanthropy and social entrepreneurship. Arizona State University is one example of where social entrepreneurship curriculum has been developed outside of its school of business. The teaching of social entrepreneurship as broadly conceived concerns itself with leadership characteristics of social entrepreneurs, the application of selected business principles to social issues, the examination of the nonprofit form and its relationship to government and business, and earned income strategies through enterprise models. Professional Development education provides a more narrow approach to the field in response to market demand for immediately useable knowledge and tools provided through short-course training workshops. Teaching social entrepreneurship outside a business school and within a defined undergraduate and graduate degree program in nonprofit and philanthropic studies, such as the program at ASU, also involves understanding the role of voluntary action and nonprofits in shaping civil society and a myriad of other social, economic and political considerations. The Nonprofit Academic Centers Council is an interdisciplinary national organization of university-based members that develops curricular guidelines at the undergraduate and graduate levels for the field, including topics related to social entrepreneurship and social enterprise.

REFERENCES

American Association of Colleges of Schools of Business (2007), *Member Schools with Social Entrepreneurship Programs*, retrieved from: http://www.aacsb.edu/members/communities/interestgrps/socialdoc.asp (14 August).

Nonprofit Academic Centers Council (2007), *Curricular Guidelines for Undergraduate Study in Nonprofit Leadership, the Nonprofit Sector and Philanthropy*, Cleveland, OH: Nonprofit Academic Centers Council.

Seton Hall University (2007), *Nonprofit Management Education: Current Offerings in University-Based Programs Site*, retrieved from http://tltc.shu.edu/npo/ (15 August).

Skoll Foundation (2007), retrieved from Skoll Foundation's Web site: http://www.skollfoundation.org/skollcentre/skoll_forum.asp (14 August).

Social Enterprise Alliance (2007), retrieved from http://www.se-alliance.org (14 August).

University Network for Social Entrepreneurship (2007), retrieved from http://www.universitynetwork.org (15 June).

APPENDIX 1: UNDERGRADUATE GUIDELINES –
2007 – NONPROFIT ACADEMIC CENTERS COUNCIL

Part I: The Role of the Nonprofit/Voluntary Sector in Society

1.0 Comparative Perspectives on Civil Society, Voluntary Action, and Philanthropy

    1.1   The structure – both formal and informal, individual and collective – of civil society and philanthropy across cultures and contexts

    1.2   How individual philanthropy, voluntary behavior and volunteerism is expressed in different cultural contexts

    1.3   The role of voluntary action and nonprofit organizations in social movements and social change

    1.4   The role of various religious traditions in shaping civil society and philanthropy

2.0 Foundations of Civil Society, Voluntary Action, and Philanthropy

    2.1   The history, role and functions of civil society and voluntary action organizations (nonprofit, nongovernmental, voluntary) across time and place

    2.2   The size, impact and trends in philanthropy and associational development throughout the world

    2.3   The diversity of forms of philanthropic action and the diversity of fields of activity

    2.4   The relationship and dynamics among the governmental, nonprofit, for-profit and household sectors

    2.5   Various theoretical explanations for the nonprofit/voluntary sector such as economic, political, sociological and anthropological

3.0 Ethics and Values

    3.1   The values embodied in philanthropy and voluntary action, such as trust, stewardship, service, voluntarism, freedom of association and social justice

    3.2   The foundations and theories of ethics as a discipline and as applied in order to make ethical decisions

    3.3   Issues arising out of the various dimensions of diversity and their implications for mission achievement in nonprofit organizations

    3.4   The standards and codes of conduct that are appropriate to professionals and volunteers working in philanthropy and the nonprofit sector

4.0 Public Policy, Law, Advocacy and Social Change

    4.1   Key public policies and their past, current and potential impact on the nonprofit sector, nonprofit organizations and philanthropic behaviors

4.2   The legal frameworks under which nonprofit organizations operate and are regulated

4.3   Legal and tax implications related to various kinds of nonprofit activity, including charitable giving, advocacy, lobbying, and any commercial activities of tax-exempt nonprofit organizations

4.4   The roles of individuals and nonprofit organizations in effecting social change and influencing the public policy process

4.5   How individuals and nonprofit organizations shape public policy through strategies such as public education, policy research, community organizing, lobbying, and litigation

5.0 Nonprofit Governance and Leadership

5.1   The role of nonprofit boards and executives in providing leadership at the organizational, community and societal levels

5.2   The history, role and functions of nonprofit governing boards and how these roles and functions compare to governing boards in the public and for-profit sectors

5.3   The role of nonprofit boards and nonprofit executives as agent(s) of and for social change and social justice at both the organizational and societal level

6.0 Community Service and Civic Engagement

6.1   The value of community service and civic engagement in the development of civil society

6.2   Direct exposure to nonprofit organizations through internships, service learning, community service and/or experiential learning

Part II: Leading and Managing Nonprofit Organizations

7.0 Leading and Managing Organizations

7.1   The steps and processes involved in establishing a nonprofit organization

7.2   Organizational theories and behavior as they apply in nonprofit and voluntary organizations including issues of work design and implications of operational policies and practices

7.3   Theories of leadership and leadership styles

7.4   The role of strategic management and organizational planning, including an understanding of ways to identify, assess and formulate appropriate strategies

7.5   The role of networks, partnerships and collaborative activity in achieving organizational missions

7.6   Methods that managers use to evaluate performance at both organizational and programmatic levels

8.0 Nonprofit Finance and Fundraising
  8.1 Theory of nonprofit finance, including the various sources of revenues in nonprofit organizations, the strategic choices and issues associated with each type of revenue, and the methods used to generate these revenues
  8.2 The relationship between and among philanthropic gifts and grants, earned income, and government funding and how they influence fulfillment of an organization's mission
  8.3 The fund development process and commonly-used fundraising strategies, such as annual appeals, special events, non-cash contributions, major gifts, capital campaigns and planned giving
  8.4 Recent and emerging trends such as social enterprise, micro-enterprise and entrepreneurship, and their implications for nonprofit performance and for mission achievement
9.0 Financial Management
  9.1 Application of accounting principles and concepts including financial and managerial accounting systems (including fund accounting) in nonprofit organizations
  9.2 Financial management including financial planning and budgeting, management of cash flows, short- and long-term financing, and endowment management policies and practices
10.0 Managing Staff and Volunteers
  10.1 Human resource processes and practices in both formal and informal nonprofit organizations and how human resource issues, as experienced in nonprofit organizations, are different from the experience in public and for-profit organizations
  10.2 Teamwork and group dynamics and their implications for supervision, staff development and organizational performance
  10.3 The role, value and dynamics of volunteerism in carrying out the work and fulfilling the missions of nonprofit organizations
  10.4 Issues of supervision and human resource management processes and systems for both staff and volunteers
  10.5 The dimensions of individual and organizational diversity within the nonprofit sector and their implications for effective human resource management
11.0 Nonprofit Marketing
  11.1 Marketing principles and techniques and their application in philanthropic and nonprofit settings, including the dynamics and principles of marketing 'mission' in a nonprofit context
  11.2 The link between marketing theories and concepts and their use in nonprofit organizations

12.0 Assessment, Evaluation and Decision-Making Methods
-   12.1   Methods and modes of assessment and evaluation
-   12.2   Decision-making models and methods and how to apply them in nonprofit organizational settings
-   12.3   The use and application of both quantitative and qualitative data in improving the effectiveness of nonprofit organizations
-   12.4   The role of information and technology in the pursuit of a nonprofit organization's mission

13.0 Professional and Career Development
-   13.1   Field experiences that are grounded in and linked to curricular goals and projected outcomes
-   13.2   The role of professional associations and mentoring in professional development
-   13.3   The ways that various professionals contribute to and are engaged with philanthropic and nonprofit sectors
-   13.4   Opportunities for service and volunteerism that exist in the community
-   13.5   The standards and context of professionalism, e.g., conduct and speech appropriate to the (respective) profession

APPENDIX 2: GRADUATE GUIDELINES – 2007 – NONPROFIT ACADEMIC CENTERS COUNCIL

Curricular Guidelines for Graduate Study in Nonprofit Leadership, the Nonprofit Sector and Philanthropy

1.0 Comparative Perspectives on the Nonprofit Sector, Voluntary Action and Philanthropy

    1.1   The impact of global social, economic and political trends on the role and function of voluntary action, civil society, the nonprofit sector and philanthropy

    1.2   How individual philanthropy, voluntary behavior and volunteerism is expressed in different cultural contexts

    1.3   The structure and regulation of philanthropic and voluntary behavior within different political contexts, including formal, informal and alternative associational forms

    1.4   The role of various religious traditions in shaping philanthropy and voluntary behavior

2.0 Scope and Significance of the Nonprofit Sector, Voluntary Action and Philanthropy

    2.1   The role and function of philanthropic, nonprofit, voluntary and civil society organizations

    2.2   The size, impact of, and trends in philanthropy, voluntarism and the nonprofit/nongovernmental sector

    2.3   The diversity of types, forms and language that is used to describe voluntary action within society

    2.4   The diversity of activity undertaken by nonprofit, voluntary and civil society organizations, including both charitable and mutual benefit organizations, as well as those formally and informally structured

    2.5   The relationship and dynamics among and between the nonprofit, government and for-profit sectors

3.0 History and Theories of the Nonprofit Sector, Voluntary Action and Philanthropy

    3.1   The history and development of philanthropy, voluntarism, voluntary action, and the nonprofit sector within particular contexts and how this experience compares to the development of comparable sectors in various parts of the world

    3.2   Civil society, social movements and related concepts that are important to our understanding of philanthropic behavior and voluntary action

3.3   Theoretical explanations of the emergence of the nonprofit sector, including (but not necessarily limited to) political, economic, religious and socio-cultural perspectives

4.0 Ethics and Values

4.1   Values embodied in philanthropy and voluntary action, such as trust, stewardship, service, voluntarism, civic engagement, freedom of association and social justice

4.2   The foundations and theories of ethics as a discipline and as applied in order to make ethical decisions

4.3   Issues arising out of the various dimensions of diversity and their implications for mission achievement

4.4   Standards and codes of conduct that are appropriate to professionals and volunteers working in philanthropy and the nonprofit sector

5.0 Nonprofit Governance and Leadership

5.1   The role of nonprofit boards and executives in providing leadership at the organizational, community and societal levels

5.2   The history and function of governance and the role of boards and executive leadership in achieving the mission and vision of nonprofit organizations

5.3   The history, role and functions of nonprofit governing boards and how these roles and functions compare to governing boards in the public and for-profit sectors

5.4   The role of nonprofit boards and nonprofit executives as leaders whose role is both to make strategic choices that will lead to greater mission achievement and advocate for those being served by the work of the nonprofit organization

5.5   The process of board development as a tool to not only create effective governing boards but also to ensure a successful board-executive relationship

6.0 Public Policy, Advocacy and Social Change

6.1   The various roles of nonprofit organizations and voluntary action in effecting social change and influencing the public policy process in both national and international contexts

6.2   Public policies of significance to the nonprofit sector and their past, current, and potential impact on the sector, nonprofit organizations, and philanthropic behaviors

6.3   How individuals as well as nonprofit organizations can shape public policy through strategies such as community organizing, public education, policy research, lobbying, and litigation

6.4   The role of board members, staff and volunteers as agents of and for social change, grounded in particular mission-driven efforts

7.0 Nonprofit Law
- 7.1 The legal frameworks within which nonprofit organizations operate and are regulated
- 7.2 The legal rights and obligations of directors, trustees, officers and members of nonprofit and voluntary organizations
- 7.3 Legal and tax implications related to charitable giving, advocacy, lobbying, political and commercial activities of tax-exempt nonprofit organizations
- 7.4 Oversight responsibilities of national and sub-national regulatory bodies

8.0 Nonprofit Economics
- 8.1 Economic theory as it applies to the nonprofit sector and as understood in multi-sector economies
- 8.2 The impact of market dynamics on the sector as a whole, within nonprofit sub-sectors and between and among the public, for-profit and nonprofit sectors

9.0 Nonprofit Finance
- 9.1 Theory of nonprofit finance, including knowledge of the various types of revenues pursued by nonprofit organizations, the strategic choices and issues associated with each type of revenue, and the methods used to generate these revenues
- 9.2 The relationship between and among earned income, government funding and philanthropic gifts and grants as sources of revenue, and how each can influence fulfillment of an organization's mission
- 9.3 The history and function of philanthropic gifts and grants as distinctive dimensions of the nonprofit sector
- 9.4 The emergence, growth and implications of government funding as a significant source of sector revenue
- 9.5 The history, expansion and implications of earned income as a significant source of nonprofit sector revenue
- 9.6 Recent and emerging trends in sources of sector revenue, e.g., micro-enterprise, social enterprise and entrepreneurship, and a critical examination of their use as a means of and for mission achievement

10.0 Fundraising and Development
- 10.1 The various forms and structures in and through which organized philanthropy occurs
- 10.2 Components and elements that are part of a comprehensive fund development process

11.0 Financial Management and Accountability
- 11.1 The role and function of financial literacy, transparency and stewardship in the effective oversight and management of nonprofit organizational resources

11.2 Application of accounting principles and concepts including financial and managerial accounting systems (including fund accounting) in nonprofit organizations

11.3 The analysis and use of accounting information in financial statements and other reports as needed for responsible stewardship, including a critical examination of social accounting

11.4 Financial management including financial planning and budgeting, management of cash flows, short- and long-term financing, investment strategies, and endowment management policies and practices

12.0 Leadership, Organization and Management

12.1 Theories of leadership and an understanding of the role of leaders in building effective and sustainable organizations

12.2 Theories of organizational development and behavior and their application to nonprofit and voluntary organizations

12.3 What it means to 'manage to the mission', i.e., how management and accountability are different within nonprofit and voluntary organizations

12.4 The role, value and dynamics of multiple stakeholders and networks in carrying out activities and fulfilling the mission

12.5 The role of strategic thinking and management, organizational planning and project management, including an ability to identify, assess and formulate appropriate strategies and plans

12.6 The role of nonprofit leaders in generating new ideas and new strategies to meet needs in the community

13.0 Nonprofit Human Resource Management

13.1 Human resource issues within both formal and informal nonprofit organizations and how human resource issues in nonprofit organizations are different from the experience in public and for-profit organizations

13.2 The role, value and dynamics of volunteerism in carrying out the work and fulfilling the missions of nonprofit organizations

13.3 Issues of supervision and human resource management systems and practices relevant to both paid and unpaid employees

13.4 The dimensions and dynamics of individual and organizational diversity within the nonprofit sector and their implications for effective human resource management

14.0 Nonprofit Marketing

14.1 Marketing theory, principles and techniques, in general, and as applied in a philanthropic and nonprofit environment (including the dynamics and principles of marketing 'mission' in a nonprofit context)

14.2 The specific application of marketing theories to the development of financial and non-financial sources of support, e.g., fundraising, social marketing and entrepreneurial ventures

14.3 The link between marketing theories and concepts and their use in nonprofit organizations, e.g., strategies in organizational communication and public relations

14.4 Stakeholder theory and its effective use and function in the nonprofit context

15.0 Information Technology and Management

15.1 Roles of information and technology in advancing the causes of civil society

15.2 The appropriate use and application of information technology in order to increase productivity and effectiveness in the pursuit of a nonprofit organization's mission

15.3 The types, sources and location of information that is useful to the effective operation of nonprofit organizations

15.4 How various technologies can be used to assess nonprofit performance and effectiveness

16.0 Assessment, Evaluation and Decision-Making Methods

16.1 Methods and modes to evaluate performance and effectiveness at both organizational and programmatic levels

16.2 Decision-making models and methods and how to apply them in nonprofit organizational settings

16.3 The use and application of both quantitative and qualitative data for purposes of strengthening nonprofit organizations, the nonprofit sector and the larger society

PART 2

Non-market entrepreneurship: society and economy

4. Non-market sources of American entrepreneurial capitalism

Zoltan J. Acs, Ronnie J. Phillips, David B. Audretsch and Sameeksha Desai

INTRODUCTION

The success of the American economy over time has been linked to its entrepreneurial spirit. Individual initiative and creativity, along with small business and wealth creation, are indelible parts of the American spirit. The recent technological revolution and resulting economic restructuring have made both the general public and government officials keenly aware of the entrepreneur's role in job and wealth creation (Hebert and Link, 1989). This critical role in economic development has fostered efforts by all levels of government to promote entrepreneurship (Hart, 2001).

However, another crucial component of American economic, political and social stability is increasingly recognized: Philanthropy. Merle Curti in 1957 advanced the hypothesis that 'philanthropy has been one of the major aspects of and keys to American social and cultural development' (Curti, 1957: 353). To this we would add that philanthropy has also been crucial in economic development. Further, when combined with entrepreneurship, the entrepreneurship-philanthropy nexus (Acs and Phillips, 2002) becomes a potent force in explaining the long-run dominance of the American economy.

A major difference between American capitalism and many other forms of capitalism[1] (Japanese, French, German and Scandinavian) is a historic focus on both the creation of wealth (*entrepreneurship*) and the reconstitution of wealth (*philanthropy*). Philanthropy is imbedded within an implicit social contract that stipulates wealth beyond a certain point should revert to society (Chernow, 1999). Although individuals are free to accumulate wealth, it must be invested back into society to expand opportunity (Acs and Dana, 2001). In this chapter, we cast the United States as the unique product of a certain type of human character and social role, one which produced the English Revolution and modern American civilization. In this character type, the agent possessed unprecedented new powers of discretion and self-reliance, yet was bound to collective ends by novel emerging forms of institutional authority and internal restraint (Dewey, 1963).[2] Much of the new wealth in the US has historically been given back to the community to build up the great social institutions that, in turn, pave the way for future economic growth.[3]

Though it is recognized that the philanthropists of the nineteenth century enabled the foundation for wealth creation and social stability, this has not been quantified within the framework of private and social costs and benefits (America, 1995). Take, for example, the challenge of calculating the *ex post* benefits of the establishment of the University of Chicago by the Rockefeller family. Certainly, there was no immediate private benefit to the donor family and contributions occurred several generations later. The number of Nobel Prize winners at the university is perhaps just one measure of social benefits that emerge from the original investment. The complexity of measuring (and even identifying) *ex post* benefits demonstrates that the entrepreneurship-philanthropy nexus has not been fully understood – neither by either economists nor the general public. This is, in part, due to an intellectually restrictive view of self-interest as a (perhaps *the*) fundamental driver of capitalism.

The purpose of this chapter is to suggest that American philanthropists – especially those who have made their own fortunes – create foundations that, in turn, contribute to greater and more widespread economic prosperity through opportunity, knowledge creation and entrepreneurship. This was Andrew Carnegie's hope when he wrote about 'the responsibility of wealth' more than 100 years ago, which has translated for today's entrepreneurs as 'giving back'. In the new global economy, philanthropy holds promise as a proponent of renewed growth and prosperity, as the new rich of the twenty-first century have the opportunity to shape American and global society. The founders of modern American philanthropy tried to provide answers to problems that were national in scope, at a time when national government was weak. Similarly, today's philanthropists have the chance to address problems that are global in scope, at a time when global institutions are even weaker (Soros, 1998). We suggest that by analyzing philanthropy, we are better able to understand both the process of economic development and an underlying reason for American economic dominance.

In the next section we examine the economics of philanthropy and altruism as individual behavior. In the third section, we provide a brief background on the origins of philanthropy in American history, and discuss some of its early contribution to economic prosperity. The fourth section outlines strengths of American capitalism – namely entrepreneurship, innovation and wealth creation. The fifth section examines philanthropy in the new 'Gilded Age' and asks how well the institutions of the philanthropic sector are meeting the goals of creating economic opportunity. We provide conclusions and implications for policymakers, foundations and the intellectual community in the final section.

THE ECONOMICS OF PHILANTHROPY AND ALTRUISM

The word philanthropy literally means 'love of mankind' and philanthropic acts depend upon the generosity of the giver. Although we do not seek to define philanthropy or evaluate competing definitions, we would like to describe the concept. In this chapter, we take philanthropy as: *Giving money or its equivalent to persons and institutions outside the family without a definite or immediate* quid pro quo *for purposes traditionally considered philanthropic.* Soloman Fabricant discussed the relationship of philanthropy to economic development (Dickinson, 1970: 8):

> in this broad sense philanthropy is a necessary condition of social existence, and the extent to which it is developed influences an economy's productiveness. For decent conduct pays large returns to society as a whole, partly in the form of a higher level of national income than would otherwise be possible. Underdeveloped countries are learning that, despite their hurry to reach desired levels of economic efficiency, time must be taken to develop the kind of business ethics, respect for the law, and treatment of strangers that keep a modern industrial society productive. Widening of the concepts of family loyalty and tribal brotherhood to include love a man 'in general' is a necessary step in the process of economic development.

Economists from Adam Smith (1937 (1776)) onwards have recognized the role of self-interest in the creation of wealth, through the assumption that self-interest is the underlying motivation behind human exchange. Critics of capitalism, notably Karl Marx, focused on negative effects, especially its resulting maldistribution of wealth. Indeed, although wealthy entrepreneurs of the nineteenth century certainly provided the impetus for Thorstein Veblen's (1899) 'leisure class', they were, at the same time, also great philanthropists (Sugden, 1982).

When economists confront philanthropic behavior, they seek the *quid pro quo* behind the act. They conclude that although behavior appears to be altruistic, it is fundamentally consistent with self-interest. Contemporary economic theory has largely ignored the possibility of purely altruistic behavior (though with notable exceptions – see Margolis, 1982; Sugden, 1982),[4] and this habit of explaining all behavior as inherently and ultimately self-interested leaves much to be clarified, specifically with respect to philanthropy.

We argue that altruism is different from[5] – and more than – enlightened self-interest. Although Adam Smith noted the centrality of self-interest in *The Wealth of Nations*[6] (1937 (1776)), he indicates a larger motivation in *The Theory of Moral Sentiments* (1969 (1759), which predates *The Wealth of Nations* by nearly two decades. Smith suggests (1969 (1759), 47):

> How selfish soever man may be supposed, there are evidently some principles of his nature, which interest him in the fortune of others, and render their happiness necessary to him, though he derives nothing from it, except the pleasure of seeing it.

The behavior described by above appears consistent with modern economics, specifically the premise that 'utility' is derived from the choices on which one's income may be spent. Starting from this, economists have generated interdependent utility functions, so that the utility ('happiness' or 'satisfaction') one person receives is dependent upon that of another (Ireland, 1969; Kaufman, 1993; Sugden, 1982; Danielsen, 1975).

However, Kenneth Boulding suggests that although 'it is tempting for the economist to argue that there are really no gifts and that all transactions involve some kind of exchange, that is, some kind of *quid pro quo*' (Boulding, 1962: 57–8), such an approach seriously misleads us because there is nothing in utility theory that requires all motivations to be alike. Indeed, in Boulding's view, the motivation leading to philanthropic behavior – where there is no *quid pro quo* – 'may be very different from that which leads us to build up a personal estate or to purchase consumption goods for our own use' (Boulding, 1962: 61). Boulding develops this further by drawing a parallel between the self-interested orientation of modern economics with its development of a theory of the firm (collection of individuals) and with individual philanthropic behavior and a theory of philanthropic foundations. There are two basic approaches of the foundations. One, like the Ford Foundation, is to give money to a variety of individuals (a large number of grantees) and projects and presumably allocates dollars so the marginal benefit is equal across all units. The other is behavior that Boulding speculates may have done more for higher education – such as the Rockefellers' establishment of a single strong University of Chicago (Boulding, 1962: 65).

Further, the neo-classical assumption of utility maximization neglects to specify what utility actually is, making it impossible to separate altruism from selfishness (Simon, 1983: 158). Simon defines altruism as 'sacrifice of fitness'. It is then possible (in principle) to determine which choices are selfish or altruistic by examining the effect of a million dollar gift, for example, on the number of progeny of the donor (Simon, 1993: 158). Simon concludes that economic theory has treated economic gain as the primary human motive, but an empirically grounded theory would assign comparable weight to other motives, including altruism and the organizational identification associated with it (Simon, 1993: 160).

Is philanthropic behavior always self-interest motivated, i.e., is there always a *quid pro quo*? Or is there also behavior, as Boulding argues, where there is no *quid pro quo*? We argue that the vitality of American capitalism is testament to the importance of non-self-interest motivated behavior, and also that altruism is superior to enlightened self-interest. Hence, an economic theory that adequately explains the real world must explicitly introduce altruistic behavior into its models of individual behavior (Simon, 1993; Budd, 1956; Giddings, 1893). We consider US history an example of the superiority of altruism over enlightened self-interest, and this has been crucial to economic prosperity over time.

THE CONTRIBUTIONS OF THE NINETEENTH CENTURY PHILANTHROPISTS

Studying philanthropy in the context of economic prosperity is not a new idea. In *Corruption and the Decline of Rome*, Ramsay MacMullen (1988) notes how charitable foundations were partly responsible for the flourishing of Rome, and that their decline coincided with the loss of the empire. The roots of American philanthropy begin in England, in the period 1480–1660. By the end of the Elizabethan period, 'it was generally agreed that all men must somehow be sustained at the level of subsistence' (Jordan, 1961: 401). Though charitable organizations at the beginning of this period were centered around religion, religious charities comprised only 7 percent of all charities by the end of the sixteenth century (Jordan, 1961: 402).

How is this philanthropic behavior explained? According to Jordan, there existed a partly religious and partly secular sensitivity to human suffering in sixteenth-century England (Jordan, 1961: 406). Another important motivating factor was Calvinism, which taught that 'the rich man is a trustee for wealth which he disposes for benefit of mankind, as a steward who lies under direct obligation to do Christ's will' (Jordan, 1961: 406–7).

The real founders of American philanthropy, then, were the English men and women who crossed the Atlantic to establish communities better than those at home[7] (Owen, 1964). Beginning with the Puritans, who regarded excessive profit-making as both a crime and a sin,[8] there is a long tradition of Americans questioning the right of people to become rich. Puritan principles of industry, frugality and humility had an enduring impact on America (Tocqueville, 1966 (1835)). In view of the popular prejudice against ostentatious enjoyment of riches, the *luxury of doing good* was almost the only extravagance the American rich of the first half of the nineteenth century could indulge in with good consciences (Tocqueville, 1966 (1835): 40; Veblen, 1899). To whatever extent this was true, things had certainly changed by the second half of the century when Carnegie, Mellon, Duke and others were making their fortunes.

Andrew Carnegie was the ideal Calvinist. Philanthropy was at the heart of his 'gospel of wealth' (Hamer, 1998). For Carnegie, the question was not only, 'How to gain wealth?' but, equally importantly, 'What to do with it?' *The Gospel of Wealth* suggested that millionaires administer their wealth as a public trust during their lives, as opposed to bequeathing to heirs or making benevolent grants by will (Carnegie, 1889). Both Carnegie (at the time) and Jordan (as a historian) suggest that a key motive for philanthropy is social order and harmony.[9]

In the past, the malefactors of great wealth were also benefactors of extraordinary generosity (Myers, 1907). In the US, much of the new wealth created historically has been given back to the community, and have built up the great social institutions *that have a positive feedback on future economic growth*. For example, many of the great private research universities (Stanford, MIT, Johns Hopkins, Carnegie-Mellon, Duke, University of Chicago) were created over a century ago by American philanthropy, and have played a critical role in recent American success (*The Economist*, 4 October 1997).

One of the greatest nineteenth-century philanthropists was George Peabody, who developed a philosophy of philanthropy that seemed to have two important considerations. One was a deep devotion to the communities in which he was reared or in which he made money. The other was a secular vision of the Puritan doctrine of the stewardship of riches: His desire, in the simplest terms, was to be useful to mankind. In his lifetime, he donated more than $8 million to libraries, science, housing, education, exploration, historical societies, hospitals, churches and other charities (Parker, 1971: 209). Peabody's most enduring influence, however, lies in the precedents and policies formulated by the Peabody Education Fund Trustees. This fund paved the way for future foundation aid to the South after the Civil War. Perhaps more importantly, it also influenced operational patterns of subsequent major foundations, including John D. Rockefeller's Education Board, the Russell Sage Foundation and the Carnegie Foundation. In this way, George Peabody is considered the founder of modern educational foundations (*Christian Science Monitor*, as cited in Parker, 1971: 208).

> George Peabody was in fact the originator of that system of endowed founda-
> tions for public purposes . . . It is interesting to consider the many ways in which
> the example set by [George Peabody] has been followed by visioned men of
> means in the United States . . . In a sense the Peabody Fund was not the only
> monument to George Peabody, for the example he set has been followed by a
> host of other Americans.

In 1867, Peabody explained his philanthropy to Johns Hopkins, a Baltimore merchant and financier: 'To place the millions I had accumulated, so as to accomplish the greatest good for humanity.' Hopkins donated his entire fortune of $8 million (an extraordinary amount of money at the time) to found the Johns Hopkins University, Medical School and Hospital (Brody, 1998). Each institution, which would have separate but closely linked boards of trustees, was given $3.5 million to establish itself. It was at the time the largest philanthropic bequest in US history. Thus Peabody, apart from his own charities, may honorably stand in the shadow of what Hopkins achieved (Offit, 1995).

The nineteenth century American model of entrepreneurship and philanthropy was followed by a period of progressivism[10] in the early twentieth-century and then by World War I. Though the 1920s was a period of technological change and prosperity, underlying economic problems resulted in the collapse of the world economy into the Great Depression of the 1930s. This period, along with World War II, changed the role of government and the philanthropic activities of the entrepreneur. It is not our point here to argue that the role of philanthropy was to provide social welfare – health insurance, social security, unemployment insurance. Indeed, the rise of the state in the twentieth century was in some ways a rise of social welfare provided by government.

This function, however, is distinct from the *pure function of philanthropy* that arises from issues of wealth accumulation. The rise of the welfare state (with its high marginal taxes, high inheritance taxes, anti-trust laws, and the abolition of private property in some societies) tried to eliminate the role of private wealth altogether. In fact, the only role for philanthropy in a socialist state might be religious giving. Interestingly, the rise of the welfare state in the United States did not coincide with a decline in philanthropy, as might be expected. In fact, according to a study by the National Bureau of Economic Research (Dickinson, 1970), total private domestic philanthropy as a percentage of Gross National Product between 1929 and 1959 increased from 1.7 per cent to 2.3 per cent. According to the Johns Hopkins nonprofit sector project, this figure is the highest in the world, followed by Spain, Britain and Hungary.[11] In the United States, almost 80 per cent of donations are made by individuals. Why did Americans continue to fund philanthropy, at least at a constant level, even as federal government stepped into the business of social security? The answer, at least in part, lies in the shared roots of philanthropy and the entrepreneurial system: American *individualism* (*Newsweek*, 29 September 1997: 34).[12] However, as we will see in the next section, the elimination of opportunities for wealth creation has social consequences that go far beyond philanthropy.

THE STRENGTHS OF AMERICAN CAPITALISM

Joseph A. Schumpeter proposed his concept of the entrepreneur against the backdrop of economic development in *The Theory of Economic Development* (1934 [1911]). The function of the entrepreneur is to reform or revolutionize the patterns of production by exploiting an invention or more generally, an untried technological possibility for producing a new commodity or producing an old line in a new way.

Six decades after this initial contribution, it is the large corporation that draws attention to Schumpeter's gloomy prospects for economic progress in *Capitalism, Socialism and Democracy* (1950 [1942]). The large corporation, by taking over the entrepreneurial function, not only makes the entrepreneur obsolete but also undermines the sociological and ideological functions of capitalist society. As Schumpeter himself wrote in a classic passage (1950 [1942]: 134):

> Since capitalist enterprise, by its very achievements, tends to automatize progress, we conclude that it tends to make itself superfluous – to break to pieces under the pressure of its own success. The perfectly bureaucratized giant industrial unit not only ousts the small or medium-sized firms and expropriates the bourgeoisie as a class which in the process stands to lose not only its income but also what is infinitely more important, *its function*.

As the large firm replaces the small- and medium-sized enterprise, economic concentration starts to have a negative feedback effect on entrepreneurial values, innovation and technological change. Technology – the means by which new markets are created – may die out, leading to a stationary state. This view of the future capitalist society was held by Keynes (1963), Schumpeter (1950 [1942]) and much of the 1960s intellectual left (Heilbroner, 1985).[13]

Schumpeter was nearly right in Sweden (Henreksen and Jakobsson, 2000), and his prognoses about economic consequences of firm-size appear true for former socialist countries, where industrial concentration has left its mark (Stiglitz, 1994). However, Schumpeter was wrong about the future of American capitalism. He erred by underestimating its deeply-rooted entrepreneurial spirit (Acs, 1984: 172):

While for Marx and Heilbroner the principle struggle is between privileged and underprivileged, for Schumpeter, as in the transition from feudalism to capitalism, the quintessential struggle is between elites and elites: That is merchants and aristocrats, entrepreneurs and bureaucrats. Schumpeter did not see – partly because of his aristocratic European background – that the entrepreneurial spirit would emerge from the nation's past and rise to challenge, engage and extinguish the embers of bureaucratic hegemony, bringing to an end the era of monopoly capitalism, heralding a new dawn.

When the Berlin Wall fell in 1989, international order shifted from issues of East versus West (Capitalism versus Socialism) to questions of global competition (Acs, 2000; Acs and Audretsch, 2001) and comparative advantage. The perceived wisdom at the time was that the United States might not be able to compete in the new global economy[14] (Garten, 1992).[15] However, after a quarter century of ups and downs following 1976, the US economy appeared to be doing extraordinarily well.[16] Unemployment in 1999 was just under 5 percent, the economy was growing at 4 percent a year, inflation was at bay, manufacturing productivity was rising, the dollar was strong and the stock market was consistently breaking records. It appeared that the US economy had restructured itself, moving from an industrial base to a knowledge base, and transitioned to the next century.

Entrepreneurs – individuals who take risk and start something new – are indispensable to economic growth and prosperity. Entrepreneurship – the process of creating a new venture and assuming the risks and rewards – has been essential in the renewal of prosperity in the US in the past two decades, just as it was at the turn of the twentieth century. There is little doubt that the dramatic increase in the number of entrepreneurial businesses in the late 1970s and early 1980s (then maintained at a high level in the 1990s) has contributed significantly to the relatively vigorous US economy in recent years.[17] And it is important to connect entrepreneurship to innovation because of their important joint contributions to creativity, growth, productivity and job creation (UK Secretary of State for Trade and Industry, 1998).

The direction of technological development is equally important because it is the way resources are channeled into industries. Each of the last three industrial revolutions was characterized by a revolution that made possible the transportation both of raw materials and finished commodities to market. During the first industrial revolution (1780–1830), a system of canals in England enabled transportation of goods at a fraction of the previous cost. During the second industrial revolution (1830–1850), the railways provided cheap transportation in England, Germany, and the US. During the third industrial revolution (1920–40), the automobile, truck, and airplane made the transportation of goods and people inexpensive. The fourth industrial revolution, now taking place (1984–?), also has a transportation revolution. However, it is a revolution in the transportation of information, not goods. Like technologies of history – the steam engine and internal combustion engine – the microprocessor does not operate within the confines of existing structures but enables a new one: The Information Age.

Much of the entrepreneurial investment to finance America's information infrastructure was made during the 1980s. According to the *Wall Street Journal* (2 March 1993) Michael Milken invested $21 billion in the information industry. His largest commitments were to MCI, Tele-communications Inc, McGraw Cellular Communications Inc, Turner Broadcasting, Time Warner Inc, and Metromedia Broadcasting. Virtually devoid of conventional sources of collateral, none of these companies could have raised comparable sums elsewhere. An original investment of $10 billion in these companies had a market value of $62 billion in 1993. This web of glass and light is today an essential resource for America's information economy. A second wave of entrepreneurial start up companies, financed in part by venture capital, is now completing the infrastructure for the information age: America On Line, Cisco Systems, Amazon.com, Oracle, Sun Microsystems, Netscape and Yahoo.

The re-emergence of entrepreneurship in the United States during the 1980s, and the positive channeling of it, must be seen as a triumph of American capitalism.[18] A clear manifestation of this entrepreneurial success is the increase in job wealth creation in the US. The accumulation of wealth in private hands is a function of the freedom that we allow individuals in an entrepreneurial society. If it is taxed away, wealth creation will cease. However, with that right is responsibility. Private wealth that was created in a community needs to be reinvested in the future growth of society, and this is as true now as it was for early American philanthropists. In fact, as enormous new wealth has been created, the role of philanthropy has similarly grown. The contribution to philanthropy in the US rose to around two per cent of GDP. The number of active private and community foundations has more than doubled since 1980. About three-fifths of the largest foundations have been created since 1980.

It has only been in the last two decades, since 1982, that a combination of political changes (Reagan Revolution), massive technological advances and the collapse of communism have enabled a return to American roots of individualism, entrepreneurship and philanthropy. However, while entrepreneurship is a *necessary* condition for the shift from industrial capitalism to an entrepreneurial society, it is not by itself sufficient for economic prosperity, opportunity and social progress.

PHILANTHROPY IN THE 'NEW GILDED AGE'

At the beginning of this chapter, we suggested that American philanthropists created foundations that, in turn, enabled greater and more widespread economic prosperity (by investing in the future of America). However, such views are not fashionable among scholars of philanthropy and more than a few professionals that staff foundations. For example, a book published by MIT Press on American foundations argues that they serve largely as vehicles for advancing the interests of their benefactors (Dowie, 2001). At an American Assembly meeting a few years ago, the participants (most were professionals from foundations and non-profit groups) produced a statement calling on philanthropists to do more to redistribute their wealth from the 'haves' to the 'have nots'. Carnegie would have been appalled since he thought that by fostering greater economic opportunities, philanthropists could prevent such redistributive schemes.

It is important to reiterate the argument. We need to distinguish redistribution of wealth from the creation of opportunity, both intellectually in academy and operationally in foundations. This distinction is similar to that between small business and entrepreneurship: small business is about lifestyle and entrepreneurship is about wealth creation. In the same sense, charity is about redistribution while philanthropy in the American tradition is about investing wealth to create opportunity. The first question is: How do we evaluate what should be done and what has gone before? What is needed is a benchmark against which to evaluate the role of philanthropy today. This clearly does not exist. However, Jeffrey Sachs articulated a position by which to judge our philanthropic activities based on past accomplishments: Creating opportunity for future generations means creating knowledge today,[19] and the model to study is the Rockefeller Foundation[20] (*The Economist*, 24 June 2000). Schramm suggests that ideas and personnel (that is internal human capital) enable foundations to work through intellectual influence (Schramm, 2006). While it is beyond the scope of this chapter to identify all wealthy entrepreneurs and to study their relative philanthropic engagement, we will briefly address four that set the standard: George Soros, Ted Turner, Bill Gates and Warren Buffett.

Soros, the financier, pledged $2 billion dollars to a global network of foundations to promote an open society.[21] The Soros Foundation supports education, children's programs, public health initiatives, contemporary art and culture programs and small-enterprise development. He has contributed to creative and unusual methods, taking great care over how the money is spent in transforming the former socialist countries. He donated $500 million to fund health and civic programs in Russia (*The Washington*

Post, 21 October 1997: A3) and another $25 million to fund after-school programs in Baltimore.[22]

Another large gift was the donation of $1 billion to the United Nations by Ted Turner, from the wealth created by his shares in the Time Warner media empire. With that gift, Turner challenged the extremely rich to give away more money.[23] The Turner Foundation is dedicated to making the earth more environment-friendly – protecting clean water and air quality, alternative forms of transportation and fuels, strategies for infill development, and soon. Goals of the foundation also include slowing population growth and preserving wildlife. The foundation has an endowment of about $350 million, but its annual giving ($50 million) is more in line with a $1 billion foundation (Maria Saporta The Atlanta Journal and Constitution 8 October 2001).

Bill Gates – who had previously promised $100 million to fight childhood disease in developing countries and $200 million for computers for libraries – created the largest philanthropic foundation in the US: The Bill and Melinda Gates Foundation, endowed with $22 billion.[24] The recent announcement that Warren Buffett will give the bulk of his $44 billion fortune to the Gates Foundation creates the largest philanthropic foundation in history (*The Economist*, 2006). To put this into perspective, the contribution is about four times as large as that created by Carnegie or Rockefeller in constant dollars. The foundation focuses on third world health issues, and will give away one billion dollars annually.

CONCLUSION

From an American perspective, the current model of entrepreneurial capitalism, with its sharp focus on entrepreneurship and philanthropy, offers continued potential to create and strengthen important institutions that seek to equalize unequal distribution of wealth. There are important implications for a range of stakeholders in the economy, and we will outline those specific to policymakers, foundation professionals and the intellectual community.

Public Policy Implications

Policy issues arise at many levels – federal, state, local – and across a range of decision-making bodies and policy arenas – taxation, small business support, education, welfare and social assistance programs, and so on. The increase in high profile philanthropic activities is occurring at a time when Americans in general are increasing their philanthropic contributions. A recent study by the Newtithing.org suggests that those areas of the country without amenities such as mountains, beaches and museums are reinventing themselves through philanthropic efforts to invest in the community. States that rank the highest are those from the Rockies through the Plains and in the Southeastern states: 'The middle of the country has developed a culture of philanthropy that the coasts and the Southwest, for all their wealth, do not have' (Leonhardt, 2006). Such philanthropy is yet another manisfestation of the entrepreneurship-philanthropy nexus in American society.

Government policies should be designed to support, or at least not hinder, the flow of money into the philanthropic sector. Legal and regulatory policy affects both the demand and supply conditions in this sector. For example, rather then constraining the rich through taxes, they may be more effective at creating social change by creating opportunity.[25] Foundations operate under complex regulatory frameworks, facing tighter restrictions than public charities – such as excise taxes on net investment income – and have gone through periods of restricted independence and operational scrutiny (Schramm, 2006). The idea of donor intent[26] is threatened by a move to blanket foundations within the realm of 'public, quasi-governmental institutions', where the notion of public purpose is mistaken for public money (Schramm, 2006).

The very strength of the American foundation is its conceptualization as an *out-market institution* (Schramm, 2006). Driven by a renewed spirit of philanthropy among the new rich, the foundation has the potential to strengthen future American economic prosperity. In addition to domestic implications, the entrepreneurship-philanthropy nexus has significant global application. Sustaining global capitalism will require vision and investment from and a spread of the ideas that indeed make American capitalism successful. The projects for philanthropy are as broad today as they were 100 years ago: Health, education, infrastructure and social values. If the new rich rise to the occasion, then prosperity will continue well into the next century as the coming 'Golden Age of Philanthropy' creates investments that will have a positive feedback on the economy.

Two realities stand out in the global economy. First, the world is getting wealthier. Second – and this counts perhaps as the greatest negative externality of market economies – the unequal distribution of wealth is growing. We have suggested in this chapter that the American model of entrepreneurial capitalism may be the only sustainable model for global development. Entrepreneurial capitalism is different from other forms of capitalism because of its historical focus on both the creation of wealth (entrepreneurship) and reconstitution of wealth (philanthropy). Both stem from what may be uniquely American constructs of individualism, agency and human nature.

In industrial capitalist wealth creation, wealth ownership and wealth distribution were, in part, left to the state. However, in an entrepreneurial society, individual initiative plays a vital role in propelling the system forward. Entrepreneurial leadership is the mechanism by which new combinations are created, new markets are opened and new technologies are commercialized. In the entrepreneurial society, entrepreneurship plays a vital role in wealth creation and philanthropy plays a crucial role in its distribution. The execution of this, as we argued earlier, was based on a new character type with unprecedented new powers of discretion but yet bound to collective ends. From a global perspective, the American model of entrepreneurial capitalism offers a sustainable and self-reinforcing means through which to encourage prosperity and advancement.

Implications for Foundations

From the perspective of those working in philanthropy, particularly those in grantmaking and mission-based foundations, the pressing question may well be: How well is the philanthropic sector meeting its obligations? Is the sector, in fact, challenging the new rich to use their wealth to 'find permanent solutions to what seem like intractable problems?' (Milken, 1999).

As with most organizations, operational efficiency is a concern[27] and it may now be time for market mechanisms to be applied to the philanthropic sector.[28] Organizational capacity may be improved by expanding beyond merely program innovation (Letts *et al.*, 1997). The challenge is not just to create solutions (Morino Institute, 2000; W.K. Kellogg Foundation; Reis, 1999) but to make them affordable, sustainable, replicable and scaleable to fulfill organizational mission. Lessons from the for-profit world,[29] such as performance-based compensation, entry and exit strategies, and financial sustainability may be useful for foundations.

Research Agendas

In addition to the immediate public policy implications and the considerations for foundation professionals, there are a number of research agendas that emerge from the new topic of the Entrepreneurship-Philanthropy nexus (Acs and Phillips, 2000). For economists and other scholars of the interaction between economic activity and its social effects, the relationship between entrepreneurship and philanthropy has at least six major paths. First, identifying wealthy entrepreneurs and measuring their philanthropic contributions. Second, identifying the extent to which wealthy entrepreneurs engage in philanthropic activities. Third, when measured by size and societal impact, how do philanthropic activities of today's entrepreneurs compare with those in the late nineteenth and early twentieth century? Fourth, how do these activities vary across countries or communities?

The remaining two questions are related to the fundamental assumptions of economics with relation to human behavior. Self-interest and altruism, though very different motives for human activity, are in fact fundamental traits of human nature that are especially crucial in maintaining economic vitality. Fifth, *why* do wealthy entrepreneurs engage in philanthropy: Is it self-interest or is it altruism? If the answer is the latter, then economic theory should alter its underlying premise of a self-interest motivation for human activity. This leads to the final research question: Are returns to society greater when the philanthropic behavior requires no *quid pro quo*?

NOTES

1. For a statement on the nature and logic of capitalism see Robert L. Heilbroner (1985). Of course it is precisely the institutional framework that differs from country to country and not necessarily the logic of the system. For a discussion of the different institutional frameworks see Michael Porter (2000) on Japan, on France see Honah D. Levy (1999) and on Sweden see Karlsson and Acs (2002, special issue on Institutions, Entrepreneurship and Firm Growth.
2. One could argue that the recent antitrust case against Microsoft was as much about anti-competitive behavior as about violating this social contract.
3. For example, John D. Rockefeller gave back 95 percent of his wealth before he died.
4. In contrast to this, a survey of theory and research on altruism by sociologists concluded that evidence points to the existence of altruism as a part of human nature (Pilavin and Charng, 1990).
5. Also see Coase (1976).
6. 'It is not from the benevolence of the butcher, the brewer, or the baker, that we expect our dinner, but from their regard to their own interest' (Smith, 1937 (1776): 14).
7. The Puritan leader John Winthrop forthrightly stated their purpose in the lay sermon, 'A Model of Christian Charity', in which he preached on the ship *Arabella* to the great company of religious people voyaging from the old world to New England in the year 1630 (Bremner, 1960: 7).
8. And punished it accordingly.
9. It is plausible that philanthropists like Carnegie took a longer term approach and realized that their interests necessitated assisting the worthy poor and disadvantaged: enlightened self interest as opposed to altruism.
10. Increasing role of government.
11. See Salamon, Ahheier and Associates (1999).
12. There's no escaping the brutal truth: the nation famous for capitalism red in tooth and claw, the epicenter of the heartless marketplace, is also the land of the handout. It's not really such a paradox. Both our entrepreneurial economic system and out philanthropic tradition spring for the same root: *American individualism*. Other countries may be content to let the government run most of their schools and universities, pay for their hospitals, subsidize their museums and orchestras, even in some cases support religious sects. Americans tend to think most of these institutions are best kept in private hands, and they have been willing to cough up the money to pay for them' (*Newsweek*, 29 September 1997: 34).

13. For an alternative view see Ayn Rand, *Return of the Primitive: The Anti-Industrial Revolution* (New York: A Meridian Book, 1999).
14. Jeffrey E. Garten, Under Secretary of Commerce, summed up this view at the beginning of the first Clinton administration (1922: 15): 'Relative to Japan and Germany, our economic prospects are poor and our political influence is waning. Their economic under-pinnings – trends in investment, productivity, market share in high technology, education and training – are stronger. Their banks and industry are in better shape; their social problems are far less severe than ours'.
15. Also see Tyson (1992) and Thurow (1992).
16. According to Lawrence H. Summers, former deputy Treasury Secretary: 'The economy seems better balanced than at any time in my professional lifetime' (*Washington Post*, 2 December 1996: 1)
17. While Americans allow entrepreneurs continually to change the economic system, the French, for example, 'are fighting to preserve what is to them one of the most successful societies and most agreeable ways of life in the world – one that other Europeans esteem and Americans still flock to, admire and even envy' *The Washington Post*, 14 April 1997, A1.
18. An enormous amount of wealth has been created in the US since the Great Depression of the 1930s. Between 1950 and 2000, household net worth in the United States increased from $130 000 to $400 000 in 2001 inflation adjusted dollars. The addition to real measured by additions to gross domestic product by decade increased by $56.2 billion in the 1980s and by $75.6 billion in the 1990s. In 1950 80 percent of wealth on the Forbes list of the richest people in America was inherited by 1990 it has fallen to only 20 percent. Between 1998 and 2001, four trillion dollars of new wealth was created in the stock market. The number of billionaires had increased from 13 in 1982 to 170 today; the number of deca-millionaires stands at 250 000 and millionaires at 4.8 million (*Economist*, 30 May 1998: 19). The impressive performance of the US in the last few years may be contrasted with the rather lackluster performance in both Europe and Japan, where GDP has grown at less than 1.5 percent per annum in the last five years. In the European Union (EU) the unemployment rate has remained stubbornly in double digits, and in Japan the stock market has been stagnant since 1992 at half its previous level (Audretsch and Thurik, 1998; Wennekers and Thurik, 1999; Acs *et al.*, 1999; Armington and Acs, 2002; Carree *et al.*, 2001).
19. For a theory of knowledge in economic growth, see Arrow (1962) and Romer (1990). For an application to the regional and global economy see Acs (2000).
20. Sachs writes: 'The model to emulate is the Rockefeller Foundation, the pre-eminent development institution of the 20th century, which showed what grant aid targeted on knowledge could accomplish. Rockefeller funds supported the eradication of hookworm in the American South; the discovery of the Yellow Fever vaccine; the development of penicillin; the establishment of public-health schools (today's undisputed leaders in their fields) all over the world; the establishment of medical facilities in all parts of the world; the creation and funding of great research centers such as the University of Chicago, the Brookings Institution, Rockefeller university, and the National Bureau of Economic Research; the control of malaria in Brazil; the founding of the research centers that accomplished the green revolution in Asia; and more' (*The Economist*, 24 June 2000: 83).
21. For treatment of the Soros perception of the global problem, see Soros (1998).
22. He described Baltimore as a miniature version of the world with much of the world's bounty, problems and promise (*The Baltimore Sun*, 16 December 1998: C1).
23. Ted Turner was awarded the 2001 Albert Schweitzer Gold Medal for Humanitarianism given by the Johns Hopkins University.
24. *New York Times*, 2 December 1998: A10 and *Newsweek*, 30 August 1999: 50.
25. In the past, the fight against slavery had some very wealthy backers. If we shut off the opportunities for wealthy individuals to give back their wealth we will also shut off the creation of wealth which has far greater consequences for an entrepreneurial society. It is the *channeling* of this wealth to socially useful and constructive activities that may offer the greatest possibility for social change.

26. And therefore, potentially the ultimate mission for which the foundation was established.
27. John Doerr, who leads the $20 million dollar New Schools Ventures Fund, argues that one of the major problems with the nonprofit sector is that there is not a mechanism to weed out inefficient organizations (*Time*, 2000: 55).
28. This is consistent with the emergence of focus on 'hybrid' management in business schools, social enterprising for nonprofits, and the 'double bottom line'.
29. The founders of Google, Larry Page and Sergey Brin, have established a 'for profit' charitable foundation. This is a new model and one that will allow the foundation to fund start-up companies, form partnerships with venture capitalists and even to lobby Congress. Unlike other foundations, the Google Foundation is not being established for tax reasons (Hafner, 2006).

REFERENCES

Acs, Zoltan J. (1984), *The Changing Structure of the US Economy*, New York: Praeger.
Acs, Zoltan J. (ed.) (2000), *Regional Innovation, Knowledge and Global Change*, London: Pinter.
Acs, Zoltan J. and David B. Audretsch (2001), 'The emergence of the entrepreneurial society', *Swedish Foundation for Small Business*, Stockholm, Sweden, May.
Acs, Zoltan J. and Leo P. Dana (2001), 'Two views of wealth creation', *Small Business Economics*, **16**(2), 63–74.
Acs, Zoltan J. and Ronnie, J. Phillips (2000), 'Entrepreneurship and philanthropy in the new gilded age: a research agenda', Working Paper, Department of Economics, Colorado State University.
Acs, Zoltan J. and Charlie Karlsson (2002), 'Institutions, entrepreneurship and firm growth: the case of Sweden', *Small Business Economics*, (special issue), **19** (3).
Acs, Zoltan J., B. Carlsson, and C. Karlsson (1999), 'The linkages among entrepreneurship, SMEs and the macroeconomy', in Z. Acs, B. Carlsson and C. Karlsson (eds), *Entrepreneurship, Small & Medium-Sized Enterprises and the Macro Economy*, Cambridge: Cambridge University Press, 3–44.
America, Richard, F. (1995), *Philanthropy and Economic Development*, Westport, CN: Greenwood Press.
Armington, Catherine, and Zoltan J. Acs (2002), 'The determinants of regional variation in new firm formation', *Regional Studies*, **36**, 33–45.
Arrow, K.J. (1962), 'Economic welfare and the allocation of resources for invention', in Richard Nelson (ed.), *The Rate and Direction of Inventive Activity*, Princeton, NJ: Princeton University Press, 609–26.
Audretsch, David B. and Roy Thurik (1998), *The Knowledge Society, Entrepreneurship and Unemployment*, Zoetermeer: EIM.
The Baltimore Sun (1998), 'A gift for all ages', 16 December C1.
Becker, Gary S. (1974), 'A theory of social interactions', *Journal of Political Economy*, **82**, 1095–117.
Boulding, Kenneth (1962), 'Notes on a theory of philanthropy,' in Frank G. Dickinson (ed.), *Philanthropy and Public Policy*, Boston, MA: NBER, 57–72.
Bremner, Robert, H. (1960), *American Philanthropy*, Chicago, IL: University of Chicago Press.
Budd, Louis, J. (1956), 'Altruism arrives in America', *American Quarterly*, **891**, 40–52.

Carree, Martin, Andre van Stel, Roy Thurik, Sander Wennekers (2001), 'Economic development and business ownership: an analysis using data of 23 OECD countries in the period 1976–1996', *Small Business Economics*, **19** (3), 271–90.

Carnegie, Andrew, 1889, 'Wealth', *North American Review*, **148** (391), 653–65.

Coase, Ronald H. (1976), 'Adam Smith's view of man', *Journal of Law and Economics*, **19**, 529–46.

Chernow, Ron (1999), *Titan: The Life of John D. Rockefeller Sr.*, New York: Random House.

Collard, David (1978), *Altruism and Economy*, New York: Oxford University Press.

Curti, Merle (1957), 'The History of American Philanthropy as a Field of Research', *The American Historical Review*, **62** (2), 352–63.

Danielsen, Albert L. (1975), 'A theory of exchange, philanthropy and appropriation', *Public Choice*, **24**, 13–26.

Dickinson, Frank, G. (1970), *The Changing Position of Philanthropy in the American Economy*, National Bureau of Economic Research, Distributed by Columbia University Press, New York.

Dowie, Mark (2001), *American Foundations*, Cambridge, MA: The MIT Press.

The Economist (1997), 'The knowledge factory', 4 October, 1–22.

The Economist (1998), 'The gospel of wealth', 30 May, 19.

The Economist (2000), 'Sachs on globalization', 24 June, 81–3.

The Economist (2006), 'The new powers in giving', 1 July, 63–5.

Fortune (1998), 'Most generous Americans', 2 February, 88.

Garten, Jeffery E. (1992), *A Cold Peace: America, Japan and Germany, and the Struggle for Supremacy*, New York: Times Books.

Giddings, Franklin H. (1893), 'The ethics of social progress', *International Journal of Ethics*, **3** (1), 137–64.

Hafner, Katie (2006), 'Philanthropy Google's way: not the usual', *New York Times*. 14 September.

Hamer, J.H. (1998), 'Money and the moral order in late nineteenth and early twentieth-century American capitalism', *Anthropological Quarterly*, **71**, 138–50.

Hart, David (2003), *The Emergence of Entrepreneurship Policy: Governance, Start-ups, and Growth in the Knowledge Economy*, Cambridge: Cambridge University Press.

Hebert, Robert F. and Albert N. Link (1989), 'In search of the meaning of entrepreneurship', *Small Business Economics*, **1** (43), 1.

Heilbroner, Robert (1985), *The Nature and Logic of Capitalism*, New York: Harper and Row.

Henreksen, Magnus, and Ulf Jakobsson (2000), 'Where Schumpeter was nearly right – the Swedish model and capitalism, socialism and democracy', Working Paper no. 370, Stockholm School of Economics.

Hickman, Larry, A. (1998), *Reading Dewey: Interpretations for a Postmodern Generation*, Indianapolis, IN: Indiana University Press.

Ireland, Thomas R. (1969), 'The Calculus of Philanthropy', *Public Choice*, **7**, 23–31.

Jordan, W.K. (1961), 'The English background of modern philanthropy', *The American Historical Review*, **66** (2), 401–8.

Karlsson, C. and Z. Acs (2002), 'Introduction to institutions, entrepreneurship and firm growth: the case of Sweden', *Small Business Economics*, **19** (2), 63–7.

Keynes, John M. (1963), *Essays in Persuasion*, New York: W.W. Norton.

Kaufman, Dennis A. (1993), 'Self-serving philanthropy and Pareto optimality', in *The Nonprofit Sector in the Mixed Economy*, Avner Ben-Ner and Benedetto Gui (eds), Ann Arbor, MI: University of Michigan Press.

Leonhardt, David (2006), 'Philanthropy from the heart of America', *New York Times*, 11 October.

Letts, Christine W., William Ryan and Allen Grossman (1997), 'Virtuous capital: what foundations can learn from venture capitalists', *Harvard Business Review*, **75** (2), 36–44.

Levy, Jonah D. (1999), *Tocqueville's Revenge: State, Society and Economics in Contemporary France*, Boston, MA: Harvard University Press.

MacMullen, Ramsay (1998), *Corruption and the Decline of Rome*, New Haven: Yale University Press.

Margolis, Howard (1982), *Selfishness, Altruism, and Rationality: A Theory of Social Choice*, Cambridge: Cambridge University Press.

Milken, Michael (1999), 'Follow your passion', *Wall Street Journal*, 4 October.

Morck, Randal K., David A. Stangeland and Bernard Yeung (1998), 'Inherited wealth, corporate control and economic growth', *in Concentrated Corporate Ownership*, Randal Morck (ed.), Chicago, IL: The University of Chicago Press, 319–69.

Morino Institute (2000), *Venture Philanthropy*, produced for the Morino Institute Youth Social Ventures by Community Wealth Ventures, Inc.

Myers, Gustavus (1907), *History of Great American Fortunes*, New York: The Modern Library.

NewTithing Group (2006), *Wealth & Generosity by State*, http://www.new tithing.org/content/sept06_tables.html.

The New York Times (1998), 2 December, A10.

Newsweek (1997), 'The land of the handout', 29 September, 34–6.

Newsweek (1999), 30 August, 50.

Offit, M.S. (1995), *Benchmark: 1990–1995*, Baltimore, MD, The Johns Hopkins University.

Owen, David (1964), *English Philanthropy 1660–1960*, Cambridge, MA: The Belknap Press of Harvard University.

Parker, George F. (1971), *Peabody*, Nashville, TN: Vanderbilt University Press.

Pilavin, Jane Allyn and Hong-Wen Charng (1990), 'Altruism: a review of recent theory and research', *Annual Review of Sociology*, **16**, 27–65.

Porter, E. Michael (2000), *Can Japan Compete?*, London: Macmillan Press Ltd.

Porter, Michael E. and Mark R. Kramer (1999), 'Philanthropy's new agenda: creating value', *Harvard Business Review*, November–December, 121–30.

Rand, Ayn (1999), *Return of the Primitive: The Anti-Industrial Revolution*, New York: A Meridian Book.

Romer, Paul (1990), 'Increasing returns and long run growth', *Journal of Political Economy*, **94**, 1002–37.

Reis, Tom (1999), *Unleashing New Resources and Entrepreneurship for the Common Good*, Battle Creek, MI: W.K. Kellogg Foundation.

Salamon, Lester M., Helmut K. Anheier and Associates (1999), *The Emerging Sector Revisited*, Baltimore, MD: The Johns Hopkins University Institute for Policy Studies Center for Civil Society Studies.

Schramm, Carl J. (2006), 'Law outside the market: the social utility of the private foundation', *Harvard Journal of Law and Public Policy*, **30** (1), 355–415.

Schumpeter, Joseph A. (1950 [1942]), *Capitalism, Socialism and Democracy*, New York: Harper and Row.

Schumpeter Joseph A. (1934 [1911]), *The Theory of Economic Development*, Cambridge, MA: Harvard University Press.

Simon, Herbert A. (1993), 'Altruism and economics', *American Economic Review*, **83** (2), 156–61.

Slate Magazine (2000), 'The Slate 60 Huffington Virtue Remix', March.

Smith, Adam (1937 [1776]), *The Wealth of Nations*, New York: Modern Library.

Smith, Adam (1969 [1759]), *The Theory of Moral Sentiments*, Indianapolis, IN: Liberty Classics.

Soros, George (1998), *The Crisis of Global Capitalism*, New York: Public Affairs.

Stiglitz, George (1994), *Wither Socialism*, Cambridge, MA: MIT Press.

Sugden, Robert (1982), 'On the economics of philanthropy,' *The Economic Journal*, **92**, 341–50.

Thurow, Lester (1992), *Head to Head: The Coming Battle Among Japan, Europe, and America*, New York: William Morrow and Company.

Time (1999), 'The century's greatest minds', 29 March.

Time (2000), 'The new philanthropists', 24 July.

Tocqueville, Alexis de (1996 [1835]), *Democracy in America*, New York: Harper and Row.

Tyson, Laura d' Andrea (1992), *Who's Bashing Whom? Trade Conflict in High Technology Industries*, Washington, DC: Institute for International Economics.

Veblen, Thorstein (1899), *The Theory of the Leisure Class*, New York: The Macmillan Company.

The Washington Post (1996), 'US sails on tranquil economic seas', 2 December, 1.

The Washington Post (1997), 14 April, A1.

The Washington Post (1997), 21 October, A3.

UK Secretary of State for Trade and Industry (1998), *Our Competitive Future: Building the Knowledge Driven Economy*. London.

Weber, Max (1958), *The Protestant Ethic and the Spirit of Capitalism*, New York: Charles Schribner's Sons.

Wennekers, Sander and Roy Thurik (1999), 'Linking entrepreneurship and economic growth', *Small Business Economics*, **13** (1), 27–55.

5. The political economy of the philanthropic enterprise

Peter J. Boettke and Christopher J. Coyne

INTRODUCTION

Warren Buffet recently pledged to donate the majority of his estimated $44 billion estate to the Bill and Melinda Gates Foundation. The pledge, valued at $37 billion, is the largest charitable donation ever. To put the magnitude of this donation in context, compare Buffet's pledged contribution to two well-known American philanthropists, John D. Rockefeller and Andrew Carnegie. Rockefeller and Carnegie's total philanthropy was $7.6 billion and $44.1 billion respectively.[1] Buffet's donation makes the Gates Foundation the largest charitable foundation in American and Europe with total assets valued at $60 billion.[2] This highlights an increasing trend in private giving by the wealthy in the United States.[3]

In 2000, *Bankers Trust* conducted a study of 112 wealthy households to examine the notion of 'wealth with responsibility'. The underlying motivation was to obtain a measure of how much the wealthy were giving to society in terms of charitable donations. Ninety percent of respondents stated that they have established an estate plan, which leaves 16 percent of their assets to charities, 47 percent to their heirs, and 37 percent goes to government in the form of taxation.

The most significant finding, for the purposes of what we wish to discuss in this chapter, is that the *Bankers Trust* study reports that 66 percent of respondents indicated that they would give *more* if they had better information on the effectiveness of their charitable donations. However, measuring the effectiveness of charitable giving is notoriously difficult to appraise. As a result, charitable giving is often more about the giver feeling good rather than actually doing good.

The actions of Warren Buffet, coupled with an increasing trend of private giving, indicate a fundamental point about Americans. Namely, they are extremely generous in their support for charitable causes – ranging from health and human welfare, to artistic endeavors, to education.[4] The

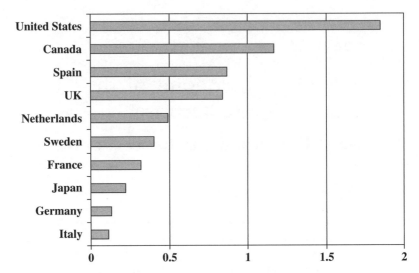

Figure 5.1   *Philanthropic giving (cash and other property gifts) as a*
                percentage of GDP 1995–2002

magnitude of this giving in the United States, relative to other developed countries, is illustrated in Figure 5.1.[5]

As Figure 5.1 indicates, as a percentage of GDP, Americans (1.85 percent) gave more than other comparatively developed countries during the 1995–2002 time period. In fact, the percentage given by Americans was more than double that donated by those in the United Kingdom (0.84 percent) and Netherlands (0.49 percent) and over four times what the citizens of Sweden (0.40 percent) and France (0.32 percent) donated.

While recognizing the philanthropic activities of US citizens, it is important to keep in mind the tremendous benefits that entrepreneurial visionaries generate via the creation of wealth. Indeed, business innovation, and the associated far-reaching benefits manifested through increasing human standards of living, far exceeds the benefits of charitable activity. To understand the basic thrust of this perspective, simply reflect on the benefits realized by the masses of people due to the introduction of mass production techniques. These production techniques lower the costs of products from automobiles to computers which, over a matter of years, transformed these products from luxuries consumed only by the wealthy to products consumed throughout society.

Americans are better off in terms of convenience, quality of services, and wide availability of products when compared to their parents let alone their grandparents (see Moore and Simon, 1999; Cox and Alm, 1999). These increases in living standards are not due to the charitable contributions of the business elite, but because of the profit-seeking activity of entrepreneurs and the positive-sum benefits they confer.

Our purpose in highlighting this fact is not to denigrate the tremendous contribution that philanthropic activity makes to society, but rather to correct the common error of overlooking the contributions of for-profit activities to the betterment of society. All too often for-profit activities are viewed as negative or zero-sum while philanthropic activities are viewed as 'giving back' to society. We wish to highlight that while charitable donations are one means of giving to society, so is the provision of jobs as well as new products and services available at decreasing costs. Of course we fully recognize not all activities can be rendered in term of profit and loss statements, and many of these activities are the most precious in our human interactions.

Even the most ardent of free market economists, Ludwig von Mises, pointed out the inability of the market economy to value the beauty of a waterfall in making a decision on whether to build a waterworks (1920: 99). Mises, in fact, is explicit on the limits of monetary calculation, and strictly restricts the role of monetary calculation to the sphere of exchange relations and production through a roundabout process. Honor, beauty, happiness all exist outside the strict delineation of exchange relations and thus monetary calculation.

Nonetheless, Mises insists that recognizing the limits to monetary calculation does not detract from its significance for everyday economic life. Honor, beauty and happiness are goods of the first order, and thus can be valued directly.[6] Individuals can incorporate these components into their decision even though they lie outside of monetary calculation. As Mises puts it:

> Sensitive people may be pained to have to choose between the ideal and the material. But that is not the fault of a money economy. It is in the nature of things. For even where we can make judgments of value without money computations we cannot avoid this choice. Both isolated man and socialist communities would have to do likewise, and truly sensitive natures will never find it painful. Called upon to choose between bread and honour, they will never be at a loss how to act. If honour cannot be eaten, eating can at least be forgone for honour. Only such as fear the agony of choice because they secretly know that they could not forgo the material, will regard the necessity of choice as a profanation. (1922: 100)

Mises follows this discussion of the limits of monetary calculation with an argument for its importance. Within its appropriate sphere monetary calculation 'does all that we are entitled to ask of it'. Without it, we would be lost 'amid the bewildering throng of economic possibilities', and thus 'all production by lengthy and roundabout processes of production would be so many steps in the dark' (1922: 101). Mises, in his emphasis on the importance of the mechanisms of profit, loss and prices, states, 'In the absence of profit and loss the entrepreneurs would not know what the most urgent needs of the consumers are. If some entrepreneurs were to guess it, they would lack the means to adjust production accordingly' (1949: 297).

Mises acknowledged the precise problem we wish to address in this chapter, namely that philanthropic activity is largely outside the realm of monetary calculation, despite the fact that gifts are provided in monetary sums. Thus, if we follow Mises and insist on the limitation of monetary calculation to the arena of exchange relations, we would expect that philanthropic enterprise would be limited to activities which can be directly valued, or else it will be characterized by endemic waste. Along these lines, Mises notes that 'whenever the operation of a system is not directed by the profit motive, it must be directed by bureaucratic rules' and these rules are characterized by 'inflexible regulations' (1949: 307). Philanthropic enterprises are indeed subject to these constraints making information difficult to assess with prices absent, and to bureaucratic rules making it difficult for nonprofits to adjust 'production' when the enterprise has misapprehended local needs and demands. There are, nevertheless, striking examples of nonprofits successfully fulfilling local demands through incentive-compatible, community-based projects in which the nonprofits maintain strict accountability to donors within a limited scope.

Our goal in this chapter is to explore the political economy of the philanthropic enterprise. Specifically, we seek to identify the mechanisms that allow philanthropic enterprises to overcome the constraints identified by Mises. In the competition between the state and philanthropic provision of goods and services not provided on the market, we argue that there are various mechanisms at work that ensure the dominance of state provision when the activity is pushed beyond very localized provision.[7]

There is a large and wide-ranging literature on the topic of philanthropy. While others have studied the history of philanthropy (Bremner, 1994; McCarthy, 2005), the factors that motivate giving and volunteering (Brooks, 2005; Dekker and Halman, 2003) and the moral issues associated with philanthropy and charity (Smith, 2005), our focus is on applying the economic way of thinking to philanthropic enterprise. Specifically, we focus on the incentive and information issues facing philanthropic enterprises which, by definition, act outside the market context. This approach is similar to that taken by Holcombe (2000), who focuses on the incentives facing foundation trustees as well as the implications of tax policy on donations to foundations and philanthropic enterprises. We build on earlier work by Boettke and Prychitko (2004) that attempts to develop an Austrian economic interpretation of nonprofit and voluntary action.

CIVIL SOCIETY VERSUS THE STATE

It has become commonplace in the last decade or so to assert that a vibrant civil society is necessary for the establishment of a working democratic state (see Almond and Verba, 1989; Ehrenberg, 1999; Putnam, 1993; Warren, 2000). Within this context, much of the literature contrasts civil society with the profit motive of the market. It is argued that the market operates on the principle of everything for sale, while civil society was based on norms and codes of behavior outside of the profit motive.

Criticism is often directed at the *laissez-fare* 'State vs. Market' dichotomy because it is argued that such a distinction fails to recognize the informal norms which underlie democratic life on the one hand and economic behavior on the other. Critics contend, in contrast, that one must view the contrast as between 'Society (which includes state and civil society) vs. Market' (see Salamon, 1987, 1995) Along these lines, critics hold that the market economy erodes the values, which underlie not only a working democracy, but ironically, the values necessary for the operation of the market economy itself.

We do not deny that a vibrant democratic society is grounded in a healthy civil society and institutions of self-governance. This is so mainly because it limits government from expanding its scope of activities. Such a limiting constraint on the scope of government is necessary to ensure that government is restricted to those activities it can do well and avoids those tasks, which in fact it lacks the knowledge and incentives to accomplish effectively. In our view, the attempt to conceptualize the market as contrasted with civil society suffers from both errors of commission and errors of omission.

First, the market versus civil society view underestimates the coercive nature of state action. The state, as Max Weber (1918) emphasized, is a geographic monopoly on coercion.[8] The state is a powerful instrument through which some parties can gain by exploiting others.

Second, this underestimates the role of civil society as a means of self-governance *against* the coercive power of the state. It was this aspect of nineteenth-century America that so captured the imagination of Alexis de Tocqueville (1835/1839). Tocqueville saw America's propensity for self-governance (what he called 'the art of association') as opposed to reliance on the formal structures of state action as a defining characterization of that society. Self-governance was seen as an alternative to the state, not as a prerequisite for a working state sector.[9]

Third, the contemporary juxtaposition omits a discussion of the importance of the self-enforcing norms and bonds of trust, which are evident in everyday economic life. Formal contracts and various less formal alternative institutional facilitators of voluntary cooperation are at work in the day-to-day operation of a market society. Benson (1990) suggests that in the United States, 75 percent of commercial disputes are settled privately through arbitration and mediation. Rubin (1997) points out that in developed economies businesses employ methods of doing substantial amounts of business without relying on contracts and the threat of legal enforcement makes private arrangements easier.

What these studies indicate is that economic actors, due to the discipline of repeated dealings, must build a reputation for trustworthiness, craftsmanship and reliability in order to be successful (Klein, 1997). As F.A. Hayek states: 'In actual life the fact that our inadequate knowledge of the available commodities or services is made up by our experience with the persons or firms supplying them – that competition is in large measure competition for reputation or good will' (1946: 97).

It is true, as Adam Smith (1776: Book I, Chapter II) stressed, that it is due to the power of self-interest, and not benevolence, that we can expect our dinner from the butcher, the baker and the brewer. But it is also true that the self-interest of the butcher, the baker and the brewer is best served by their recognition of the desires and demands of others in the market. Absent certain background of institutions (formal and informal rules), markets will not operate effectively to coordinate production and exchange (Boettke and Coyne, 2003). In short, market activity is embedded within a larger context of rule-governed behavior.

Instead of the distinction that sees the profit motive standing at odds with civil society, we believe that the more appropriate contrast would be the traditional state versus civil society dichotomy, where civil society is divided into non-market and market activity, as can be seen in Figure 5.2.

The contrast that we postulate is built on the basic recognition of the coercive nature of state action versus the voluntary nature of civil society. In the arena of civil society, whether in the local bridge club or the grocery store, interactions are based on consent – mutually beneficial interactions occur even though they are not recorded in profit and loss statements. State activity, on the other hand, is built on the foundation of force – the ability

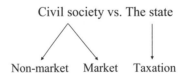

Civil society vs. The state

Non-market   Market   Taxation

Figure 5.2   Civil society–state dichotomy

of one entity to dictate to another the terms of interaction are to be as empowered through the power to tax.

Civil society and self-governance in our framework are near synonyms, while state action is by definition an enforced order. The self-governing properties of a market economy are a function of the institutions of private property, monetary prices and profit and loss accounting. These institutions provide the incentives for economic to husband resources effectively by communicating information regarding the relative scarcities of various goods and services. They also provide the incentive for economic actors to innovate and improve in their economic decision-making. Current inefficiencies in economic relations are quickly translated through the informational mechanisms of the price system into profit opportunities for those entrepreneurs who can eliminate inefficiencies and realize the gains from exchange that were previously unexploited (Kirzner, 1973; Leeson *et al.*, 2006).

Entrepreneurship within the context of a market economy serves both the function of arbitraging within the existing array of economic decisions to ensure efficiency in exchange and production, and innovating in exchange and production to realize previously unrecognized, and therefore unexploited, economic opportunities. The institutions of property, prices and profit and loss continually work to prod economic actors to adjust and adapt their behavior to realize the mutual gains from exchange until no further gains can be exploited. But what are the analogous institutions in the non-market sector of civil society?

THE PHILANTHROPIC ENTERPRISE: ENTREPRENEURSHIP IN NON-MARKET SETTINGS

The incomplete knowledge of the available commodities and services that Hayek stressed is not only felt by consumers but also by entrepreneurs. Entrepreneurs in the market setting, working within the context of property, prices and profit and loss, face incomplete knowledge regarding the desires and demands of consumers. As such, one would expect the issue of incomplete knowledge to be further exacerbated in the arena of nonprofit ventures where by definition prices and profit and loss are absent.

Given this realization, the central question becomes: by what mechanisms can we ensure that actions undertaken are not merely to feel good, but actually to do good? Stated differently, what mechanisms, if any, guide the behavior of entrepreneurs in the non-market setting to ensure that they are allocating resources to those that need them the most? To begin to answer these questions let us consider the notion of entrepreneurship, and the disciplinary mechanisms that exist in the market context, in more detail.

Entrepreneurship is fundamentally an act of dissent. The entrepreneur sees the situation differently than his contemporaries and engages in an action, which is directed at changing the situation in direct opposition to how his contemporaries are currently viewing the scene (Kirzner, 1973). If everyone saw the existing situation the way the entrepreneur saw it, there would be no entrepreneurial profits to be gathered. In short, a profit opportunity known to all is realized by none. The entrepreneur's ability to see the situation differently is the very essence of entrepreneurship whether it is in the activity of buying low and selling high (arbitrage) or the building of a better mouse trap (innovation).

Stated differently, entrepreneurship is a bold and wishful conjecture made by an economic actor. Within the context of the market economy these wishful conjectures are the prime mover of progress precisely because we have clear mechanisms for sorting among these conjectures. Not all wishful conjectures are correct. Most, in fact, go by the wayside and are revealed as little more than wishes through the operation of the price system.

Through the market process, entrepreneurs are redirected in their activity either to make conjectures that are more in line with the underlying tastes and preferences of their fellow citizens or to lose the monetary resources which enable them to finance their wishful conjectures. Nobody's financial resources are unlimited. What spurs entrepreneurship is the lure of profit, and what disciplines entrepreneurs is the penalty of loss. The property rights structure provides the incentives and establishes the issue of the residual claimant, and the price system provides economic actors with the information to act on the bases of those incentives to utilize resources effectively. To understand the importance of disciplinary devices to ensure that resources are being effectively allocated, consider the various market mechanisms that have evolved to deal with the principal-agent problem.

When ownership is separated from control, the principals (owners) can be exploited by the agents (those entrusted to manage the assets) unless these agents are monitored effectively. The principals, however, by the nature of the problem we are setting up, cannot directly monitor the activities of the agents. In the context of a market economy, various impersonal market mechanisms emerge to provide a corporate governance structure and effectively monitor that behavior of agents.

For instance, there is both the market for corporate control through takeovers and mergers, and the market for managerial labor. The evolution of the modern corporation provided a means for financing expansion in business while not incurring all the risk. By selling shares in its business entity, an enterprise could raise needed financial capital.

However, with the creation of the corporation, a chasm exists between the owners (shareholders) and the managers – between principals and agents. The share price of a firm is a reflection of the expected future profitability of the firm. If the firm's assets are not highly valued and its expected future earnings are low, its share price will fall and in the limit the firm will be driven out of existence. If, on the other hand, the firm's assets are highly valued, but its current earnings do not match that expectation, the share price will fall and others will have an incentive to buy those shares at the lower price in order to reorganize the firm to realize the potential earnings of those assets. Managers who do not realize the potential of the firm's assets will be displaced through the process of mergers and acquisitions in the market for corporate control.

Additionally, a vibrant market for managerial labor exists and individuals compete vigorously to establish themselves as being qualified to realize the full potential of a firm's assets through their organizational and leadership skills. The impersonal forces in a market economy, found in this example in the markets for corporate control and for managerial labor, discipline the behavior of agents so it aligns with the interests of the principals. This is accomplished by the institutional functions of property, prices and profit and loss.

But can we say anything in alternative contexts where market forces are absent? How is the principal-agent problem to be addressed in non-market settings? How can the philanthropic enterprise sort between alternative projects to avoid waste? These are the central questions when considering the political economy of the philanthropic enterprise.

First, let us consider the state sector and in particular the effectiveness of democracy in assuring that agents act in the interest of the principals. In this example the agents are elected officials, and the principals are the voting public (Ferejohn, 1986). Is the vote mechanism as effective in disciplining the behavior of the agents in relation to the demands of the principals, as what we argued was the case in the market setting? Our argument is that it is not.

The voting mechanism is governed by the logic of concentrated benefits and dispersed costs. The interaction in democratic politics is one characterized by rationally ignorant voters, specially interested votes, and vote-seeking politicians. The bias of this interaction is for the politician to concentrate benefits on the well-organized and well-informed special interest voters and to disperse the costs on the unorganized and ill-informed mass of voters (see Mitchell and Simmons, 1994: 39–84). This is why good economics is not necessarily good politics, and thus policies can be chosen which are counter-productive from the perspective of overall economic growth. It is this basic examination of the logic of democratic discipline that underlies the argument for government failure theory, which is juxtaposed with market failure theory, in modern political economy. The state cannot be viewed as a better provider of a service even in the face of a market failure simply by hypothesis.

Does the non-profit sector avoid the pitfalls of the state sector? The non-market component of civil society certainly avoids the pitfall of coercion, but it does not have recourse to the institutions of property, prices and profit and loss to the same extent as the market component does. Instead, the non-market sector relies on face-to-face interaction and the disciplinary devices most appropriate for that sort of interaction, namely reputation.

Philanthropic enterprises emerge to help the needy and increase human welfare where state bureaucracy and the vagaries of the market have failed. As mentioned above, the central issue is how the philanthropic enterprise knows if it is doing the right thing in its choice of project A or project B? How does the enterprise calculate the use of scare time and financial resources? We contend that it can do this only by limiting its activities to those initiatives that can be directly monitored and disciplined on the basis of face-to-face mechanisms of self-governance. This is due to the fact that philanthropic enterprise does not have recourse to the anonymous mechanisms of self-governance that exist in a market economy.

The example of micro-finance provides a clear illustration. In the standard story, members of a society who are denied access to normal financial markets can be aided through micro-lending programs to start small businesses that improve their lot in life. These micro-lending programs are run as follows. Since the individuals in question do not have access to traditional forms of collateral to put up against the loans, they must put up their reputation as collateral. For example, five non-family members of the community must vouch for them and be willing to pay their debt if they default. Small loans are made on the basis of this 'reputational collateral', and businesses are started which otherwise would not have been. This is an example market mechanism of self-governance based in part of the norms of face-to-face interaction and reputation.

We suggest that the philanthropic enterprise is most effective when modeled along these lines. In making grants to educational institutions, health care facilities, or artistic endeavors, if the granting foundation has personal knowledge of the grantee and can monitor closely to make sure that the agent (recipient) is acting in the interest of the principal (giver), then the entrepreneurial innovation is more likely to be truly effective in accomplishing its goal. Since the reputational capital of the recipient is what is being held as collateral, the recipient has a strong incentive to accomplish the task for which he has received the grant.

In fact, we would argue that given the necessity of reputation as the main self-governing mechanism (if our goal is effectiveness) that the entrepreneurial activity of the philanthropic enterprise is really a function of betting on people, not on projects. Grant giving organizations should identify people they trust and these people must put their reputation on the line each time. Projects can be attractive, but unless the feedback loops are well established even the most promising project can be poorly executed.

COMPETITION BETWEEN THE PRIVATE AND STATE SECTORS

A case study in the provision of student loans serves to illustrate the ideas discussed above. Indeed considering the philanthropic provision of student loans shows that philanthropic enterprises can fail in the face of competition from the government, which provides student loans via coercive taxation of the citizenry. Richard Cornuelle and colleagues created the United Student Aids Fund, Inc. (USAF) in an attempt to compete with federally subsidized student loans. They assessed that there was a demand for student loans that existed among college students. At the time, the costs of college were increasing and the biggest need was among low-income families attempting to send their children to college who were high risk and had no collateral.

The first task of these entrepreneurs was to identify who needed loans and how much they needed. Cornuelle and associates attempted to identify the neediest students to ensure the loans went to those that needed them the most. The problem faced by these philanthropic entrepreneurs was twofold. First, the philanthropic entrepreneurs associated with USAF had to acquire capital from private organizations. To do so, they had to convince donors that their donations were necessary and would be directed to the goal of putting the neediest students through college. What made this problem especially difficult is that USAF was attempting to privately provide a service that the government was already in the business of providing. This made the problem of convincing private donors to donate money all the more difficult (Cornuelle, 1965: 80–4).

Within this context, USAF had to rely on reputational collateral as the main means of obtaining capital. The philanthropic entrepreneurs had to convince the private donors that the government provided service had failed to meet the needs of low-income students. Further, they had to indicate that the money donated to USAF would better enable needy students to attain student loans and that the receipts would complete their education. Of course convincing private donors that their money will be put to use effectively is not always easy given that the nature of any nonprofit is that it operates under the structure of a bureaucracy and as such is subject to 'soft budget constraints' (Kornai, 1980). Along these lines, Cornuelle noted that, 'fund-raising was difficult. The program was untested. Worst of all, donors felt the government had already preempted the field. It was a hard sale all around' (1965: 85).

In order to overcome some of these issues, the USAF coordinated banks, colleges, students and contributors (the loans were made through banks). For every dollar that was deposited into the bank the bank agreed to lend $12.50 at a nonprofit rate. The money was to be held in a security fund. Students could borrow up to $1000 per year for undergraduate and $2000 per year for graduate students with a maximum of $4000 to be borrowed which was to be repaid starting four months after the student graduated with three years total to repay the loan (Cornuelle, 1965: 84).

After overcoming the first problem of securing capital, the second issue was finding the 'best' recipients for the funds. While reputational collateral on the part of the members of the philanthropic enterprise was necessary to secure the required capital, the enterprise had to seek out potential recipients who possessed adequate reputational capital. Recall that the activities of the philanthropic enterprise take place absent the price mechanism. In the context of school loans, the market was unable to facilitate exchange in the face of government provision of such services and thus assessing willingness to pay through the price mechanism was not possible. In other words, the government provision of loans had 'crowded out' the potential for the market provision of such loans. When the government program failed to generate the desired effect, it was philanthropic enterprises, acting in the non-profit sector, which had to fill the gap.

Market prices convey information among buyers and sellers. Without the price mechanism there was no clear means of exchanging information and determining willingness to pay. In the absence of prices, the task of USAF was to determine which students wanted to college and which were truly committed to completing their educations. Picking the 'best' candidates was important not just in terms of effectively utilizing current funds but also to ensure future donations from private donors.

Of course the USAF was competing with a government program that did not need to prove the value added of the final product. This is because government loans were the result of taxes and the logic of the political decision-making process is such that the cost of the program to each individual taxpayer was small while the benefits to society are vaguely measurable at best. What is the value added to any one individual of one more person attaining a college education? Infinitesimal. Yet in the aggregate political agents assure citizens that society is better off when more of its citizens have college educations. Thus, the government program that provided loans was not subject to the same rigorous tests of value added as philanthropic enterprises are.

This becomes clear when one considers the manner in which the government distributes student loans as compared to the manner in which USAF distributed loans, including the conditions under which they were repaid. The federal government appropriates funds each year to be dispersed by the Student Loan Marketing Association (SLMA), which is a government-sponsored enterprise created by a 1972 federal charter. There is no minimum amount. The only qualifications for student applicants are that they are enrolled full- or part-time, are US citizens or eligible non-citizen residents, and have a satisfactory credit history. The only real limit on the loan is that a student may borrow only up to the total cost of education less any other grants the student is receiving.

The federal program has additional funds that it allows students to borrow, in addition to the student loans, each year. Students do not have to repay the borrowed funds until a year after they graduate and they have ten years to repay the loan. Students pay no interest on the portion of their loan that is subsidized and on the unsubsidized portion they pay no interest while they are in school. At the time that the program was in place, students paid 3 percent interest on the government loans. To default or get forbearance in the federal program is also much easier and if the student is studying for certain government sanctioned professions as much as half of the total loan amount may be forgiven (Cornuelle, 1965: 85–6).

A central dilemma facing USAF was that they had to assess a willingness to pay criterion for the students who have no ability to pay. Thus the standards for providing services by philanthropic enterprises is relatively rigorous because capital to fund the project is scarce, particularly when compared to the government's ability to sequester capital and redistribute it at will. Members of the philanthropic enterprise must not only establish their own reputational collateral in attempting to acquire capital *to* loan to students, but also must acquire reputational collateral *from* the students as a proxy for their willingness to repay their loans.

To establish this reputational collateral among students, USAF required specific levels of academic achievement from the students receiving loans. Ultimately, USAF was better able to provide student loans to the neediest students with the lowest default percentages. They did this through setting up the strict requirements of academic achievement and repayment methods. For instance, a 1964 survey by the General Accounting Office indicated a 16.6 percent delinquency rate on loans provided through the federal program which was about 20 times the delinquency rate on USAF loans (Cornuelle, 1965: 86–9). In other words, the federal program involving low interest rates and extended repayments encouraged delinquencies.

This case highlights the central problem facing philanthropic enterprises. Specifically, they must attempt to determine and assess proxies for market prices. In doing so they face the challenge of acquiring capital through reputational collateral which requires face-to-face knowledge of donors on the one hand and the needs and desires of the communities it strives to help on the other hand. Philanthropic enterprises cannot use market prices to convey information regarding willingness to pay and therefore have high search costs for acquiring information regarding community needs.

The government, in providing student loans at below-market costs, does not concern itself with assessing willingness to pay and therefore does not face the same search costs as philanthropic enterprises. Thus the government enables students to attain low-interest loans with little cost for poor academic performance and little cost for default. Thus, those who would not have otherwise desired a college education are encouraged to do so because of relatively low costs.

The phenomena of dispersed and tacit knowledge in society can make search costs high, yet the government is not confined by such costs (Hayek, 1945: 77–8). The coercive nature of government allows it to relax standards for assessing who needs the loans the most and gives loans to almost anyone. As such, there are weak or non-existent monitoring mechanisms because the associated costs would be exorbitant with little associated benefit for the government. While the private sector faces much higher search costs, it often more correctly identifies the needs of the community it strives to serve due to local, community-based initiatives that require strict donor accountability. Therefore, although fewer loans are distributed, the loans that are distributed are given to those students most likely to succeed and actually be made better off by the assistance.

This problem of overcoming the dispersed knowledge makes philanthropic activity a local phenomenon. As discussed, the primary goals of the philanthropic enterprise are to accurately assess the needs of the community and to acquire reputational collateral. This is best achieved at the local level.

The Habitat for Humanity project, which provides housing for those who live in substandard housing and cannot obtain a mortgage, requires reputational capital on the part of individuals they attempt to help. According to Millard Fuller, the founder of Habitat for Humanity, every Habitat affiliate has a 'family selection committee' comprised of local residents. Further, the people desiring a house must fill out an application and invest what Fuller calls 'sweat equity', which means that the family must help build the house, and once they move in they are required to pay the money back. If the people cannot make the payments due to irresponsibility, Habitat will take the house back (Philanthropy Roundtable, 2001). Thus there is both an end product and a monitoring mechanism. This is only possible on the local level, where the reputations of potential recipients are known, or can be easily discovered, by the family selection committee.

To reiterate, in order to be effective the philanthropic enterprise can only operate effectively on a local level because acquiring the disbursed knowledge and understanding the needs of the community is infinitely costly at the federal level. This is precisely why the government, when providing any type of welfare assistance, generalizes the requirements for distribution and lacks effective feedback mechanisms. At the extreme, these programs can harm the very people they aim to assist by eliminating market exchange and crowding out philanthropic enterprises.

CONCLUSION

The non-profit sector plays a vital role in a society of free and responsible individuals. Without the activities of associations such as churches, community groups, and the like, which provide not just support for those in need but also a sense of community and identity, a key aspect of a free society will be diminished. It is our contention that nothing discourages the development and maintenance of healthy communities quite like the coercive powers of the state. The state has grown in size and scope with the consequence of distorting, and in many instances displacing, the self-governing properties of civil society.

The problem often overlooked in examining civil society is that market forces work in anonymous situations, whereas non-market self-governance is based on face-to-face relations. Face-to-face relationships and anonymous relationships are essential for a vibrant civil society, but each has a different set of limitations. Market forces tend to disturb us when applied to areas of life typically thought of as requiring face-to-face transactions. But we should be just as concerned when the self-governing norms of face-to-face society are pushed into situations, which require the self-governing institutions of anonymous interaction.

Our argument is that non-market activity, such as the philanthropic enterprise, are most effective when limited to local action where the 'reputational collateral' of the recipient is clearly on the line and the services can be directly monitored and valued. When pushed beyond this local level, the philanthropic sector either gets crowded out or co-opted by state activity. The state cannot manage its affairs any better than the non-market sector when pushed beyond a certain level of complexity, but through the power to tax it avoids to a considerable extent the financial constraint impacting more harshly non-market activities that cannot rely on tax financing.

Given these constraints, state and non-market activities geared toward helping those in need and providing a sense of community and identity, when pushed beyond that face-to-face level, are characterized by waste and ineffectiveness. Effective large-scale projects must be coordinated through various impersonal forces as provided through the monetary price system; effective small-scale projects can be coordinated through the face-to-face forces of reputation and community membership. A vibrant civil society will limit state intrusion as much as possible and instead rely on the self-governance of both the non-market and market variety and most importantly understand the proper delineation between state and civil society.

ACKNOWLEDGMENTS

This chapter is partially based on Boettke and Rathbone (2002), a previously unpublished working paper. The current version has been significantly revised and edited by the current authors. Financial assistance from the Mercatus Center is acknowledged. Coyne was a visiting fellow at the Mercatus Center during the writing of this chapter. The usual caveat applies.

NOTES

1.   Rockefeller and Carnegie contributions measured in 2006 dollars.
2.   Source of Buffet, Rockefeller and Carnegie donation information, 'The new powers in giving', *Economist*, 1 July 2006.
3.   See, 'A survey of wealth and philanthropy: the business of giving', (2006), *The Economist*, 25 February 2006, pp. 3–16.
4.   For a categorical breakdown of US philanthropy, see American Association of Fundraising Council (2006).
5.   Source of philanthropic giving data: Johns Hopkins Comparative Nonprofit Sector Project. Available at: http://www.jhu.edu/cnp/pdf/comptable5_dec05.pdf.
6.   First order goods refer to final consumer goods while second, or higher, order goods are those that contribute to the production of first order goods.
7.   However, we argue that the effectiveness of state provision cannot be inferred from its survivorship in this competition in the same way that the survivorship of an economic organization can be taken as evidence of certain efficiency properties in that organization. The main reason for this asymmetry in assessment is because of the important distinction between finance through voluntary means and finance through the coercive means of taxation.
8.   Weber defined the state as a monopoly on violence in a specific geographic region in his 1918 speech, *Politik als Beruf* (*Politics as a Vocation*). A version of this speech is available online, http://www2.pfeiffer.edu/~lridener/DSS/Weber/polvoc.html.

9. According to Tocqueville, associations stand between the government, or the public sector, and the market, or the private sector. Associations allow individual members of a society to come together to solve common problems without relying on the government. As such, on the one hand civil society protects American society as a whole from the extreme individualism of markets, and on the other hand, from arbitrary rule and the abuse of power by political actors.

REFERENCES

Almond, Gabriel A. and Sidney Verba (1963) [1989], *The Civic Culture. Political Attitudes and Democracy in Five Nations*. Newbury Park, CA: Sage.

American Association of Fundraising Council (2006), *Giving USA 2006*, Glenview, IL: American Association of Fundraising Council.

Bankers Trust (2000), *Wealth With Responsibility Study 2000*, New York.

Benson, Bruce L. (1990), *The Enterprise of Law*, San Francisco, CA: Pacific Research Institute.

Boettke, Peter J. and Christopher J. Coyne (2003), 'Entrepreneurship and development: cause or consequence?', *Advances in Austrian Economics*, **6**, 67–88.

Boettke, Peter J. and David L. Prychitko (2004), 'Toward an Austrian school interpretation of nonprofit and voluntary action', *Conversations on Philanthropy*, **I**, 1–40.

Boettke, Peter J. and Anne Rathbone (2002), 'Civil society, social entrepreneurship, and economic calculation', Working Paper, George Mason University Department of Economics.

Bremner, Robert (1994), *Giving: Charity and Philanthropy in History*, Somerset, NJ: Transaction Publishers.

Brooks, Arthur C. (2005), *Gifts of Time and Money: The Role of Charity in America's Communities*, Lanham, MD: Rowman & Littlefield.

Cornuelle, Richard (1965), *Reclaiming the American Dream*, New York: Random House.

Cox, W. Michael and Richard Alm (1999), *The Myths of Rich and Poor*, New York: Basic Books.

Dekker, Paul and Loek Halman (eds) (2003), *The Values of Volunteering: Cross-Cultural Perspectives*, New York: Springer.

Economist (2006a) 'A survey of wealth and philanthropy: the business of giving', *The Economist*, 25 February, Special Section, pp. 3–16.

Economist (2006b) 'The new powers in giving', *Economist*, 1 July, 63–5.

Ehrenberg, John (1999), *Civil Society: The Critical History of an Idea: The Critical History of an Idea*, New York: NYU Press.

Ferejohn, John (1986), 'Incumbent performance and electoral control', *Public Choice*, **50**, 5–26.

Hayek, F.A. (1946) [1948], 'The meaning of competition', in F.A. Hayek *Individualism and Economic Order*, Chicago, IL: University of Chicago Press, pp. 92–106.

Hayek, F. A. (1948), 'The use of knowledge in society', in F.A. Hayek *Individualism and Economic Order*, Chicago, IL: University of Chicago Press, pp. 77–91.

Holcombe, Randall G. (2000) *Writing Off Ideas: Taxation, Philanthropy and America's Non-Profit Foundations*, Somerset, NJ: Transaction Publishers.

Klein, Daniel B. (1997), *Reputation: Studies in the Voluntary Elicitation of Good Conduct*, Ann Arbor, MI: University of Michigan Press.

Kirzner, Israel M. (1973), *Competition and Entrepreneurship*, Chicago, IL: The University of Chicago Press.

Kornai, Janos (1979), 'Resource constrained versus demand constrained systems', *Econometrica*, **47**(4), 801–19.

Leeson, Peter T., Christopher J. Coyne and Peter J. Boettke (2006), 'Does the market self-correct? Asymmetrical adjustment and the structure of economic error', *Review of Political Economy*, **18**(1), 79–90.

McCarthy, Kathleen D. (2005), *American Creed: Philanthropy and the Rise of Civil Society, 1700–1865*, Chicago, IL: University of Chicago Press.

Mises, Ludwig von (1920) [1935], Economic calculation in the socialist common-wealth', in F.A. Hayek (ed.), *Collective Economic Planning*, London: George Routledge & Sons, pp. 87–130.

Mises, Ludwig von (1922), *Socialism: An Economic and Sociological Analysis*, New York: Macmillan Co.

Mises, Ludwig von (1949), *Human Action*, New Haven, CT: Yale University Press.

Mises, Ludwig von (1952), 'Profit and loss', in L.von Mises, *Planning for Freedom*. Grove City, PA: Libertarian Press, pp. 103–43.

Mitchell, William C. and Randy T. Simmons (1994), *Beyond Politics: Markets, Welfare, and the Failure of Bureaucracy*, Boulder, CO: Westview Press.

Moore, Stephen and Julian L. Simon (1999), *The Greatest Century That Ever Was – 25 Miraculous Trends of the Past 100 Years*, 15 December, Washington, DC: The Cato Institute.

Philanthropy Roundtable (2001), 'New powers in giving', January.

Putnam, Robert D. (1993), *Making Democracy Work*, Princeton, NJ: Princeton University Press.

Rubin, Paul H. (1997), 'Promises, promises: contracts in Russia and other post Communist economies', *The Shaftesbury Papers*, **11**, Cheltenham, UK and Brookfield, VT: Edward Elgar.

Salamon, Lester M. (1987) 'Of market failure, voluntary failure, and third-party government: toward a theory of government-nonprofit relations in the modern welfare state', *Journal of Voluntary Action Research*, **16** (1–2), 29–49.

Salamon, Lester M. (1995), *Partners in Public Service: Government-Nonprofit Relations in the Modern Welfare State*, Baltimore, MD: Johns Hopkins University Press.

Smith, Adam 1776 [1904], *An Inquiry into the Nature and Causes of the Wealth of Nations*, 5th edn, Edwin Cannan (ed.), London: Methuen and Co. Ltd.

Smith, David H. (ed.) (2005) *Good Intentions: Moral Obstacles and Opportunities*, Bloomington, IN: Indiana University Press.

Tocqueville, Alexis de (1835/1839) [1969], *Democracy in America*, J.P. Mayer (ed.), translated by George Lawrence. New York: Doubleday & Co., Inc.

Warren, Mark E. (2000), *Democracy and Association*, New Jersey: Princeton University Press.

6. Indigenous communities, entrepreneurship, and economic development in the New Economy

Robert B. Anderson, Scott W. MacAulay, Bob Kayseas and Kevin G. Hindle

INTRODUCTION

Around the world Indigenous Peoples are struggling to rebuild their 'nations' and improve the socioeconomic circumstances of their people. Depending on the figures used this constitutes an emerging market of 500 million people (Peredo *et al.*, 2004; Indigenous Peoples' Human Rights Project, 2003). Participation in the global economy through entrepreneurship and business development is widely accepted as the key to success by most Indigenous People. However, importantly most Indigenous groups want this participation to be 'on their own terms' – terms in which traditional lands, history, culture and values play an important role (Anderson, 2006; Dana *et al.*, 2005; Peredo *et al.*, 2004, Hindle and Lansdowne, 2005; Galbraith *et al.*, 2006). What is emerging is a version of non-market entrepreneurship consistent with the definition used by the editors of this work, which is that ' "non-market entrepreneurship" consists of all forms of entrepreneurship not being undertaken solely for purposes of profit maximization or commercialization, which encompasses entrepreneurial activities such as social enterprise and entrepreneurship, public sector entrepreneurship, policy entrepreneurship, nonprofit entrepreneurship, and philanthropic enterprise, among many others'. Perhaps Indigenous entrepreneurship, or even a more general category called community entrepreneurship, could be added to the 'other' categories in this list.

In the next section, we provide a description of the development aspirations and activities of other Indigenous People and a description of the approach to economic development that is emerging among them, using Canada as a particular example, but also considering others. We also describe the successful efforts of the world's Indigenous Peoples to gain recognition of their rights to their traditional lands and resources as a very important element of their approach to 'non-market entrepreneurship'; one which provides capacity to participate in the global economy one their own terms, some of which are decidedly non-market driven.

Following the overview of Indigenous People (particularly their approach to development and the increasing recognition of their right to their traditional lands and resources), we use regulation theory to explore the feasibility of the emerging Indigenous approach to development including the critical role of entrepreneurship in the process. As a result of this review, we conclude that the approach is theoretically sound. We argue that successful participation in the global economy by a particular Indigenous group is the manifestation in a particular context of the evolving relationship between business (the regime of accumulation, RA) and society (the mode of social regulation, MSR) that produces a mode of development (MD). Further we argue that such an MD emerges from the 'very specific articulation of local social conditions with wider coordinates of capitalist development in general' (Scott, 1988: 108). Importantly, these local conditions include 'economic structures, values, cultures, institutions and histories' (Dicken, 1992: 307).

Having made the theoretical argument, in the third section we present a case study on the Osoyoos First Nation that illustrates one instance of the emergence of a successful MD that is allowing an Indigenous community to participate in the broader economy 'on its own terms' including the role of traditional lands and resources in the process. Then in the fourth and concluding section, we re-examine the Aboriginal approach to development the lens of the Osoyoos experience.

THE PROBLEM AND THE RESPONSE

According to the World Bank 'Indigenous Peoples are commonly among the poorest and most vulnerable segments of society' (World Bank, 2001). Confronted with these depressing economic statistics, many, but certainly not all, modern nation states have recognized the plight of their Indigenous communities. In response, throughout the middle decades of the twentieth century, Indigenous Peoples, along with other poor populations of the world, were the target of a wide range of initiatives, efforts and programmes to assist in economic development. In large part, these top-down, externally developed, modernization-based efforts failed to improve the economic circumstance of the world's poor including Indigenous Peoples, while at the same time often damaging their traditional economies leaving communities less self-reliant and therefore worse of than before.

Agrawal says that the failure of neo-liberal (market) and authoritarian and bureaucratic (state) approaches to development has lead to a 'focus on Indigenous knowledge and production systems' (Agrawal, 1995: 414). He goes on to say that these efforts are an attempt 'to reorient and reverse state policies and market forces to permit members of threatened populations to determine their own future' (Agrawal, 1995: 432). For the most part, these efforts are not taking place outside the global economy, but within it. As Bebbington suggests, 'like it or not, Indigenous Peoples are firmly integrated into a capricious and changing market. Their well-being and survival depends on how well they handle and negotiate this integration' (Bebbington, 1993: 275). He goes on to say that the Indigenous approach to negotiating this integration is not to reject outright participation in the modern economy:

> But rather to pursue local and grassroots control . . . over the economic and social relationships that traditionally have contributed to the transfer of income and value from the locality to other places and social groups. (Bebbington, 1993: 281)

This is certainly the approach to development among Aboriginal people in Canada. They have not been standing idly by accepting the status quo. Instead over recent decades they have been developing and successfully implementing an approach to development. Aboriginal people intended to achieve the outcome described by Bebbington. This approach is described in Box 6.1. Entrepreneurship – the identification of unmet or undersatisfied needs and related opportunities, and the creation of enterprises, products and services in response to these opportunities – lies at the heart of the Aboriginal economic development strategy. Through entrepreneurship and business development they believe they can attain their socioeconomic objectives. These objectives include (a) greater control of activities on their traditional lands; (b) an end to dependency through economic self-sufficiency; (c) the preservation and strengthening of traditional values and the application of these in economic development and business activities; and of course (d) improved socioeconomic circumstance for individuals, families and communities. Others have found this approach among Indigenous People outside Canada, for example among the Maori in New Zealand and Aborigines in Australia (Hindle and Lansdowne, 2005; Frederick and Foley, 2006; Lindsay, 2005), the Sámi Northern Europe (Dana and Remes, 2005; Gernet, 2005), Native Americans in the United States (Pearson, 2005) and in Africa (Ndemo, 2005; Serumaga-Zake *et al.*, 2005). But it is far from the only approach as we discuss in the next section on theory.

BOX 6.1: THE CHARACTERISTICS OF ABORIGINAL ECONOMIC DEVELOPMENT

The Aboriginal approach to economic development is:

1. A predominantly collective one centered on the community or 'nation'.

For the purposes of:
2. Ending dependency through economic self-sufficiency.
3. Controlling activities on traditional lands.
4. Improving the socioeconomic circumstances of Aboriginal people.
5. Strengthening traditional culture, values and languages (and reflecting the same in development activities).

Involving the following processes:
6. Creating and operating businesses that can compete profitably over the long run in the global economy to
   a) Exercise the control over activities on traditional lands
   b) End dependency through economic self-sufficiency.
7. Forming alliances and joint ventures among themselves and with non-Aboriginal partners to create businesses that can compete profitably in the global economy.
8. Building capacity for economic development through: (a) education, training and institution building and (b) the realization of the treaty and Aboriginal rights to land and resources.
9. Strengthening bonding and building social capital.

Adapted from Anderson (1999).

The Emerging Indigenous Market

Events during the final decades of the twentieth century and the opening decade of the twenty-first resulted in Indigenous People becoming an emerging market of some consequence to all players in the global economy. These events can only be covered briefly. We will do so by focusing on three things: (a) ILO 169 of 1989 of the International Labour Organization; (b) the United Declaration on the Rights on Indigenous

People finally going before the General Assembly in the fall of 2006 for a ratification vote; and (b) the policy of the World Bank toward Indigenous Peoples revised in 2005.

It is essential to understand the reason for the emergence of these three things. They are not the result of the benevolent action of the countries of the word coming together to decide to grant something to Indigenous People. If fact, the truth is just the opposite. They are the outcome of a centuries-long struggle by Indigenous People around the world to have their rights recognized, in the face of immense resistance by the states in which Indigenous People have found themselves. This resistance by states (as well as other players such as multinational corporations) has ranged from arguably well-meant efforts at modernization to genocide on a huge scale. Yet Indigenous People have succeeded to a remarkable extent in forcing the world to acknowledge their rights.

International Labor Organization Convention 169
In 1989, the International Labor Organization (ILO), which at the time was the only UN agency with a special convention in relation to Indigenous Peoples, revised its Convention 107 of 1957 and created a new Convention (ILO Convention 169). In response to pressure from Indigenous People, the new convention dropped the 'integrationist' or 'assimilationist' philosophy of the previous one and recognises the rights of Indigenous People 'to retain their own customs and institutions, where these are not incompatible with fundamental rights defined by the national legal system and with internationally recognized human rights' (ILO Article 8).

ILO 169 Article 14 address land rights and Article 15 addresses resource rights. Relevant excerpts from both follow.

Article 14
1. The rights of ownership and possession of the peoples concerned over the lands which they traditionally occupy shall be recognised. In addition, measures shall be taken in appropriate cases to safeguard the right of the peoples concerned to use lands not exclusively occupied by them, but to which they have traditionally had access for their subsistence and traditional activities. . . .

2. Governments . . . identify the lands which the peoples concerned traditionally occupy, and to guarantee effective protection of their rights of ownership and possession.

Article 15
1. The rights of the peoples concerned to the natural resources pertaining to their lands shall be specially safeguarded. These rights include the right of these peoples to participate in the use, management and conservation of these resources.

2. In cases in which the State retains the ownership of mineral or sub-surface resources or rights to other resources pertaining to lands, governments . . . shall consult these peoples, . . . The peoples concerned shall wherever possible participate in the benefits of such activities, and shall receive fair compensation for any damages which they may sustain as a result of such activities.

United Nations Declaration of the Rights of Indigenous Peoples[1]

For more than two decades, efforts have been underway in the United Nations to develop international standards to address the widespread discrimination and marginalization that has forced Indigenous Peoples worldwide into situations of extreme poverty and cultural destruction. After many years of discussion within the UN's Sub commission on Human Rights, on 29 June 2006

> *the Working Group brought forward a proposed final text that offers both an inspiring affirmation of the rights of Indigenous Peoples and an assurance that 'the human rights . . . of all shall be respected.'* (http://www.iwgia.org/graphics/Synkron-Library/Documents/Noticeboard/News/International/PublicstatementAmnesty.htm)

In the preamble the Declaration recognizes the importance of land and resources to Indigenous Peoples saying that they have suffered as a result of the loss of their lands and resources (PP5), that these rights are inherent to their existence as Peoples (PP6), and that these rights are essential to rebuilding Indigenous communities as Indigenous People wish to rebuild them (PP8)

> PP5 Concerned that Indigenous Peoples have suffered from historic injustices as a result of, inter alia, their colonization and dispossession of their lands, territories and resources, thus preventing them from exercising, in particular, their right to development in accordance with their own needs and interests,

> PP6 Recognizing the urgent need to respect and promote the inherent rights of Indigenous Peoples which derive from their political, economic and social structures and from their cultures spiritual traditions, histories and philosophies, especially their rights to their lands, territories and resources;

> PP8 Convinced that control by Indigenous Peoples over developments affecting them and their lands, territories and resources will enable them to maintain and strengthen their institutions, cultures and traditions, and to promote their development in accordance with their aspirations and needs,

A series of statements about specific rights follow the preamble. Excerpts from those most relevant to land and resource rights and development on their own terms follow.

A21 Indigenous Peoples have the right to maintain and develop their political, economic and social systems or institutions, to be secure in the enjoyment of their own means of subsistence and development, and to engage freely in all their traditional and other economic activities.

Indigenous Peoples deprived of their means of subsistence and development are entitled to just and fair redress.

A26 Indigenous Peoples have the right to the lands, territories and resources which they have traditionally owned, occupied or otherwise used or acquired. . . .

A27 Indigenous Peoples have the right to redress, by means that can include restitution or, when this is not possible, of a just, fair and equitable compensation, for the lands, territories and resources which they have traditionally owned or otherwise occupied or used, and which have been confiscated, taken, occupied, used or damaged without their free, prior and informed consent.

The World Bank policy on Indigenous Peoples

In 2005 the World Bank instituted a new policy with respect to Indigenous Peoples, BP4.10. This policy replaces the previous one, OD4.2, dated September 1991. While only pertaining to the activities of the Bank itself and the projects it funds, the new policy is another reflection of the success of the struggle by Indigenous Peoples for recognition of their rights, including those to land and resources. One of the center-pieces of the new policy is the concept of 'free, prior and informed consultation'. The Bank's policy says

2. Free, Prior, and Informed Consultation. When a project affects Indigenous Peoples, . . . assists the borrower in carrying out free, prior, and informed consultation with affected communities . . . taking into consideration the following:
(a) . . . consultation that occurs freely and voluntarily, without any external manipulation, interference, or coercion, . . . parties consulted have prior access to information on the intent and scope of the proposed project in a culturally appropriate manner, form, and language;
(b) . . . recognize existing Indigenous Peoples Organizations (IPOs), including councils of elders, headmen, and tribal leaders, and pay special attention to women, youth, and the elderly;
(c) . . . starts early, since decisionmaking among Indigenous Peoples may be an iterative process, and there is a need for adequate lead time to fully understand and incorporate concerns and recommendations of Indigenous Peoples into the project design

In addition to free, prior and informed consultation, the Bank's policy requires a social assessment

(d) An assessment . . . of the potential adverse and positive effects of the project . . . an analysis of the relative vulnerability of, and risks to, the affected Indigenous Peoples' communities given their distinct circumstances and close ties to land and natural resources . . .

(e) The identification and evaluation . . . of measures necessary to avoid adverse effects, or if such measures are not feasible, the identification of measures to minimize, mitigate, or compensate for such effects, and to ensure that the Indigenous Peoples receive culturally appropriate benefits under the project.

Finally, the policy requires the development of an Indigenous Peoples Plan which includes

(c) A summary of results of the free, prior, and informed consultation . . . that led to broad community support for the project.
(d) A framework for ensuring free, prior, and informed consultation . . . during project implementation.
(e) An action plan of measures to ensure that the Indigenous Peoples receive social and economic benefits that are culturally appropriate, including, if necessary, measures to enhance the capacity of the project implementing agencies.
(f) When potential adverse effects on Indigenous Peoples are identified, an appropriate action plan of measures to avoid, minimize, mitigate, or compensate for these adverse effects.

Concluding comments on the international context

While the ILO Convention and the UN Declaration are not binding on states and the World Bank policy applies only to projects in which the organization is involved the emergence of the three indicates that the world is listing and responding to the just demand of Indigenous People. According to the International Working Group on Indigenous Affairs (IWGIA) of the United Nations (speaking about the UN Declaration but equally true of the other two):

While the Declaration is not binding to governments, it is a positive step which puts pressure on governments to live up to the objectives of the Declaration and would serve to reinforce such universal principles as justice, democracy, respect for human rights, equality, non-discrimination, good governance and good faith. (IWGIA, 2006)

And they put similar pressures on the other major global player, particularly multinational corporations. Indigenous People are emerging as players on consequence in the global economy.

In the section that follows, we explore the theoretical feasibility of Aboriginal people (or any other Indigenous People) negotiating their integration into the global economy in a manner that leaves them a reasonable level of control over the terms, conditions and outcomes of such an integration, and how this might be accomplished and the role of entrepreneurship in this process. In doing so, we will pay particular attention to the role that alliances between Indigenous and non-Indigenous enterprises might play in the process.

THEORETICAL PERSPECTIVE

The modernization and dependency perspectives have dominated development thinking throughout the middle decades of the twentieth century. The former has been the operational paradigm driving the development agenda, giving the state a central role in the process; while the latter has emerged as a critique of the failure of this modernization agenda to deliver the anticipated development outcomes, often casting the corporation as the villain. Even as modified in recent years, the two perspectives present incompatible views of the relationship between a developing people/region and the developed world. In particular circumstances, one or the other of these approaches can often adequately explain what happened. However, when applied in any particular circumstance to offer insight into what might happen, the two produce conflicting answers. Similarly, they provide contradictory guidance to groups searching for a path to development as they perceive it.

In the closing three decades of the twentieth century, the conflict between the modernization and dependency perspectives led many to conclude that both are incomplete (as opposed to wrong) with each describing a possible but not inevitable outcome of interaction between a developing region and the global economy. In this vein, Corbridge says that there has been a powerful trend towards 'theories of capitalist development which emphasize contingency . . . a new emphasis on human agency and the provisional and highly skilled task of reproducing social relations' (Corbridge, 1989: 633). As Tucker states, this allows 'for the possibility of incorporating the experience of other peoples, other perspectives and other cultures into the development discourse' (Tucker, 1999: 16). Development need not be as defined by the 'developed world' and the interaction between a particular people and the global economy need not be as envisaged by the modernization or dependency perspectives; it can be something else entirely. Why not that which is being sought by Indigenous Peoples – development as they define it?

Regulation theory is one of the new approaches to development that emphasizes contingency and human agency. Hirst and Zeitlin say that it executes:

> a slalom between the orthodoxies of neo-classical equilibrium theory and classical Marxism to produce a rigorous but nondeterministic account of the phases of capitalist development that leaves considerable scope for historical variation and national diversity. (Hirst and Zeitlin, 1992: 84)

Expanding on this notion of variation and diversity, Elam says that on one hand, national and regional units are constantly in a state of flux as they adjust to the influences of the global economy. All must accommodate themselves at least to some extent to its hegemony. At the same time, these broader global influences 'are seen as having essentially local origins' (Elam, 1994: 66). This translates into a counter-hegemonic potential in terms of the activities actually undertaken by people as they negotiate their way locally through the global economy. It is not simply a case of conform or fail.

Regulation theory analyzes the global economy 'in terms of a series of *modes of development* based on combination of the currently ascendant *regime of accumulation* and a variety of *modes of social regulation*' (Hirst and Zeitlin, 1992: 84–5). The regime of accumulation determines the general possibilities for the economy. Scott says it 'can be rather simply defined as a historically specific production apparatus . . . through which surplus is generated, appropriated, and redeployed' (Scott, 1988: 8). Importantly, with respect to geographic scale, the regime of accumulation is a 'relationship between production and consumption defined at the level of the international economy as a whole' (Hirst and Zeitlin, 1992: 85).

If the world were Adam Smith's, peopled by the universal perfectly rational 'economic man', no regulation of the global economy beyond the 'invisible hand' of perfectly functioning markets would be required. But the world is not Smith's; people are far from perfectly rational and they are driven by many things not economic. Further, they are far from universal in the nature of their variations from the 'perfect'. As a result, Scott says that stability in the economic system is:

> dependent on the emergence of a further set of social relations that preserve it, for a time at least, from catastrophic internal collisions and breakdowns. These relations constitute a mode of social regulation. They are made up of a series of formal and informal structures of governance and stabilization ranging from the state through business and labor associations, to modes of socialization which create ingrained habits of behaviour, and so on. (Scott, 1988: 9)

Hirst and Zeitlin agree saying that a mode of social regulation (MSR)

> is a complex of institutions and norms which secure, at least for a certain period, the adjustment of individual agents and social groups to the over arching principle of the accumulation regime. (Hirst and Zeitlin, 1992: 85)

While regulation theory does not prescribe the exact nature of a particular mode of social regulation, it is generally agreed that:

1. A regime of accumulation does not create or require a particular mode of social regulation, 'each regime, in short, may be regulated in a multiplicity of ways' (Scott, 1988: 9).

2. Because modes of social regulation are based on such things as 'habits and customs, social norms, enforceable laws and state forms' (Peck and Tickell, 1992: 349) unique modes 'can exist at virtually any territorial level – local, regional, national, global' (Storper and Walker, 1989: 215).

Another aspect of regulation theory – its historicity – adds further strength to the argument that modes of social regulation, and therefore modes of development differing considerably one from another, can and do emerge at every geographic scale.

Corbridge (1989) says regulation theory indicates that the global economic system has gone through four stages in the twentieth century. In stage one, the system was in equilibrium. Stage two was a period of crisis or disequilibrium resulting from a shift from the extensive to the Fordist regime of accumulation. Equilibrium returned in stage three when suitable modes of social regulation emerged. The fourth (current) stage is also one of crisis caused by a failure of the monopolistic mode of social regulation (in all it variants) to accommodate a 'selective move from mass production [the Fordist regime accumulation] to various forms of flexible production' (Norcliffe, 1994: 2).

Forces resulting in the shift to the new flexible regime of accumulation include: (a) technical limits to rigid fixed capital production techniques; (b) working class resistance to Taylorist and Fordist forms of work organization (Jessop, 1989); (c) a change in consumption patterns 'toward a greater variety of use values . . . [that] cannot be easily satisfied through mass production' (Amin, 1984: 12); (d) the increasing mobility of capital and the resulting ability of transnational corporations (TNCs) to move among spatially-bounded regulatory jurisdictions in the pursuit of greater profits (Leyshon, 1989); and (e) in the face of this internationalization of capital, the inability of national Keynesian policies [all variants of the monopolistic mode of social regulation] to avert crisis (Komninos, 1989).

Everywhere and at every geographic scale – community, subnational region, national, supranational region and globally – people are struggling to develop modes of social regulation that will allow them to interact with this new flexible regime of accumulation on their terms. As they do this, they are building the 'new economy', not simply reacting to it.

As a result, there has been a shift in who companies consider stakeholders and how they behave toward these groups. Nowhere is this truer than in the relationship between companies and communities. In spite of globalization and information technology, everything a company does it does somewhere, every employee and every customer lives somewhere, and inputs of raw material and capital goods come from somewhere; and all these somewheres are communities in some sense of the word. Because of this, as companies forge networks of suppliers, subcontractors and marketing channel partners and seek to control them through 'collective social and institutional order in place of hierarchical control' (Storper and Walker, 1989: 152), they are much more likely to see communities as valued members of networks rather than something external to these networks.

This increase interest in communities by companies is particularly significant for those communities interested in economic development as many are. If an Indigenous community (or any other) can show that it can become a valued member of a network it is likely to find that the companies that make up the network will in turn be supportive of the community's development aspirations, not for charitable reasons but out of economic self-interest, a far more enduring motive. A sense of this can be found in Hewlett-Packard's 'New Framework for Global Engagement'.

> our global-citizenship and business strategy is about doing good and doing well in the same activities – as opposed to doing well in order to do good.
> A few years ago . . . realized . . . philanthropic efforts . . . results suboptimal. Could achieve much more if doing good and doing well were mutually reinforcing (and with recent world events we felt that we needed to do more). At the same time, we thought we could achieve more for HP's business in the process – a vital consideration for our shareholders as well as our competitiveness. (Dunn and Yamashita, 2003: 53–4)

HP is not alone in this view. Other corporations have reached the same conclusion, which flows naturally from the demands of the new flexible regime of accumulation. As a result, in recent years many Aboriginal communities have been able to forge lasting mutually beneficial relationships with corporate partners with views similar to HP's. Examples include the Osoyoos Indian Band with Vincor Canada's largest wine producer (explored later in this chapter, the La Ronge First Nation with Cameco the world's largest uranium mining company and with Trimac a multinational trucking firm (Hindle *et al.*, 2005), and the Meadow Lake Tribal Council with Millar-Western Pulp (Anderson, 2002) to name just a few.

This leads us to a discussion of the modes of social regulation emerging in response to the demands of the flexible regime of accumulation. The 'new economy rhetoric' has been stressed deregulation. But, in fact, what is being touted as deregulation is not; it is re-regulation. The nature of the regulation is changing but regulation continues, as it must. What is happening is a shift in the locus of regulation from the 'nation state' in two directions – to the supra-national and to the local – as a number of authors attest. For example, Amin and Malmberg (1984: 222) say the crisis in the global economy has resulted in 'new opportunities for the location of economic activities' and that 'the geography of post-Fordist production is said to be at once local and global'. Scott (1988: 108) agrees saying that new industrial spaces result from a 'very specific articulation of local social conditions with wider coordinates of capitalist development in general'. Finally, Dicken (1992: 307) emphasizes that successful participation in the global economic system 'is created and sustained through a highly localized process' and that 'economic structures, values, cultures, institutions and histories contribute profoundly to that success'.

With the shift in locus of regulation, the differentiating role of the state at the national level has decreased (from what it was when the national Keynesian modes of social regulation ruled in partnership with the Fordist regime of accumulation) and the homogenizing role of the state at the supranational level has increased – the European Economic Community, the North American Free Trade Agreement, the General Agreement on Tariffs and Trade, and so on. This 'globalization' of regulation is a reality; it, along the global flexible regime of accumulation, is the face of the global economy that communities see. Those who chose to participate in this global economy must accommodate themselves to this reality. But, and this is the key, they can do so 'on their own terms' so long as these term do not conflict with the global 'rules of the game'. So the Osoyoos Indian band can grow grapes and make and sell wine in a manner consistent with their history, culture, values and objectives, so long as they follow the sub-national, national and international 'rules of the wine game'. Further, over time by their actions they can influence the nature of these rules. Similarly, the La Ronge First Nation can and has established a business to harvest, dry and export organic wild mushrooms to Europe and Japan. How they chose to manage the land and compensate the pickers is up to them, but the product must meet organic standards and food safety regulations at the national and international level. As these and other communities do this, the global mode of social regulation acquires local flavors, and distinct modes of development emerge that are at the same time local and global.

The state at all levels and the 'local' do not have the mode of social regulation field to themselves. There is another important player – the civil sector. This is a diverse category consisting of an almost limitless number of non-state organizations ranging from non-governmental aide agencies, through groups espousing a variety of causes such as the environment (for example Green Peace and the Sierra Club) and human rights (for example Amnesty International), to groups speaking for a particular group of people (for example the World Council of Indigenous People), and so on. These groups, too, operate at the subnational, national and international levels. Directly through their actions and indirectly through the pressure they bring to bear on government and companies, the organizations of the civil sector play an influential part in the shaping of the mode of social regulation and in its evolution over time.

In the Indigenous context, a case in point would be the outcry by civil groups in response to the destruction of the rainforests not only from an environmental perspective but also in response to the displacement of Indigenous communities. The campaign has had an impact. Pressure on states has resulted in some of them addressing both environmental and Indigenous concerns. Perhaps more telling, publicity and the resulting market pressure on the forestry companies has resulted in at least some companies adopting more environmentally appropriate forest practices and more responsive and inclusive approaches to working with Indigenous communities in regions where they operate. This story repeats itself in other areas; for example, the growing support by many groups for: (a) Indigenous land rights and the right to self determination; and (b) the Indigenous right to 'ownership' of their traditional environmental and 'medical' knowledge, and the related right to participate in decision about the appropriate use of this knowledge and to share in the benefits from its commercialization. These and other actions by the civil sector have served to create aspects of the emerging and evolving mode of social regulation that increase the strategic importance for Indigenous communities in the networks of corporations.

Not all communities elect to participate uncritically or at all in the global economy. As a result, local modes of social regulation can be, in Gramscian terms, both hegemonic and counter-hegemonic in their policies and programs according to the extent to which they consent to capitalist global economy, attempt to transform it or dissent from it. These three responses are associated with three different analytical/intuitive starting-points with respect to the global capitalist economy. This approach is inspired by Schuurman's (1993) discussion of Eugenio Tironi's analysis of social movement discourses in Santiago, Chile. The first is an analysis that claims that peripheral (Indigenous or other) communities have been excluded from capitalism and that the objective is to remedy this by removing whatever barriers are responsible for this exclusion, and the prescribed solution is usually 'modernization'. The second is an analysis that claims that capitalism is at least in part culturally alien and that it is necessary to transform the 'alien' aspects of it as part of the process of participating in it. The third is an analysis that claims that capitalism is exploitative and beyond redemption and that the need is to exclude or resist it. These analytical/intuitive starting points are not simply abstract concepts. They and the beliefs about the capitalist economy associated with them are present in varying combinations and varying strengths among the members of all communities. So, it is quite possible for an Indigenous community to arrive at an approach to participation in the global economy that acknowledges the need for some modernization

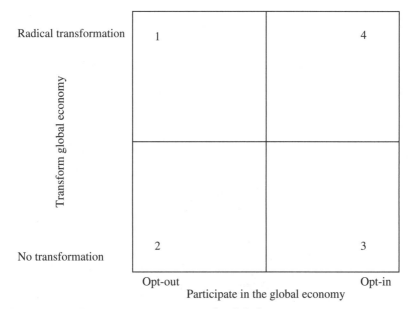

Figure 6.1   Community responses to the global economy

(for example managerial education and technical education), while maintaining certain highly valued traditional traits (for example a communal
rather than individual land holding system) and resisting certain things the
system might seek to impose on them (for example rejecting one person one
vote democracy in favour of clan and/or hereditary leadership).

Figure 6.1 captures these possibilities by considering a group's response
to the global economy on two continuums. The first is the degree to which
a group opts into the global economy, or opts out. The second addresses
the nature of this opting in or opting out. Is the approach to accept the
terms of the global economy 'as is', or is it to attempt to transform it in
some fashion. A combination of the continuums results in four extreme
possibilities. The first two occur when a group chooses to opt out of the
economy. At one extreme the opting out can be passive; that is choosing not
to participate and instead seeking isolation and even protection from the
impact of the global economy. Alternatively, the opting out can be active
and aggressive where a group rejects the global economy and seeks to resist
it or overthrow it through protest and even 'revolution'. The other two
extreme positions (numbers 3 and 4) occur when a group chooses to 'opt
in' and actively participate in the global economy. Again that participation
can be characterized further by the degree to which the group passively
accommodates itself to the requirements of the global economy, or not.

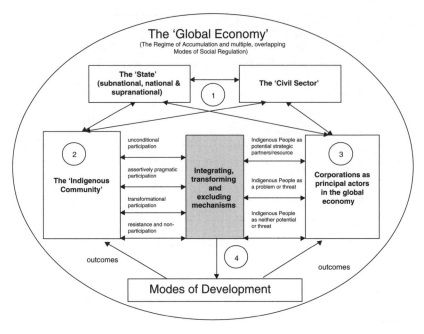

Figure 6.2   Modes of development

The Aboriginal approach in Canada (see Box 6.1) has been of the opt-in variety, but it has not been passive. Participation in the economy has been accompanied by an ongoing struggle for land and other rights to allow this participation to be 'on their own terms'. Indigenous responses elsewhere cover the entire spectrum of possibilities from rejection and violent revolution to passive acceptance and willing assimilation.

It follows that the mix of integrating, transforming and excluding mechanisms adopted by a particular community in its approach to the global economy, and therefore the mode of development that emerges, is heavily influenced by the particular 'face' of the state, the civil sector and corporations that that community sees now and has seen in the past. What Osoyoos 'sees' as its particular collage as it develops its Nk'Mip Project is many respects the same as what other winery and eco tourism operators in the Okanagan Valley see, but in some important respects it is not. Finally, this face is ever evolving not static. The face of the corporation seen by communities 30 years ago is not the same face as they see today, and that new face offers promise.

Figure 6.2 attempts to illustrate the complex relationship among Indigenous communities, corporations, the state at all levels and the civil sector, as all work together (consciously or unconsciously, willingly or unwillingly) in the formation and evolution of modes of social regulation in response to the flexible regime of accumulation. In any particular case a complex set of factors interact to influence the outcome of the interaction of a group of people (in this case that follows an Aboriginal community, but it need not be) with the forces of the global economy as they seek to develop 'on their terms'. These include (numbered 1, 2 and 3 in the model)

1. The impact of the 'state' at all levels and the 'civil sector' on the multiple overlapping modes of social regulation and therefore on participants in the global economy, and the influence of these participants on the 'state' and the 'civil sector'.
2. The community-in-question's approach to economic development (in this case Aboriginal) including history, current circumstances, objectives, approach to participation in the global economy including strategies for participation, transformation and exclusion (and these are not mutually exclusive categories), and actual outcomes.
3. Corporate (as the usual representative of the regime of accumulation encountered by communities) responses to the community-in-question particularly motivating forces (including but not limited to the community's control over critical natural, human and financial resources and/or community members attractiveness as a market), strategies and objectives, and actual outcomes.

And as both an outcome and ongoing feedback to the process

4. The expected mode of development and the actual mode that emerges in the particular circumstances.

Indigenous groups that choose to 'opt in' to the global economy are not at the end of the process, they are at the beginning. To successfully 'opt in', on their own terms or not, they must identify business opportunities and then marshal resources and develop organizations to realize the potential that these opportunities have to satisfy their economic and other development objectives. This is the process of entrepreneurship. Not the entrepreneurship that is narrowly conceived of as a small business operated and/or a new business created by an entrepreneur, but the entrepreneurship that is broadly conceived of as an economy-building process – Schumpeterian entrepreneurship. Morris (1998) captures the nature of this process by stating, 'entrepreneurship is a universal construct that is applicable to any person, organization (private or public, large or small), or nation' and that 'an entrepreneurial orientation is critical for the survival and growth of companies as well as the economic prosperity of nations' (Morris, 1998: 2).

Similarly, Kao *et al.* (2002) define entrepreneurism as, 'not just a way of conducting business; it is an ideology originating from basic human needs and desires . . . entails discovering the new, while changing, adapting and preserving the best of the old' (Kao *et al.*, 2002: 44). Other authors, including Blawatt (1998), Drucker (1985), Fiet (2000) and Moran and Ghoshal (1999) agree. Description of the entrepreneurial process, however, does not address the issue of agency. What factors contribute to initiating, negotiating and maintaining the process in the first place? We argue that social capital and mediating structures are essential agents of change in successful Indigenous modes of economic developments.

Produced capital, human capital, and natural capital, while critical ingredients of economic development, require organization and integration if they are to produce wealth. The term 'social capital' conceptualizes this requirement and gives considerable scope to the range of modes of development that are possible. 'Social capital is the glue that holds societies together and without which there can be no economic growth or human well-being' (Serageldin in Grootaert, 1998: iii). More technically:

> Social capital includes the social and political environment that enables norms and shapes social structure. In addition to . . . largely informal, and often local, horizontal and hierarchical relationships . . . [it] also includes the more formalized institutional relationships and structures such as government, the political regime, the rule of law, the court system, and civil and political liberties. (Grootaert, 1998: 3)

For Indigenous communities, as the Osoyoos case will demonstrate, the roles, powers and capacities of local, formal institutions are indicators of how successful, from sustainability and cultural perspectives, economic development will be. Indeed, as Newman and Dale (2005: 477) argue, 'much of the practical movement toward sustainable development is occurring at the community level. Many communities are attempting to resolve conflict surrounding multiple uses of land, where values are often tightly held'. Borrowing from the work of the other social capital theorists, Newman and Dale distinguish between bonding social capital and bridging social capital.

For local economic development, bonding social capital is generated by strong social and cultural ties between members of a community. It allows for the creation of a common view of the community and the values it holds. It can 'reinforce exclusive identities and homogeneous groups' (Newman and Dale, 2005: 479). For Indigenous communities working to maintain and enhance their cultures, strategies to articulate culture with economic development are essential if the juggernaut of the dominant regime of capitalist accumulation is not to totally impose its own cultural values. This requires strong bonding social capital and the political will and power to express the common aspirations of the community. This is one of the main functions of local or band government.

Bridging social capital, on the other hand, consists of ties with institutions outside of the community. In many Indigenous communities, community development corporations assess and enhance economic development opportunities by negotiating deals and joint-ventures with businesses well outside the network of bonding social capital. In this sense, the ties created by bridging social capital are weak in that they are subject to negotiation and are evaluated, in economic development terms, according to profitability. Profitability, however, is just one of the terms set by Indigenous Peoples. A long-term view of sustainability must be factored in as well as provisions to ensure collective benefit to all members of the community. It is important that both types of social capital be in balance. Indigenous communities' cultures can be maladaptive if they are not open to change and innovation. Culture is a strategy for survival by setting norms and values appropriate to existing conditions. If bonding social capital is such that change is not accepted, opting out of capitalist economic development may well be the choice, albeit one that is rife with dangers of being short-lived. Should bonding social capital be too weak, bridging social capital has the potential to overwhelm any cultural values that are at odds with mainstream values.

This is where conceptualizing Indigenous band governments and community development corporations as mediating structures is helpful. MacIntyre defines mediating structures as 'organizations that stand between individuals and the larger entities of society' (MacAulay and MacIntyre, 1998: 35). The structures, especially community development corporations, negotiate bridging social capital for economic development. There are also structures such as band governments that can mediate conflict in communities, facilitating the growth of bonding social capital (MacAulay and MacIntyre, 1998). Couto and Guthrie see the 'democratic potential' of 'community-based mediating structures [to] adapt capitalism to serve families, communities, and their broad social purposes' (1999: 4). Mediating structures can be dynamic agents of change and can provide and enforce policies that set the environment for economic growth, In terms of regulation theory, Gendron argues that:

> The new system in which economic activities are embedded is characterized by institutions that are the result of a compromise between social actors originally in conflict . . . When they are in alignment, these institutional forms result in a new regulation mode offering a certain degree of order that enables social and economic action. (2003: 487)

Based on regulation theory in general and the characteristics of the current moment in the cycle of crisis and equilibrium of the capitalist system in which we find ourselves, it is reasonable to conclude the Aboriginal approach to development described in Box 6.1 is theoretically sound. They, and others, can participate in the global economy 'on their terms' with an important proviso. That proviso is that 'their terms' cannot be in fundamental conflict with the requirements of the currently dominant flexible regime of accumulation and the pervasive global mode of social regulation that is emerging. This condition still leaves considerable room for local variations of the mode of social regulation reflecting a particular community's objectives, culture and values, and history. The key is to have mediating structures that foster both bridging and bonding social capital. The activities of the Osoyoos Indian Band described in the next section illustrate this.

THE OSOYOOS INDIAN BAND

The Osoyoos Indian Band (OIB) is located in the province of British Columbia, Canada. It has 567 members (370 of whom live 'on reserve') on a land-base of 32 000 acres (13 000 ha) in the southern Okanagan Valley. The land of the OIB is among the most environmentally sensitive in Canada, containing part of the country's only desert ecosystem. More than 60 percent of this unique ecosystem has been completely destroyed, and less than 10 percent remains relatively undisturbed, much of this on Osoyoos land. This ecosystem provides habitat for a third of Canada's endangered species; among them, half the vertebrates considered at risk, more than 100 rare plants and 300 rare invertebrates. Yet it is this land that is the foundation for much of the OIB's wine/tourism-related economic development activity described in the following pages. As Stephen Hume says, this seems to suggest

> two colliding realities – the carefully manicured fields of industrial scale viniculture . . . and the dusty, dishevelled sweep of prime rattlesnake habitat that hasn't changed since some Okanagan warriors rode south to fight the Americans on the side of Chief Joseph and the Nez Perce. (Hume, 2001)

To Clarence Louie, current Chief of the OIB, the appearance of colliding realities is deceiving. Instead, these disparate pieces are not only compatible; they are complementary, so much so that one cannot exist without the other. For Chief Louie, economic development and the self-sufficiency it creates is the best way to secure the right of his people to be who they are, to take pride in their heritage and to protect the fragile desert landscape in which a good part of their cultural identity is forever rooted. The Nk'Mip Project is the product of this belief. In other words, development but on their own terms in which control over traditional lands and resources plays a key role, as do traditional culture and values.

Before describing the Nk'Mip Project in some detail it is useful to take a brief look at the other economic development activities of the OIB. Through the Osoyoos Indian Band Development Corporation (OIBDC), the band owns and operates nine profitable enterprises – a construction company, a sand and gravel company, a forestry company, a campground, a recreational vehicle park, a golf course, two housing developments and a grocery store. The Band also leases land to several corporations and in most cases these corporations provide more than just lease revenue; there is often also a related business alliance.

The motto of the Osoyoos Indian Band Development Corporation is 'working with business to preserve our past by strengthening our future'. Two of the development objectives of the band and the OIBDC are: (a) to achieve full employment for its members; and (b) become economically self-sufficient by 2010. These and OIB's other goals are presented in Box 6.2. All five are consistent with the Aboriginal approach to development described in Box 6.1. Clearly the people of the OIB are opting into the global economy, but attempting to do so on their own terms.

The OIBDC is governed by a Board of Directors. The voting members of the board are the OIB Chief and Councillors, who are elected by the

---

BOX 6.2   OSOYOOS INDIAN BAND GOALS

- To increase the level of education in the following areas: academic, athletic, vocational and cultural – and that this responsibility will be shared by the Band, parents and students to be motivated to life long learning.
- To decrease the dependency on government funding through increased level of self-generated income, joint ventures, leasing, land and resource development so that economically we can one day be self-sufficient.
- To develop programs that reduce dependency and create community involvement that brings back the traditional Indian concepts of honour, caring, sharing and respect.
- To promote a well disciplined organization that will reduce the political influence within the Band and its agencies.
- To increase the standard of living opportunity for every Osoyoos Indian Band member.

Source: http://www.oib.ca/mission.htm.

community. At election time and throughout their terms in office they are accountable to the community for their actions including the decisions they make about the activities of the OIBDC, and the results they achieve. This ensures that the cultural vision and values of the community are represented and defended.

As evidence of the quality of the governance to date the current Chief has served continuously for 20 years with the exception of one two-year term. As the chart indicates there are six non-voting advisors to the Board selected for their expertise. While they are non-voting, the opinions of the advisory board members are respected and the elected voting directors rarely make decisions which fly in the face of this advice. Further, most issues do not reach the board until they have passed through a committee or committees made up of voting and non-voting Board members and others who thoroughly review issue or proposal. This is particularly true with respect to the evaluation of new business opportunities and/or the expansion of existing ones. This eliciting of outside expertise builds bridging capital.

As the chart indicates, the elected Chief of the OIB is also the Chief Executive Officer (CEO) of the development corporation. The CEO along with the Chief Operating Officer (COO) form the senior management of the corporation. The day-to-day operation of each of the OIBDC businesses is the responsibility of that business manager. The operating departments are supported by two support groups, finance and human resources.

The OIBDC is a corporation and like any corporation it reports to its shareholders and stakeholders quarterly and annually. However, because of its governance structure its accountability to the community (its shareholder and major stakeholder) is much closer. Issues relating to OIBDC come up regularly at the meetings of the Chief and Council in their role as government, and many of these meetings are public. In addition, according to Chris Scott the development corporation holds regular meetings with groups of stakeholders about activities, current and proposed, that will have an impact upon them to keep them informed and to elicit their advice. Bonding social capital is both required by the consultative process and is generated through it. Comprehensive consultation is not as challenging as it might first seem because of the size of the community. With only a few hundred members every one does literally know everyone else and, as with all small communities, there are few secrets. And finally, with elections every two years the election campaign and related scrutiny is virtually continuous and the ultimate moment of accountability for the voting Directors never very distant. As the results describe in the following paragraph show, the system seems to be working.

Table 6.1   Source of income

	1986	2001	Numeric increase (%)	Change (%)
Employment income (percentage of household income)	28.1 %	44.5%	16 %	58 %

Source: 2001 Canadian Census.

In 1994, the OIB had revenues from commercial activities of $1.3 million. By 2002 revenues from its ten commercial activities had increased to $12 million, an almost ten-fold increase. In 2003, the OIBDC businesses reported a profit of $1 000 000. It is expected that these profits will grow by 20 percent per year (Matas, 2005). In 1994, the value of payments received from the federal government exceeded self-generated commercial revenues. By 2003 self-generated revenues greatly exceeded the $3.7 million received from the federal government. This success prompted Chief Clarence to say 'if all the federal funding dried up, we could still run programs at the same level of service' (Matas, 2005: E7). This later statement serves to illustrate the uses to which the profits of the OIBDC are put. Fully 60 percent go to fund community programs of various types. The remaining 40 percent is reinvested in business operations.

Source of income data (Table 6.1) from the 1986 and 2001 census confirms the increasing importance of employment income as a percent of total household income. In 1986, employment income accounted for only 28.1 percent of total household income among members of the OIB. By 2001, it had increased to 44.5 percent, an absolute increase of 16 percentage points and a percent increase of 58 percent. Not yet self-sufficient, but clear progress toward the goal and a considerable accomplishment.

Success on the employment front has been equally impressive as confirmed by selected census data (Table 6.2). Between 1986 and 2001, the OIB participation rate increased from 34.6 percent to 46.2 percent, the unemployment rate fell from 29.6 percent to 9.3 percent and the employment rate increased from 25.6 percent of the potential labour force (those 15 and older) to almost 42 percent.

While the gains made by the people of the OIB between 1986 and 2001 as a result of their development efforts have been impressive, much remains to be done if the people of the OIB are to achieve parity with the non-Aboriginal people of British Columbia as illustrated by the comparative data presented in Table 6.3. For example, while OIB employment income as

Table 6.2   Employment data

	1986	2001	Numeric change	Change (%)
All 15 years and over	390	465	75	19%
In the labour force (all 15 years and over)	135	215	80	59%
Employed (all 15 years and over)	100	195	95	95%
Unemployed (all 15 years and over)	40	20	−20	−50%
Participation rate (all 15 years and over)	34.6%	46.2%	12%	33%
Unemployment rate (all 15 years and over)	29.6%	9.30%	−20%	−69%
Employment rate	25.6%	41.9%	16%	64%

Source: 2001 Canadian Census.

a percentage of total income improved between 1986 and 2001, the resulting level of 44.5 percent is still very low compared to the 75.8 percent level for the province as a whole. The same is true for the participation rate and employment rates. While the OIB increase is a major achievement, the 2001 participation rate of 46.2 percent is far below the provincial rate of 65.2 percent. The 2001 employment rate of 42 percent, while a great improvement over the 1986 rate of 25.6 percent, is still short of the provincial rate of almost 60 percent. Realizing the challenge that they still face, the OIB are continuing their development efforts. The Nk'Mip Project, described in the next section is the centerpiece of their ongoing efforts.

THE NK'MIP PROJECT

To begin our discussion of the Nk'Mip project, we will first examine wine and Aboriginal tourism in general and in the Okanagan Valley. A third tourism – eco tourism – could have been included but we feel we can accomplish our purposes without doing so. Examining wine and Aboriginal tourism will help us understand the regime of accumulation and multifaceted mode of social regulation that the OIB faced and faces as it identifies and exploits business opportunities in pursuit of its development objectives.

Wine Tourism

Globally, wine tourism continues to increase in popularity as wine lovers seek opportunities to taste and buy wine in unique settings. Successful wine tour operations are not limited to old world producers. In fact, new world

Table 6.3   Comparative performance – 2001 conditions

	Osoyoos	British Columbia
Employment income (as a percentage of household income)	44.5%	75.8%
Participation rate (all 15 years and over)	46.2%	65.2%
Unemployment rate (all 15 years and over)	9.3%	8.5%
Employment Rate	41.9%	59.6%

Source: 2003 Canadian Census.

wineries have enjoyed considerable success. In 1995, Australia wineries had 5 million visits, as did the Napa Valley in California (Getz *et al.*, 1999: 20). Robert Mondavi Winery alone has over 300 000 visitors annually.

The wine tourism industry is more than just wine tasting at a winery. Hall and Macionis define it as the 'visitation to vineyards, wineries, wine festivals and wine shows for which grape wine tasting and/or experiencing the attributes of the grape wine region are the prime motivating factors for visitors' (Hall and Macionis, 1998). Successful wine tourism regions have three things in common: (a) a well-deserved reputation for quality wines (b) a critical mass of wineries catering for the wine tourist and (c) complimentary services and events.

As wine tourism grows some areas, particularly the Napa Valley, are experiencing high volumes of tourists causing congestion, and in the opinion of some, over-commercialization. According to Halliday 'It (Napa Valley) witnessed exponential proliferation of wineries and cellar operations which were in fact more concerned with selling cheap tourist baubles than wine' (Halliday, 1999). As a result, it has become a 'victim of its own success' at least in the minds of those wine tourists for whom a quality wine experience is important. This creates an opportunity for other wine regions to attract tourists interested in quality wines and quality wine tours. A large number of such tourists is not essential. A small number of high-yield tourists can support a region. High-yield customers are those who travel to a region specifically for wine-related reasons and stay for an extended time. These customers are looking for the complete wine experience.

Okanagan Valley wine Industry and tourism
The Okanagan Valley is located in the south central part of the province of British Columbia, Canada. The 124-mile long valley begins at the town of Osoyoos in the south and runs north to Salmon Arm between the Cascade

Mountains on the west and the Monashee Mountains on the east. The valley has distinct microclimates that range from the hot, sandy, desert in the southern valley to the cooler vineyard sites in the northern part of the valley. Chardonnay, Merlot, Cabernet Sauvignon, Pinot Gris and Pinot Noir are commonly grown in the south, while Pinot Blanc, Pinot Noir, Pinot Gris, Riesling and Gewürztraminer are grown in the mid- and northern regions. The mid- and northern areas also produce the region's famed ice wines.

Wine production is a growing industry in the Okanagan Valley. Len Bykowski, president of the British Columbia Wine Institute in Kelowna, is quoted in the *Calgary Herald* newspaper as saying 'In 1990, we harvested 4800 tons of British Columbia grapes, producing 2.9 million litres of wine. This year it's anticipated to be 16 000 tons of grapes and 9.6 million litres of wine' (Dolphin, 2002). As production has increased, so have the number of wineries. In 1990 the Okanagan Valley had 14 wineries; today there are 72, compared to 200+ in the Napa Valley. The region grows 15 to 25 percent of all grapes produced in Canada and has 10 percent of all country's wineries.

The relatively small size of the wine producing sector in British Columbia forced the vintners to recognize the need to differentiate themselves from Californian and European operations. Many have sought to do so by producing high quality, distinctive wines. Ice wine is an example of this differentiation strategy. In addition to high quality wine, the wineries of the Okanagan strategy includes the construction of top-end facilities to attract potential customers who may have gone to Napa Valley in the past.

For wine tourists, the Okanagan Valley is divided into the north tour and the south tour. The north tour begins in the city of Kelowna and includes: Sumac Ridge Estate Winery, Hainle Vineyards Estate Winery, Mission Hill Winery, Quails' Gate Estate Winery, Pinot Reach Cellars and Gray Monk. The largest winery of the north tour is Mission Hill, which had 100 000 visitors in 2001. The company is forecasting an annual 25 percent visitor growth rate. For the past 22 years, the city of Kelowna has hosted the Okanagan Fall Wine Festival. In 2002 the Festival attracted 125 000 people; a 44 percent increase from the previous year.

The south tour begins 35 minutes south of the city of Penticton passing through the towns of Okanagan Falls and Oliver and eventually ending in Osoyoos. The wineries most commonly visited include; Inniskillin Okanagan Valley Vineyards, Hester Creek Estate Winery, Gehringer Brothers Estate Winery, Tinhorn Creek Vineyards, Blue Mountain Vineyard and Cellars and Hawthorne Mountain Vineyards. The town of Oliver is the self-appointed 'wine capital of Canada'. The claim has some credibility as Oliver is surrounded by 13 wineries. Fifty percent of British Columbia's wine production comes from wineries located between Osoyoos and Oliver.

Nk'Mip Cellars is the southern-most winery on the south tour. It is strategically located at the junction of the valley's north-south highway (the wine route) and a major east-west transportation route leading from recreation areas in eastern British Columbia and the rest of Canada to Vancouver on British Columbia's Pacific coast. Nk'Mip Cellars is the first winery travellers will encounter entering the Okanagan Valley from the south, the last they can visit leaving the valley to the south and it is the only winery directly accessible to travellers on the east-west route. An ideal location.

It is not just the award-winning wines and quality wineries that draw people to the Valley, but also the beautiful scenery, agreeable climate and numerous outdoor adventure opportunities such as horseback riding, bicycle tours, mountain biking, golfing and hiking. The region, without the wineries, is considered an ideal vacation destination. This leads us to a discussion of Aboriginal/eco tourism, the second opportunity being pursued by the OIB.

Aboriginal tourism

According to the Government of Canada Department of Industry, in 2000 the tourism industry in Canada was valued at $54.1 billion and employed almost 550 000 people. Aboriginal tourism accounted for less than 1 percent of this total generating $300 million annually and employing 16 000 people in an estimated 1500 Aboriginal owned and operated businesses. Forecasts predict that Aboriginal tourism annual revenue will rise to $1.9 billion within a decade. In comparison, in New Zealand there are 150 Maori-owned tourism businesses, while in Australia there are 200 Aborigine-owned businesses with annual sales totalling $130 million.

Currently, the vast majority of tourists utilizing Aboriginal tourism businesses are from Canada and the United States. However, recently Canadian Aboriginal tourism has been generating significant interest from travelers in Europe (Williams and Richter, 2002). This European interest in Aboriginal sites and attractions, while promising, is constrained by limited market awareness of Aboriginal tourist destinations and poor access to effective distribution intermediaries.

In spite of the general low awareness level of Canadian Aboriginal tourist destinations in the European market, there are 30 tour operators in France that include Aboriginal destinations in the packages they offer to customers, and another 30 in Germany. These tour operators indicate some difficulty selling stand-alone Aboriginal destinations. Instead, they find that such destinations can be an important as value added component of larger tour packages that include non-Aboriginal attractions as well. This issue is a significant concern because 70 percent of Europeans, when traveling internationally, employ the services of a tour operator (Williams and Richter, 2002). To generate awareness of Aboriginal tourist destinations among European tourists, marketing efforts must be directed at tour operators and through them to their customers. These marketing efforts should highlight the Aboriginal lifestyle and culture, in conjunction with the themes of nature, history and adventure in Canada; and this is the intention of the OIBDC as it markets its tourism attractions, especially the Nk'Mip Desert and Heritage Interpretive Centre and Nk'Mip Cellars.

The Project

Building on the foundation provided by its successful development activities to date, the OIB's current activities and future plans centre on a group of business activities together called the Nk'Mip Project. Included in this $25 million project are: (a) Nk'Mip Cellars, and associated vineyards; (b) a recreation vehicle park and campground; (c) the $5-million Nk'Mip Desert and Heritage Interpretive Centre; (d) a residential resort that provides ownership, in whole or in part, of 30 Villas and 64 Suites; and (e) a new golf course opened in May 2004. These ventures will be located on a 1200-acre parcel of band land that adjoins the town of Osoyoos and fronts on Osoyoos Lake:

The success of the project depends on successful participation in the wine tourism and eco/cultural tourism market segments. Nk'Mip Cellars and the Nk'Mip Desert and Heritage Interpretive Centre are the primary vehicles being developed to pursue this success.

The $5-million Nk'Mip Desert and Heritage Interpretive Centre is being developed to appeal to the growing Aboriginal/eco tourism market by educating visitors about 3000 years of Osoyoos band history and the unique nature of the community's desert environment. Chief Clarence Louie says

> The Desert and Heritage Centre is probably going to be our biggest business venture, and it's going to combine all of those things that you see in a first class desert interpretive centre – the educational stuff, the scientific stuff, the desert trails, the walks, the scientific interpretive stuff . . . the other major component of it, which is really special, is the uniqueness of the Okanagan First Nations, with the language and the heritage and the cultural component to it.

As part of the appeal to that cultural/eco tourism market, the centre will preserve up to 1000 acres of the unique dessert ecosystem. It will also work to restore habitat, and reintroduce to the area species at risk.

The center began operation in the temporary facility on 13 June 2002 with the gift shop half-stocked and admission by donation. By 15 July, the retail store was fully stocked and the center began charging full admission. Construction of the permanent building began in early 2005 with plans for it to be open for the 2006 season. As well, a start has been made on the interpretive trails and a traditional Okanagan village has been built.

Nk'Mip Cellars, opened in September 2002, is the culmination of almost 35 years of Osoyoos Indian Band involvement in the wine industry. The story begins in 1968 when in association with Andres Wines Ltd; the OIB planted its first vineyard. This has grown into the 230-acre (93 ha) Inkameep Vineyard, which provides high quality vinifera grapes to many of the wineries in the Okanagan valley and some further afield. There are another 1000 acres (400 ha) of vineyard on Osoyoos land most in partnership with Vincor International Inc. Vincor is Canada's largest wine producer and OIB's joint venture partner in Nk'Mip Cellars. By the end of 2003, almost 25 percent of the vineyard acreage in the Okanagan valley was on Osoyoos land.

The next phase of the OIB's involvement in the wine business began in 1980 with the erection of a building near the Inkameep Vineyard. T.G. Bright & Co. (now Vincor) leased for 25 years and equipped it as a winery. The lease has since been extended and the winery is undergoing a $10-million renovation. Speaking of the company's ongoing relationship with the Osoyoos Indian Band, Donald Triggs, Chief Executive Officer of Vincor says:

> We have a very long and important relationship with the Band. Two-thirds of the employees in the Oliver winery are from the band. Our relationship goes back 25 years. Our winery is on band land. We now have vineyards developed on band land of over 800 acres. Our future in the Okanagan is very much intertwined with the future of the band. (Schreiner, 2002)

According to Julianna Hayes, the relationship between Vincor and OIB is:

> a business partnership pure and simple. Vincor get access to vineyards in one of the hottest and richest growing climates in Canada. The Osoyoos Band gets the resources to develop their land and obtain a piece of an emerging industry. (Hayes, 2002)

Nk'Mip Cellars opened on 13 September 2002. The $7-million project includes the 18 000 square foot (1700 m^2) winery and a 20-acre (8 ha) vineyard. It is North America's first Aboriginal winery, and the second in the world (a Maori-owned winery opened in New Zealand in 1998). The OIB provided an operating line of almost $1-million and $2-3 million from various federal agencies, and for this investment owns 51 percent of the venture. Vincor invested $3 million and owns 49 percent. At least as important as the money is Vincor's expertise. As Don Triggs, Vincor's chief executive says. 'We have shared with them everything that we know in design of the winery, in processing and in managing hospitality' (Schriener, 2002). Vincor will be the managing partner in Nk'Mip for ten years, after which it can sell its interest to the OIB.

With a capacity of 18 000 cases, the Nk'Mip winery is not large. As Don Triggs says 'we've not targeted it to make large quantities of wine. The real objective here is to make small quantities of very high-end wine' (Schriener, 2002). Nk'Mip currently produces Chardonnay, Pinot Blanc, Pinot Noir and Merlot, exclusively from grapes from the Inkameep Vineyard. Nk'Mip expects to sell at least 40 percent of this output to wine tourists visiting the winery. Most of the remaining production will be distributed through Vincor's marketing channels to restaurants and specialty wine stores and the international market.

The Band has developed a strategic alliance with Bellstar Hotels & Resorts to develop the Spirit Ridge Vineyard Resort and Spa, a $22 million-dollar four star resort – one of only nine four star rated resorts in British Columbia (Spirit Ridge 2005: electronic source). Located adjacent to the winery and interpretive centre, it will play an integral role in the success of the Nk'Mip Project. Construction is underway. The resort and spa opened 30 villas for operation in the fall of 2005 and completely sold out in late 2005. The project now consists of 34 villas and 64 suites.

Results to Date

From its opening in June 2002 to 30 September; the Nk'Mip Desert and Heritage Interpretive attracted 3865 visitors. Nk'Mip Cellars did not open until September 2002, six months later than planned, so the visitors that came were attracted solely by the centre. Total revenue for the period was $52 000, 61 percent ($31 700) from the gift shop. There were approximately 7000 visitors to the Centre during the 2003 season in spite of serious forest fires, which limited tourism in the region in late summer, and 9000 in 2004. Projections were for 20 000 visitors in 2006 when the new building opened.

Between 13 September 2002 (opening day) and 31 December 2002, Nk'Mip Cellars received 5642 visitors. During the 2003 season, the winery hosted more than 20 000 increasing to 34 000 visitors in 2004. In addition to its success in attracting visitors, Nk'Mip Cellars had won recognition for the quality of its wines. In 2002, its pinot noir and chardonnay both won gold medals at the All Canadian Wine Championship in Ontario and at Vignobles Nationaux in Montreal. In 2004, its 2002 merlot won a silver medal at an international competition at the Los Angeles County Fair

(Matas, 2005). And as mentioned earlier, the Spirit Ridge Vineyard Resort and Spa opened and completely sold out 30 villas by late 2005.

Finally, it is important to note that the people of the OIB are not the only ones benefiting from their successful development efforts. There are important spillovers to the surrounding non-Aboriginal communities, and the region as a whole.

CONCLUSION

As described, the development activities of the OIB have been a great success. The community is central to this success in many ways. The land that is the foundation of the project is community-owned. The OIBDC's businesses are also community-owned and while the management of the business is in the hands of the OIBDC, the OIBDC is under the direct and close control of the community leaders – the Chief and Council – thus ensuring that bonding and bridging social capital work in harmony. This translates into an effective local mode of social regulation.

It is also clear that the process the OIB has adopted to achieve their purposes involves 'opting in' to the global economy. The OIB is creating and operating businesses that can compete profitably over the long run in the global economy to exercise the control over activities on traditional lands and build the economy necessary to preserve and strengthen communities and improve socioeconomic conditions. To do so they have formed alliances and joint ventures with non-Aboriginal partners, particularly Vincor and Bellstar Hotels & Resorts, to create businesses that can compete profitably in the global economy.

The result has been the emergence of a mode of development that includes an effective mode of social regulation that permits the OIB to participate successfully in the global regime of accumulation, on their own terms. Or to switch terminology, they have developed and are practicing a very effective form of non-market entrepreneurship And if OIB can do so; why not for other Indigenous communities; indeed all communities?

We can answer this question with a qualified yes they can and are based on the activities and outcomes of other Indigenous communities in Canada and elsewhere (Anderson, 2002; Dana *et al.*, 2005; Hindle and Lansdowne, 2005; Camp *et al.*, 2005; Hindle *et al.*, 2005; Anderson *et al.*, 2004; Galbraith *et al.*, 2006). And, we are exploring this question in greater depth by conducting a multi-case study of communities in Norway, Russia, Sweden, Canada, the United States, Africa, Mexico, Latin America, Australia and New Zealand. Taken together these activities are evidence of an emerging Indigenous market that is as distinct as any other, larger than many, and like all others inextricably intertwined in the broader global economic system.

ACKNOWLEDGMENTS

Funding for this research came in part from a series of grants from the Social Sciences and Humanities Research Council of Canada. A preliminary version of this chapter was presented at the 2006 Annual Conference of the American Academy of Management. The research was funded by grants from the Social Sciences and Humanities Research Council of Canada.

NOTE

1. A plain text version of the Declarations is available at http://www.iwgia.org/sw1592.asp.

REFERENCES

Agrawal, A. (1995), 'Dismantling the divide between indigenous and scientific knowledge', *Development and Change*, **26**(3), 413–39.

Amin, Ash (1984), 'Post-Fordism: models, fantasies and phantoms of transition', in Ash Amin (ed.), *Post-Fordism: A Reader*, Oxford: Blackwell Publishers, Ltd, 1–40.

Amin, A. and A. Malmberg (1984), 'Competing structural and institutional influence of the geography of production', in Ash Amin (ed.), *Post-Fordism: A Reader*, Oxford: Blackwell Publishers, Ltd, 227–48.

Anderson, Robert B. (1997), 'First Nations economic development: the role of corporate/aboriginal partnerships', *World Development*, **25**(9), 1483–503.

Anderson, Robert B. (1999), *Economic Development among the Aboriginal Peoples of Canada: Hope for the Future*, Toronto: Captus University Press.

Anderson, Robert B. (2002), 'Economic development and aboriginal Canadians. A case study in economic development', *The Journal of Developmental Entrepreneurship*, **7**(1): 45–65.

Anderson, Robert B., Benson Honig and Ana Maria Peredo (2006), 'Communities in the New Economy: where social entrepreneurship and indigenous entrepreneurship meet', in C. Steyaert and D. Hjorth (eds), *Entrepreneurship as Social Change*, Cheltenham, UK and Northampton, MA, USA: Edward Elgar, pp. 56–78.

Anderson, Robert B., Kevin Hindle, Leo Paul Dana and Robert Kayseas (2004), 'Indigenous land claims and economic development: the Canadian experience', *American Indian Quarterly*, **28**(3&4), 634–48.

Bebbington, A. (1993), 'Modernization from below: an alternative indigenous paradigm', *Economic Geography*, **69**(3), 274–92.

Blawatt, K. (1999), *Entrepreneurship: Process and Management*, Scarborough, ON: Prentis Hall Canada.

Camp II, Ronald D., Robert B. Anderson, Robert Giberson (2005), 'Aboriginal land rights and development: corporations and trust', *International Journal of Entrepreneurship and Small Business*, **2**(2), 134–48.

Corbridge, S. (1989), 'Post-Marxism and development studies: beyond the impasse', *World Development*, **18**(5), 623–39.

Couto, Richard A. and Catherine S. Guthrie (1999), *Making Democracy Work Better: Mediating Structures, Social Capital, and the Democratic Prospect*, Chapel Hill, NC: University of North Carolina Press.

Dana, Leo Paul, Teresa Dana and Robert B. Anderson (2005), 'A theory-based empirical study of entrepreneurship in Iqaluit, Nunavut', *Journal of Small Business and Entrepreneurship*, **18**(2) (Special Issue on Indigenous Entrepreneurship), 143–52.

Dana, Teresa E. and Liisa Remes (2005), 'Entrepreneurship among the Sami People of Finland', *Journal of Small Business and Entrepreneurship*, **18**(20), 189–200.

Dicken, P. (1992), 'International production in a volatile regulatory environment', *Geoforum*, **23**(3), 303–16.

Dodd, Tim H. (1999), 'Attracting repeat customers to wineries', *International Journal of Wine Marketing*, **11**(2), 18–28

Dolphin, Ric (2002), 'The hearty bouquet of real democracy', *Calgary Herald*, 28 November, A3.

Drucker, P.F. (1981), *Innovation and Entrepreneurship*, New York: Harper and Row.

Dunn, Debra and Keith Yamashita (2003), 'Microcapitalism and the megacorporation', *Harvard Business Review*, **81**(8): 46–54.

Dunning, J. H. (2003), *Making Globalization Good: The Moral Challenges of Global Capitalism*, Oxford: Oxford University Press.

Elam, M. (1994), 'Puzzling out the post-Fordist debate', in Ash Amin (ed.), *Post-Fordism: A Reader*, Oxford: Blackwell Publishers, Ltd: 43–70.

Fiet, J.O. (2002), *Systemic Search for Entrepreneurial Discoveries*, Westport, CT: Quorum Book.

Frederick, Howard H. and Dennis Foley (2005), 'Indigenous populations and disadvantaged entrepreneurs in Australia and New Zealand', *The International Indigenous Journal of Entrepreneurship, Advancement, Strategy and Education*, **11**(2), 1–16.

Galbraith, Craig S., Carlos L. Rodriguez and Curt S. Stiles (2006), 'False myths and indigenous entrepreneurial strategies', *Journal of Small Business and Entrepreneurship*, **19**(1), 1–20.

Gendron, Corinne (2003), 'Business, economy, and the environment: Toward a new development paradigm', *Business and Society*, **42** (4), 485–95.

Gertnet, Katharina (2005), 'Reindeer herding in Central Kamchatka', *Journal of Small Business and Entrepreneurship*, **18**(20), 201–6.

Getz, Donald, Ross Dowling, Jack Carlsen, Donald Anderson (1999), 'Critical success factors for wine tourism', *International Journal of Wine Marketing*, **11**(3), 20–42.

Goldman, S. (1995), *Agile Competition: The Emergence of a New Industrial Order*, Hamilton, Ontario: The Society of Management Accountants.

Grootaert, Christaan (1998), 'Social capital: the missing link?', *Social Capital Initiative Working Paper No. 3*, Washington, DC: Social Development Department Publications, The World Bank.

Hall, M. and N. Macionis (1998), 'Wine tourism in Australia and New Zealand', in R. Butler, M. Hall and J. Jenkins (eds), *Tourism and Recreation in Rural Areas*, Chichester: Wiley.

Halliday, J. (1999), 'Wine tourism – a personal perspective', unpublished.

Hayes, Julianna (2002), 'Winery makes North American history', *Okanagan Sunday*, September.

Hindle, Kevin and Michele Lansdowne (2005), 'Brave spirits on new paths: toward a globally relevant paradigm of indigenous entrepreneurship research', *Journal of Small Business and Entrepreneurship*, **18**(20), 131–42.

Hindle, Kevin, Robert Kayseas, Robert B. Anderson, and Robert G. Giberson (2005), 'Relating practice to theory in indigenous entrepreneurship: a pilot investigation of the Kitsaki Partnership Portfolio', *American Indian Quarterly*, **29**(1&2), 1–23.

Hirst, P. and J. Zeitlin (1992), 'Flexible specialization versus post-Fordism', in Michael Storper and Allen Scott (eds), *Pathways to Industrialization and Regional Development*, London: Routledge: 70–115.

Hume, Stephen (2001), *Growing Success in the Desert: Economic Freedom, National Post*, 4 August, A17.

Indigenous Peoples' Human Rights Project (2003), *The Rights of Indigenous Peoples*, University of Minnesota Human Rights Center, viewed 9 June 2004, http://www.hrusa.org/indig/studyguide.htm.

International Working Group on Indigenous Affairs (IWGIA) (2006), accessed at http://action.web.ca/home/narcc/attach/CERD%20Report%20Feb%20 2007.pdf.

Jessop, Bob (1989), 'Conservative regimes and the transition to post-Fordism', in M. Gottdiener and N. Komninos (eds), *Capitalist Development and Crisis Theory*, New York: St Martin's Press: 261–99.

Kao, R.W.Y., K.R. Kao and R.R. Kao (2002), *Entrepreneurism for the Market Economy*, London: Imperial College Press.

Komninos, Nicos (1989), 'From national to local: the Janus face of crisis', in M. Gottdiener and N. Komninos (eds), *Capitalist Development and Crisis Theory*, New York: St Martin's Press: 348–64.

Leyshon, Andrew (1992), 'The transformation of a regulatory order', *Geoforum*, **23**(3), 347–63.

Lindsay, Noel J. (2005), 'Toward a cultural model of indigenous entrepreneurial attitude', *Academy of Marketing Science Review*, (5), 1–17.

MacAulay, Scott and Gertrude Anne Macintyre (1998), 'The University College of Cape Breton as a mediating structure for community economic development', paper presented at the *Canadian Association for University Continuing Education '98 Conference*, Sydney, Nova Scotia, 14–17 June.

Matas, Robert (2005), 'I think we are on our way', *Globe and Mail*, 2 March, E7.

Moran, P. and S. Ghoshal (1999), 'Markets, firms, and the process of economic development', *The Academy of Management Review*, **24**(3), 390–12.

Morris, M. (1998), *Entrepreneurial Intensity: Sustainable Advantages for Individuals, Organizations and Societies*, Westport, CT: Quorum Books.

Newman, Lenore and Ann Dale (2005), 'The role of agency in sustainable local community development', *Local Environment*, **10**(5), 477–86.

Ndemo, Bitange (2005), 'Maasi entrepreneurship and change', *Journal of Small Business and Entrepreneurship*, **18**(20), 207–20

Norcliffe, Glen (1994), 'Regional labor market adjustments in a period of structural transformation: the Canadian case', *The Canadian Geographer*, **38**(1), 2–17.

OIB (2003), http://www.oib.ca/mission.htm.

Pearson, J. Diane (2005), 'Native American teamsters', *Journal of Small Business and Entrepreneurship*, **18**(20), 153–70

Peck, J. and Adam Tickell (1992), 'Local modes of social regulation', *Geoforum*, **23**(3), 347–63.

Peredo, Ana Maria, Robert B. Anderson, Craig Galbraith, Benson Honig and Leo Paul Dana (2004), 'Toward a theory of indigenous entrepreneurship', *International Journal of Entrepreneurship and Small Business*, **1**(1), 1–20.

Petten, Cheryl (2001), 'Economic development meets cultural preservation in project', *Windspeaker*, **19**(5), BG1.

Petten, Cheryl (2002), 'First Aboriginal-owned winery opens for business', *Windspeaker*, **20**(6), 13, 29.

RCAP (1996), *The Report of the Royal Commission on Aboriginal People*, Ottawa: Government of Canada.

Robinson, M. and E. Ghostkeeper (1987), 'Native and local economies: a consideration of economic evolution and the next economy', *Arctic*, **40**(2), 138–44.

Robinson, M. and E. Ghostkeeper (1988), 'Implementing the next economy', *Arctic*, **41**(3), 173–82.

Schreiner, John (2002), 'Grape expectations: Osoyoos Indian Band thought to have first Aboriginal winery in North America', *National Post*, 18 July, FP9.

Schuurman, Frans J. (1993), 'Modernity, post-modernity and the new social movements', in Frans J. Schuurman (ed.), *Beyond the Impasse: New Directions in Development Theory*. London: Zed Books.

Scott, A.J. (1988), *New Industrial Spaces: Flexible Production Organization and Regional Development in North America and Western Europe*, London: Pion Ltd.

Serumaga-Zake, P A.E., D Kotze, R. Anab, J.N. Sihawu, Y. Depha, M. Gaba and T. Bangani (2005), 'Poverty alleviation: South Africa', *Journal of Small Business and Entrepreneurship*, **18**(20), 221–30

So, A.Y. (1990), *Social Change and Development: Modernization, Dependency, and World-System Theories*, Newbury Park, CA: Sage Publications.

Storper, M. and R. Walker (1989), *The Capitalist Imperative: Territory, Technology and Industrial Growth*, New York: Basil Blackwell.

Tucker, V. (1999), 'The myth of development: a critique of a Eurocentric discourse', in Ronald Munck and Denis O'Hearn (eds), *Critical Development Theory: Contributions to a New Paradigm*, London: Zed Books, 1–26.

Williams, P.W. and C. Richter (2002), 'Developing and supporting European tour operator channels for Canadian Aboriginal tourism development', *Journal of Travel Research*, **40**(4), 404–15.

World Bank (2001), accessed at http://Inweb18.worldbank.org/ESSD/sduext.nsf/PrintFriendly/16E4344C3551CFO28525604E005A35D5?Opendocument.

PART 3

Entrepreneurship in public affairs

7. Intrapreneurship in the public sector

Roger R. Stough and Kingsley E. Haynes

INTRODUCTION

The notion of public sector entrepreneurship may initially seem to be an oxymoron. Entrepreneurship is associated with private sector economics and the singular pursuit of profit (albeit pure profit), whereas the public sector is motivated by various objectives other than profit in the business meaning of the term. However, we argue herein that the attributes of entrepreneurship, though definitive from a private sector perspective, also offer a meaningful construct for the public sector. In fact, entrepreneurial behavior already exists in the public sector. We discuss different types of public sector entrepreneurship and derive a model of intrapreneurship in the public sector. We provide examples to articulate the role and practice of entrepreneurship in the public sector; we offer initial guidelines for the formulation of a public sector training program for agencies and individual public officials.

The chapter begins with a discussion of the definition of entrepreneurship, followed by an examination of the ways entrepreneurship has found expression in the public sector. We conclude from this discussion that existing approaches lack a conceptual framework to guide the application of entrepreneurship to public sector operations. It is then argued that the private sector concept of intrapreneurship provides one possible conceptual framework for the study and practice of public sector entrepreneurship. An analysis of this concept follows with an assessment of its applicability to the public sector. It is concluded that this is a useful way to proceed but with some exceptions. In the next part of the chapter, we examine the changing nature of public sector organizations and their dynamics. We conclude intrapreneurship may be more relevant for operationalizing public sector entrepreneurship when a strong central government may act (on behalf of the society) without significant stakeholder involvement. This means that the public sector is vertically organized with minimal stakeholder collaboration in the planning, creation and delivery of services and goods.

However, modern public sector agencies often subscribe to a model of governance that is highly interactive and is comprised of multiple stakeholders. As such, the public agency guides policy development and implementation (Osborne and Gabler, 1993) and often outsources service delivery to the private or nonprofit sectors. We suggest that sustainable public planning and operations in developed or advanced economic systems tend to involve a wide and highly diverse set of actors, motivated by a range of goals and objectives (that can be in serious conflict), who have some stake in the outcome of decisions. Goals may overlap, but usually imperfectly (Salamon, 2002), and thus alliances develop unpredictably and only partially among stakeholders. This means that an intrapreneurship model for the public sector may be more complex than simply creating a subsidiary or parallel organization to undertake or test innovative approaches or models. This chapter concludes with a discussion of how entrepreneurship may be fostered for the individual and the relevant agency in the public sector. Conclusions and directions for future research follow.

ON THE NATURE OF ENTREPRENEURSHIP

At a very simple level, entrepreneurship is often defined as behavior that results in the start of a new venture. Such behavior is argued to be motivated by the promise of pure profits that result from ideas for new products or improvements to existing products. These ideas when developed throw the existing economic order out of equilibrium and thus, the entrepreneur becomes a disequilibrating economic agent (Schumpeter, 1934) inducing economic growth as new products and markets are created. Alternatively, Kirzner (1973) argues that by creating new opportunities and methods, the entrepreneur helps drive economic systems toward equilibrium and is thus an equilibrating agent. This illustrates the importance of the basic conception of profit as the foundation upon which theories of entrepreneurship are erected. In short, entrepreneurship has been derived strictly within the context of the profit motive in the private sector. How can this become relevant to a part of society that generally does not operate on profit or market related principles despite the public choice perspective that public sector agents may engage in rent-seeking behavior (Buchanan and Tullock, 1962)? The answer lies in the nature of the 'currency' of the public sector, or what motivates the search for innovative solutions and outcomes. This can be seen as the goal of achieving positional power and leadership roles in the public sector. Later in the chapter we provide some examples including the development of public works authorities by Robert Moses and William Mulholland in New York City and Los Angeles, respectively, to illustrate this point. These examples provide cases where public officials have discovered or envisioned new ways to produce public sector goods and services and have guided their implementation to bear exceptional fruit for public good. In some cases, of course, public sector innovations through entrepreneurial behavior have produced both benefits and costs. Concern in the public sector is, however, how the benefits and costs are distributed across stakeholder groups and is that distribution defensible on fairness or justice grounds.

INTRAPRENEURSHIP

'Intrapreneurship' may be defined as the formation of a new venture from an existing company (Antoncic and Hisrich, 2001). Overlapping terms include 'intrapreneuring' (Pinchot, 1985), 'corporate entrepreneurship' (Burgelman, 1983; Vesper, 1984; Hornsby *et al.*, 1993) and 'corporate venturing' (Vesper, 1990).

Intrapreneurship can be a useful part of corporate strategy to fortify competitiveness at the firm level (Carrier, 1994; Hamel, 1996) and is considered to be an important source of growth as a private sector activity. Why is intrapreneurship viewed as an important element of corporate strategy? It provides a channel for the established firm to encourage innovation, while still operating under the necessary organizational bureaucracy. The established firm is bureaucratic, slow to change and erected on processes that support repetitive functions directed at economies of scale. At the same time, the firm is large and has accumulated a great deal of resources and capital. Intrapreneurship enables the large established firm to support innovation needed to remain competitive.

Theories of entrepreneurship offer hypotheses on how large firms use entrepreneurial talent within their labor forces and how entrepreneurial motivation can be channeled to fruitful outcomes as explained by Pinchot (1985; 1986). Intrapreneurship is how entrepreneurs within an organization are enabled to pursue innovative ideas and projects and harness resources within the corporation. As such, intrapreneurship provides the capital and manpower that would otherwise be difficult or prohibitively costly for entrepreneurial employees to acquire outside of the corporation. With these resources, new ventures have a higher probability of success than do independent startups. The corporation benefits by maintaining ties to the new venture and often first rights of access to its products or services. Consequently, intrapreneurs are employees that behave as entrepreneurs, but within an existing corporate framework. They develop innovations and can be principal agents of change inside the firm.

Intrapreneurship has been received positively in the field of business or corporate strategy, but literature on this specific topic is relatively new and only first began to appear in the early 1980s (see Vesper, 1984; Schollhammer, 1982; Burgelman, 1983; Kanter, 1984; Rule and Irwin, 1988).

Antoncic and Hisrich (2001) suggest four parts of a theory of intrapreneurship. First, a new business-venturing dimension means a new venture becomes linked to existing products and markets. This new venture can be within the originating corporation or be a separate firm. In this case, termed 'incubative entrepreneurship', the new venture is separate or autonomous from the corporation (Schollhammer, 1982). Second, the innovativeness dimension means that the creation of new products, services or technologies results from changes in process. Third, the self-renewal dimension is organizational flexibility in the business model, based on the ability to adapt with changes in strategy and structure of the corporation (Muzyka *et al.*, 1995). The fourth dimension is the ability of the firm to be proactive – that is, responsiveness to competition, new initiatives and risk. For example, proactive firms experiment and take risks (Stopford and Baden-Fuller, 1994), are aggressive against competitors (Knight, 1997) and pursue opportunities to lead the industry (Covin and Slevin, 1991).

By nature, intrapreneurs locate slack resources in the corporation (Cyert and March, 1967) and can free them up for entrepreneurial pursuits including product, service and market innovations. This contributes to improved performance, competitiveness of existing firms (Burgelman, 1983; Kanter, 1984; Rule and Irwin, 1988) and enables satisfying the four dimensions of intrapreneurship (see above Antoncic and Hisrich, 2001).

Like entrepreneurship, there is considerable effort to find a defensible measure of intrapreneurship. Two index type measures that have been developed are ENTRESCSALE (Khandwalla, 1977; later used by Knight, 1997 and Covin and Slevin, 1989) and the Corporate Entrepreneurship Scale (Zahra, 1991).

There are a variety of examples of well-known and referenced intrapreneurs. Jack Welch (ex-GE Board Chairman) is one based on the early part of his career when he built the engineering plastics division of GE. Another is ex-3M Board Chairman, Lew Lehr, who, in his early career, led 3M into the health care sector and thus created a highly successful line of new business there.

INTRAPRENEURSHIP IN THE PUBLIC SECTOR

While it is interesting to hypothesize that the concept or theory of intrapreneurship, invented and applied in the private sector organization, may also be applicable in the public sector, it is not at all clear where this argument is supported and where it is not. For sure, like most other efforts to stretch the range of applicability of a theory, there will be areas where the original theory applies and others where it does not or does so imperfectly. The following discussion is an attempt to assess the similarities between the private sector firm (organization) and the public sector government (agency). If the similarity is strong, then the potential for portability is strong.

The public and private sector organization have a number of similarities in the way they can relate to and/or support entrepreneurial initiatives. References above as well as Pizaro-Moreno *et al.* (2007) provide references for this part of the chapter. Also, the authors found a recent paper by Alder (2007) quite useful because of its attempt to identify similarities between public and private sector organizations, realizing of course that the way the profit motive is treated is different.

1. *Vertical organizational structure*: The approach to complex problems in both organizations is through vertical structures and committees. This approach is often adopted on an assumption that efficiency and effectiveness are best achieved through functional specialization and a minimization of dependency. One can find shades of the thinking of Adam Smith and the principles of Taylorism and scientific management here.

2. *Control and predictability*: Control and predictability, not experimentation and innovation are fundamental goals of both the public and private sector organization. Planning and minimizing deviation from plans are more important than seeking or trying to implement new ideas or opportunities.

3. *Organizational inertia*: Both the private and public sector organization have histories that are remembered by their leaders and that were built on an accumulation of solutions to historic problems in their special contexts. Consequently, there are strong defensive barriers in place toward using solutions to problems that have worked in the past, not new approaches.

4. *Legacy*: The lure of opportunities to organization leaders is often outweighed first by the weight of doing as in the past with 'tried and true' legacy approaches and second by the risks of adopting a different approach. In short, leaders for both private and public sector organizations are conservative decision makers. Making mistakes or committing acts that could be construed as errors are seen as costly. Consequently, even when new opportunities are recognized or discovered in some part of the organization they will seldom be pursued or receive resources needed to promote their development.

5. *Boundaries*: With hierarchical structure being the most common organizational form for both public and private sector organizations, it should be no surprise that these organizations have numerous and distinct boundaries with relatively impervious borders. For example, responsibility and accountability, expectations, decision making, resource allocation and evaluation all are often conducted within bounded sub-parts of the organization. Thus even when breakthroughs and innovations are discovered they most often occur at the boundaries and/or interaction across the boundaries separating divisions within the organizations.

6. *Lack of incentives*: There are few incentives for challenging dominant, tried and accepted practices and structures. However, there are many incentives, as noted above, to protect accepted ways, approaches, forms and structures.

It is interesting to find that there are many similarities and quite important ones as they relate to operations within the public and private sector organization. However, there are also several distinct differences. These are:

1. *Organizational objectives*: The public sector organization is a multi-objective seeking entity (for example, safety, fairness, equity, efficiency, effectiveness, and transparency) compared to the single goal of profit that characterizes the private sector organization. The notion of maximization is foreign to the public sector organization where incremental the paradigm of change and muddling through is dominant.

2. *Locus of control*: Decision making in the public sector organization is often depicted as a function of its executive-level leaders. And, while this may be true to an extent, it is much less so than in the private sector organization. Over the last two decades due to a variety of factors the role of policy and thus decision making has been broadening to include an ever increasing band of stakeholders. Consequently, the public sector executive has less and less control over decisions because of stakeholder involvement (sometimes if not often conflictual in nature) in the process. This also leads to the third and a similar difference between the public and private sector organization.

3. *Accountability*: The private sector executive is accountable ultimately to the owner or stockholder in public-owned firms. In the public sector accountability is ultimately to some amorphous entity or group called 'the public'. But the public is made up of 'owners' who are not always known, have highly diverse preferences and consequently align differently on their expectations for the public executive both individually and in their roles in stakeholder groups.

While there are surely other similarities and differences between the public and private sector organization relating to their ability to be innovative and entrepreneurial, these seem to us to be the primary ones. This assessment suggests that there appears to be a sufficient overlap or similarity for continuing the investigation of the appropriability of the private sector organization concept intrapreneurship for a conceptual frame of analysis for entrepreneurial activity in the public sector. Next, we provide some examples from the public sector of where intrapreneurship applies to various actions taken on behalf of the public.

EXAMPLES OF INTRAPRENEURSHIP IN THE PUBLIC SECTOR

Seemingly there are many examples of public sector intrapreneurship. Here we focus on a few exceptional cases and one of more recent and lesser renown.

Robert Moses

Robert Moses, also more commonly known as the 'pawn broker', was born in 1888 and died in 1981 after rising to a number of significant roles in the New York City (NYC) bureaucracy mostly focused on parks and public works. He was educated in premier higher education institutions on both sides of the Atlantic majoring in political science in areas that would later come to be known as public administration. He lived and worked during a time when merit, economic efficiency and effectiveness were seen as central goals of the public sector all rationalized by the rise of Taylorism and the notion of scientific management. This was an era that objectified these tenets. It was also the era that included Roosevelt's New Deal and the notion that government should have a broader role in people's life than experienced in the earlier days of American history. In this milieu and with his several decades of public works experience Moses saw an opportunity to produce and maintain certain public works functions by operating more like private organizations and in a way that made them self-financing by requiring no funding from public sector sources. The first and perhaps the most celebrated of his ventures was the creation of the Triborough Bridge Authority (TBA) that assumed responsibility for both the construction of the bridges linking the Bronx, Manhattan and Queens through issuing bonds and their maintenance costs through tolling. This soon became a model used in other bridge and park ventures in NYC and elsewhere. The autonomy enjoyed by the parks and bridge public works function in NYC soon spread to region-wide independence of action that spanned the public works areas of parks, airports, ports and bridges. This evolution eventually led to the formation of the New York–New Jersey Ports Authority, one of the most celebrated and successful of all intergovernmental mission type agencies. This case can be explained as an illustration of intrapreneurship in that it satisfies a number of attributes of the concept as outlined in the early part of this chapter:

1. was initiated inside the New York City bureaucracy;
2. created a new organizational form, the authority;
3. led to the growth and expansion of services at no cost to the general public;
4. enabled an innovation that spread to other parts of the bureaucracy and to other city regions;
5. used NYC to legitimize the offering and sale of bonds, thus creating resources;
6. found and utilized a type of 'slack' organizational resources;
7. residents of NYC benefited by enhanced and improved public services at minimal or no additional cost;
8. developed new markets both in NYC and later more broadly throughout the urban community of the US and abroad; and
9. created a new 'business'.

William Mulholland

William Mulholland was born in 1855 and died in 1935. He was a self-educated engineer who became superintendent of the Los Angeles Water Company and later headed the Department of Water and Power for the city until 1928. Early in his career he recognized that Los Angeles would need water to become a major city. He organized the Owens River diversion to bring water from the mountainous interior to the San Fernando Valley where the City of Los Angeles was located. He led the development of a series of authorities, much like Moses did in NYC, to organize additional diversions of water to the region and financed these much as Moses did issuing city-legitimized bonds to construct the diversions and related infrastructure in the name of the City of Los Angeles. Changes or fees for water used by consumers were used to pay off the bonds. These projects were often derided and led to serious confrontations with various impacted groups including those resident in regions from where the water was diverted and, also, those whose land was subject to intense development pressure when the water supply was increased. One such project was the St Francis Dam that led to Mulholland's downfall. The Mulholland case bears much similarity to the NYC experience of Robert Moses and may be rationalized as another example of intrapreneurship in the public sector, much as with Moses' experience.

Franklin Delano Roosevelt

The rise of the New Deal erected and rationalized with the Keynesian argument of government's role to create demand through the provision of services beyond those that would normally be provided as a result of market conditions was a response to the Great Depression in the US. Similar policies simultaneously evolved in Europe. This historical development of policy laid the foundation for another case of intrapreneurship but on a much broader and deeper scale. The New Deal was an enormous departure from traditional values in the US of strong individualism and weak government institutions (Lipsett, 1996). Thus it is not surprising that after World War II the debate continued on the proper role of government in society. This debate was strongest in the US and as a consequence increasing support began to emerge, and also in Britain, to limit the role of government. Margaret Thatcher in Britain and Ronald Reagan in the US were both elected on the basis of their vision of a reduced role of government in society. This led to dramatic changes. In the US a strong policy position aimed at reducing the role of government in society was adopted and implemented through reductions in government employment and increased privatization and/or outsourcing of government goods and services to the private sector. This may be viewed as policy entrepreneurship[1] as it embodies many of the attributes of intrapreneurship, although the analogy is not as strong as with the cases of Robert Moses and William Mulholland. The interested reader is referred to some of the policy entrepreneurship literature (Ostrom, 1964; Wagner, 1966; Frohlich and Oppenheimer, 1972; Riker, 1980, 1982, 1986; Baumgartner and Jones, 1993; Kingdon, 1995; Shockley *et al.*, 2006) but this field is somewhat tangential to the focus here on the operations of the public sector organization than the policy making function per se. Policy entrepreneurship is of course an alternative way to conceptually organize a framework for the study of entrepreneurship in the public sector. However, in our estimation, the theory of intrapreneurship provides more potential. Thus, we stay with our focus here on intrapreneurship.

CapWIN

A final case is the Capital Wireless Integrated Network (CapWIN) established in the late 1990s. A group of local public safety officials (police, fire and emergency services) become increasingly concerned that their ability to manage incidents that involved multiple jurisdictional response in the Washington metropolitan region were compromised by a limited ability to communicate in real time across jurisdictional boundaries. Experience with jurisdictional authority and response issues was varied. One incident originated from a suicide attempt on a major bridge that supports north-south traffic flow through the region to the 9/11 attack (at a later time) on the Pentagon that houses the US Department of Defense.

The Washington metropolitan region is located in two states (Maryland and Virginia) in addition to the District of Columbia at its geographic core. The two states have elements of independence and autonomy under the US constitution that provides for separation of powers between the federal and state governments. The Federal District has elements of autonomy also that are reinforced with congressional involvement in its management. Problems in management of the above referenced incidents as well as many others often occurred in incidence response because of the nature of the distribution of authority in the region and some degree of territorial control that often resides at the local level. The region is home to 23 local government units and numerous state and local authorities as well as a host of federal agencies and installations. The problem was how to manage incidents when conflict across government entities or uncertainty regarding who had authority arose.

The local officials had a vision of a system that would provide seamless communication across all agencies in the region and seamless access to their data bases in a common infrastructure. This is the CapWIN vision (see Cheng *et al.*, 2005 for more background on CapWIN and the institutional barriers it faced). The local officials were unable to convey the necessity of the CapWIN concept to their senior officials and to create cross-regional planning and budgeting needed to build a CapWIN type system. So they approached the US Congress with an urgent plea for funds to begin work on the concept. Funds were appropriated for a start-up grant to support a project that would be housed at the University of Maryland as it was considered to be an experimental effort. The project received additional rounds of Congressional funding over several years and now offers a range of services (but not the total range envisioned) today that provides partial funding through fees for service. CapWIN is still partly dependent on congressional funding but with a plan to become self-sufficient through expanded services and thus fees from constituent users.

Is CapWIN an example of intrapreneurship? In many ways, Yes. It was spun off from the regional governments in a bottom-up fashion and set up in a way that it was not subject to the daily constraints and requirements of government. It did make a convincing argument to the US Congress, thus accessing 'slack' resources there (at least 'slack' from the view of local government agencies). It is an innovation and it is creating enhanced and improved emergency response services, other regions are beginning to emulate the model and thus a new market may be developing. It used the legitimacy of the idea and of the US Congress to obtain resources needed for development and implementation.

DISCUSSION

The chapter has formulated a thesis that the private sector concept of intrapreneurship could be fruitfully applied in the public sector. It has given a skeleton analysis of the similarities between the public and private sector organization and found the similarities to far outweigh the differences. It then offered some case examples in an effort to offer some evidence illustrating that intrapreneurship exists in the public sector. There is now a need to discuss and qualify the range of convenience or applicability of the concept in the public sector.

The Robert Moses and William Mulholland examples are strong and clear-cut examples of intrapreneurship in the public sector. One of the reasons for this is that they lived at a time when public sector organizations, especially in the area of public works, resembled in many ways the stereotypical private sector firm in the sense that local governments were hierarchically structured, increasingly subject to efficiency and effectiveness criteria, yet had most of the innovation constraining attributes of the private sector organization. CapWIN is included because it is a messier case. There was no central leadership or authority that served as the innovator. Rather, agency or division heads in public safety were at best the leaders while the group organized around the functional problem in public safety – not a specific office or group of executive level leaders – was the innovator. As such it was an effort underlain by multiple stakeholders and it was more an evolutionary effort than a planned one.

From the intrapreneurship view, there certainly was for sure technical, value and governance uncertainty and risk associated with the vision and its possible implementation. Benefits of the concept could be envisioned and so could portability as the benefit of seamless communication in crisis situations or in assessing criminality in real time would be considerable improvements over current capabilities. In short, CapWIN seems to be a good example of intrapreneurship in the public sector. However, it is more complicated and shows the difficulty of creating innovative solutions in contemporary government systems that place what some call an excessive emphasis on accountability, emphasizing mistake minimization and on accommodating an increasing number of stakeholders. As a consequence, intrapreneurship in the public sector would seem to be a far more complex process in contemporary government management contexts where governance and the participation of an ever-increasing number of actors and groups in producing and delivering government services and policy making is growing rapidly.

Intrapreneurship in the public sector today is undoubtedly more complicated than 40 or 50 years ago. This is because the business of government is now called governance (Skelcher, 2000) or the 'new governance' model (Salamon, 2002) where participation in the process has been expanded to include ever increasing numbers of stakeholders and advocacy groups. These groups have different preferences and thus their participation slows down decision making thus adding to the inherent tendencies of all bureaucracies to act conservatively in a risk averse and protective manner. Consequently, a topic of a future paper will be to further develop the application of intrapreneurship in the context of the new governance model and one that is more in keeping with community reference group participation.

SOME IDEAS ON EDUCATION AND TRAINING FOR PUBLIC SECTOR ENTREPRENEURSHIP

While it may be premature to discuss the education and training implications of this initial effort to examine the applicability of the concept of intrapreneurship in the public sector, we believe that the analysis does provide some insight. To begin, it appears that public sector entrepreneurship is more widespread than one would have expected and that much of this activity may be understood from the perspective of intrapreneurship. Thus, some careful case studies of examples of intrapreneurship in the public sector are needed to gauge more fully how well the principles of intrapreneurship are satisfied or not satisfied. This could begin with a full examination of the cases that were briefly described in this chapter. Such an exercise would produce case studies that could be used to undertake several types of training or education.

1. Executive-level officials in the public sector.
2. Agencies in the public sector (federal, state and local including public authorities).
3. Individual employees on how to be entrepreneurial in a context that is often not very entrepreneurial – in short, how to be an entrepreneur.

Having more deeply researched case studies completed will help to provide a better understanding of how well the intrapreneurship concept applies in the public sector. Assuming that the overlap between its application in the public sector is well-grounded, then many of the precepts, rules and arguments that work in the private sector can be incorporated into an educational element on the principles of intrapreneurship and how they work in a public sector organization.

Despite the above-referenced potentials, there remains a need for a full curriculum for teaching intrepreneurship in the public sector. This requires theoretical knowledge about its application in the public sector. It also requires a body of how to knowledge: how to motivate intrapreneurship; how to execute it (at the individual level and at the agency level); how to find slack organizational resources; how to create new markets in the public sector; how to manage resistance; and so on. These, then, are questions showing the need for more research in order to have a better-informed training and education program.

CONCLUSIONS

This chapter has conducted an initial assessment to consider the applicability of the intrapreneurship concept in the public sector. The concept was explicated and further examined to consider its portability to the public context. Some of the similarities and differences between the private and public sector organization concerning barriers to implementing intrapreneurship were outlined and examined. It was concluded that there are more similarities than differences in the two types of organizations and both carry many of the problems of adopting new ideas that result where corporatization has occurred. Then some examples of intrapreneurship in the public sector were presented showing that there are significant cases that match up quite well with the concept and at the same time others such as the CapWIN case that are more complicated institutionally and thus pose questions about applicability in a more stakeholder intensely influenced public policy and program environment. Examination of this more complicated case where Salamon's new governance model seems to be more applicable than the centralized and vertically controlled organization found in many of the less advanced economies is needed to better understand the range of applicability of the entrepreneurship concept. This is, however, left to future research. The last part of the paper considers some preliminary implications of the findings in this chapter for education and training, especially from the perspective of executive education.

Finally, future research needs to consider broader testing of the applicability and portability of the concept and practice of entrepreneurship in the public sector. An initial and interesting approach to accomplishing this might be the use of intrapreneurship measurement scales such as ENTRESCALE (Khandwalla, 1977) and the Corporate Entrepreneurship Scale (Zahra, 1991). For sure some of the scales or questions would need to be adjusted for a public sector context but with that modification public sector individuals and, in fact, employees in agencies could be surveyed. Given that these instruments have been used there is likely to be some reliability and validity data available to help interpret the resulting parameter estimates of such analyses. The results, if the questions are meaningfully restructured for the public sector organization and worker, could reveal embedded patterns offering the further possibility of comparing findings in the public sector to existing data and results for the private sector. Finally, this might help to show where the applicability of the intrapreneurship concept breaks down when applied in the public sector.

NOTE

1. The field of policy entrepreneurship is quite well developed and therefore has more than one dimension. On the one hand Riker's (1980) policy entrepreneur has the ability to disrupt the status quo while on the other Kingdon's (1995) policy entrepreneur 'practices the artful connection of solutions to problems' and thus has a more equilibrating function. As such the policy entrepreneurship model probably more effectively provides an explanation of the Thatcher/Reagan policy change than would intrapreneurship.

REFERENCES

Alder, N. (2007), 'The role of public and private interests in the innovation process and in the financing of innovations', paper presented at the International Conference on 'Building innovative capabilities of regions in a globalizing world', 13 June 2007, Uddevalla, Sweden (arranged by the Hogskolan Vast, Hogskolecentrum Bohuslan och Innovatum Teknikpark, Trollhattan, Sweden).

Antoncic, B. and Hisrich, R.D. (2001), 'Intrapreneurship: construct refinement and cross-cultural validation', *Journal of Business Venturing*, **16**, 495–527.

Baumgartner, F.R. and Jones, B.D. (1993), *Agendas and Instability in American Politics*, Chicago, IL: The University of Chicago Press.

Buchanan, J.M. and G. Tullock (1962), *The Calculus of Consent*, Ann Arbor, MI: University of Michigan Press.

Burgelman, R.A. (1983), 'Corporate entrepreneurship and strategic management: Insights from a process study', *Management Science*, **29**(12), 1349–64.

Carrier, C. (1994), 'Intrapreneurship in large firms and SMEs: a comparative study', *International Small Business Journal*, **12**(3), 54–61.

Cheng, S., M. Thibault and R. Stough (2005), 'Regional cooperation and management in public safety', in B.S. Sahay, R. Stough and G.D. Sardana (eds), *Cases in Management*, New Delhi: Allied Publishers PVT Ltd, 694 pages.

Covin, J.G. and D.P. Slevin (1989), 'The developing and testing of an organizational-level entrepreneurship scale', in R. Rondstadt, R. Peterson and K. Vasper (eds), *Frontiers of Entrepreneurship Research*, Wellesley, MA, Babson.

Covin, J.G. and D.P. Slevin (1991), 'A conceptual model of entrepreneurship as firm behavior', *Entrepreneurship Theory and Practice*, **16**(1), 7–25.

Cyert, R.M. and J.G. March (1963), *A Behavioral Theory of the Firm*, Englewood Cliffs, NJ: Prentice Hall.

Frohlich, N. and J.A. Oppenheimer (1972), 'Entrepreneurial politics and foreign policy', *World Politics*, **24**(Supplement: Theory and Policy in International Relations), 151–78.

Hamel, G. (1996) 'Strategy as revolution', *Harvard Business Review*, July/August, 69–71.

Hornsby, J.S., D.W. Naffziger, D.F. Kuratko and R.V. Montagno (1993), 'An interactive model of the corporate entrepreneurship process', *ETP*, **17**(2), 364–82.

Jones, G.R. and J.E. Butler (1992), 'Managing internal corporate entrepreneurship: an agency theory perspective', *Journal of Management*, **18**(4), 733–49.

Kanter, R.M (1984), *The Change Masters*, New York: Simon and Schuster.

Khandalwalla, P.N. (1977), *The Design of Organizations*, New York, HBJ.

Kingdon, J. (1995), *Agendas, Alternatives, and Public Policies*, New York: Addison-Wesley.

Kirzner, I.M. (1973), *Competition and Entrepreneurship*, Chicago, IL: University of Chicago Press.

Knight, G.A. (1997), 'Cross-cultural reliability and validity of a scale to measure firm entrepreneurial orientation', *JBV*, **12**(3), 213–25.

Lipset, S.M. (1996), *American Exceptionalism: A Double Edged Sword*, New York: W.W. Norton.

Muzyka D.F., A.J. de Koning and N.C. Churchill (1995) 'Entrepreneurial transformation: A descriptive theory', in W.D. Bygrave, R.H. Brockhaus, Sr and N.C. Churchill (eds), *Frontiers of Entrepreneurship Research*, Babson Park, MA: Babson College.

Osborne, D. and T. Gabler (1993), *Reinventing Government: How the Entrepreneurial Spirit is Transforming the Public Sector*, New York: Penguin Books.

Ostrom, E. (1964), *Public Entrepreneurship: A Case Study in Ground Water Basin Management*, unpublished dissertation, University of California, Los Angeles, Los Angeles, CA.

Pinchot, G. (1985), *Intrapreneuring: Why You Don't Have to Leave the Corporation to Become an Entrepreneur*, New York: HarperCollins.

Pinchot, G. (1996), *The Intelligent Organization: Engaging the Talent and Initiative of Everyone in the Workplace*, San Franciso, CA: Berret-Koehler.

Pizarro-Moreno, I., J.C. Real and E. Sousa-Ginel (2007) 'Corporate entrepreneurship: building a knowledge based view of the firm', working paper, Department of Business Administration, Pablo Olavide University, Seville, Spain, 19 pages.

Riker, W.H. (1980), 'Implications from disequilibrium of majority rule for the study of institutions', *American Political Science Review*, **74**(2), 432–46.

Riker, W.H. (1982), *Liberalism Against Populism: A Confrontation Between the Theory of Democracy and the Theory of Social Choice*, San Francisco: W.H. Freeman and Co.

Riker, W.H. (1986), *The Art of Political Manipulation*. New Haven, CT: Yale University Press.

Rule, E.G. and D.W. Irwin (1988), 'Fostering entrepreneurship: the new competitive edge', *JBS*, **9**(3), 44–7.

Salamon, L.M. (2002), *The Tools of Government: A Guide to New Governance*, Oxford: Oxford University Press.

Schumpeter, J.A. (1934), *The Theory of Economic Development*, Cambridge, MA: Harvard University Press.

Schollhammer, H. (1982), 'Internal corporate entrepreneurship', in C.A. Kent, D.L. Sexton and K.H. Vesper (eds), *Encylopedia of Entrepreneurship*, Englewood Cliffs, NJ: Prentice Hall, 209–29.

Shockley, G.E., P.F. Frank, R.R. Stough and K.E. Haynes (2006), Toward a theory of public sector entrepreneurship, *International Journal of Entrepreneurship and Innovation Management*, **6**(3), 205–23.

Skelcher, C. (2000), 'Changing images of the state: overloaded, hollowed-out, congested', *Public Policy and Administration*, **15**(3), 3–19.

Stopford, J.M. and C.W.F. Baden-Fuller (1994), 'Creating corporate entrepreneurship', *Strategic Management Journal*, **15**(7), 521–36.

Vesper, K.H. (1984), 'Three faces of corporate entrepreneurship', in J.A. Hornaday, J.A. Timmons and K.H. Vesper (eds), *Frontiers of Entrepreneurship Research*, Wellesley, MA, Babson.

Vesper, K.H. (1990), *New Venture Strategies*, Englewood Cliffs, NJ, Prentice-Hall.

Wagner, R.E. (1966), 'Pressure groups and political entrepreneurs: a review article', *Public Choice*, **1**, 161–70.

Zahra, S.A. (1991), 'Predictors and financial outcomes of corporate entrepreneurship: an exploratory study', *JBV*, **6**(4), 259–85.

8. Policy entrepreneurship: reconceptualizing entrepreneurship in public affairs

Gordon E. Shockley

INTRODUCTION

Through the middle two quarters of the twentieth century, Ludwig von Mises, Israel Kirzner, and Joseph Schumpeter conceived of the pair of insights that partially form the basis of what might be called the 'classical view'[1] of entrepreneurship in economics. Mises conceived of and Kirzner developed the first insight of the classical view of entrepreneurship: 'the ubiquity of entrepreneurship in all human endeavors'. At mid-century, Mises, who along with Nobel laureate Friedrich Hayek are commonly acknowledged as the two most prominent economists in the Austrian School of Economics, placed entrepreneurial activity front and center in his general conception of human action. Mises writes in his magnum opus *Human Action* ([1949] 1996), '[Entrepreneurship] is not the particular feature of a special group or class of men; it is inherent in every action and burdens every actor' (pp. 252–3). Misesian entrepreneurship thus holds that entrepreneurship is a universalistic key to comprehending all human action because of, in Mises' words, 'the uncertainty inherent in every action' (p. 253). Twenty-five years later, Israel Kirzner, widely regarded as Mises' most important student and successor in the Austrian School, deliberately extended and refined the universalism of Misesian entrepreneurship. Kirzner argues in his seminal work *Competition and Entrepreneurship* (1973), 'there is present in all human action an element which, although crucial to economizing activity in general, cannot itself be analyzed in terms of economizing, maximizing, or efficiency criteria' (p. 31). Taking up Mises' theme, Kirzner maintains that the ubiquitous element 'in all human action' is nothing other than entrepreneurship.

All three economists – that is, Mises and Kirzner as well as Schumpeter – arrived at the second crucial insight of the classical view of entrepreneurship in economics: 'the priority of the process of entrepreneurship over individual entrepreneurial actors'. Often neglected in contemporary discussions or applications of entrepreneurship is that entrepreneurship describes first and foremost an activity, not an actor. Tracing its origins back to the thirteenth-century Old French verb *entreprendre*, which means 'to undertake something', the term 'entrepreneurship' unambiguously refers to an activity, process, or function. By contrast, the term 'entrepreneur' did not arise until centuries later to refer to the individuals 'doing' or 'undertaking' something. When Schumpeter in the early twentieth century posited entrepreneurship as the driver of economic development in capitalism, he explicitly separated the function of entrepreneurship from the individual entrepreneur. Schumpeter writes in his timeless *The Theory of Economic Development* ([1934] 2002), 'The carrying out of new combinations we call "enterprise"; the individuals whose function it is to carry them out we call "entrepreneurs"' (p. 74). To Schumpeter, individual entrepreneurs are the instruments of the entrepreneurial function of economic development. In fact, individual entrepreneurs in Schumpeter's thought are incidental to the aggregate, macro effects of entrepreneurship in a capitalist economy. Recent commentators Schneider *et al.* (1995) observe that, in Schumpeter's theory, the fate of individual entrepreneurs are inconsequential relative to the sum of all entrepreneurial activity occurring in an economy. 'Despite the success or failure of individual entrepreneurs,' they write, 'their actions generate considerable benefits for the society as a whole' (p. 7). Similarly, Mises[2] and Kirzner[3] also clearly distinguish the function of entrepreneurship from entrepreneurial actors. Therefore, taking the work of Mises, Kirzner, and Schumpeter collectively, one might argue that the priority of the function of entrepreneurship over individual entrepreneurs and the ubiquity of entrepreneurship activity in all human endeavors comprise two of the major premises of the classical view of entrepreneurship in economics.

The logic of this chapter rests on these two insights of the classical theory of entrepreneurship in economics. My task is to reconceptualize the idea of policy entrepreneurship previously offered by preeminent political scientists such as John Kingdon (1995) and William Riker (1982; 1986) both by adapting the insights of the classical entrepreneurship theorists to policy studies and by critiquing extant theories of various forms of entrepreneurship in public affairs. Based on the first classical insight (the ubiquity of entrepreneurship in all human endeavors), I reclassify entrepreneurship in public affairs as policy entrepreneurship with the explicit aim of being more ecumenical than prior theories (for example Mintrom, 2000; Osborne and Gaebler, 1992; M. Schneider and Teske, 1992; M. Schneider *et al.*, 1995). Faithful to the second classical insight (distinguishing between the function of entrepreneurship and entrepreneurial actors and the primacy of the former), the reconceptualization of entrepreneurship in public affairs as policy entrepreneurship emphasizes not the descriptive power of identifying individual policy entrepreneurs as has been preferred in prior research (for example Carpenter, 2001; Doig and Hargrove, 1987; Frohlich *et al.*, 1971) but rather the explanatory power of entrepreneurship in public policy (Sheingate, 2003). Moving beyond the description of entrepreneurs *in* public policy, I seek to reconceptualize the entrepreneurship in public affairs by developing a theory of policy entrepreneurship that looks for the effects of entrepreneurship *on* public policy. Thus, the reconceptualization of entrepreneurship in public affairs that I undertake in this chapter is a functional theory of policy entrepreneurship.

RECONCEPTUALIZING ENTREPRENEURSHIP IN PUBLIC AFFAIRS

As for general entrepreneurship research (Shane and Venkataraman, 2000), there is a distinct need for an empirically robust, yet theoretically consistent, theory of entrepreneurship in public affairs for policy research. Here I lay the groundwork for such a theory by utilizing the work of the classical entrepreneurship theorists Joseph Schumpeter and Israel Kirzner[4] (though Ludwig von Mises is consciously everywhere in Kirzner's work) in order to critique[5] available theories of 'public sector' entrepreneurship and then to derive a theory of policy entrepreneurship.[6] The theoretical thrust of the tripartite theory of policy entrepreneurship is *causality*, that is, the effects of policy entrepreneurship on public policy. My ambition is that policy entrepreneurship *qua* entrepreneurship be recognized as having considerable analytical and explanatory power in policy studies. At the end of the first four sections I derive at least one requirement for a theory of policy entrepreneurship that is consistent with the classical theorists Schumpeter and Kirzner. In the final section I develop each of the requirements as I discuss many of the prominent theories of entrepreneurship in public affairs generally and policy entrepreneurship specifically.

Entrepreneurship and Rational Calculation

Early conceptions of entrepreneurship in public affairs recognized that there is significant public sector activity with real political and policy impact not being adequately accounted for with the available stock of political science and public administration terminology and conceptual apparatus. Among the earliest theorists, Curry and Wade (1968) advanced a kind of proto-public choice conception of political entrepreneurs as 'fiduciaries', who as 'as a catalytic political agent' in a purely rational allocative exercise 'will balance the value of a new member [to a policy coalition] against the units of policy that must be allocated to each new member'. Wagner in his review of Mancur Olson's *The Logic of Collective Action* identified political entrepreneurs as the broad group of individuals that supply collective benefits for an unspecified 'political profit' (Wagner, 1966). The research of Jones (1978) and Frohlich, Oppenheimer, and Young (Frohlich and Oppenheimer, 1972; Frohlich *et al.*, 1971) in the 1970s amplified, wittingly or not, Wagner's public choice conception of entrepreneurship by arguing that these public sector entrepreneurs should be considered economic actors, rationally calculating the personal costs and benefits of providing public goods hoping for an ambiguous political payoff. Also in the 1970s, Walker (1977) observed that public sector entrepreneurs play an important function in the political process as 'the energy of political entrepreneurs' (p. 445) often determine which policy problems are placed on the political agenda (also see Walker, 1975). These early conceptions introduced the idea of entrepreneurship in public affairs to political science discourse.

These early conceptions of entrepreneurship in public affairs, however, also propagated a certain imperfection that was corrected by the classical entrepreneurship theorists. This imperfection is that public sector entrepreneurs are simply economic actors (*homo economicus*) with (nearly) perfect rationality and (almost) complete information in the quasi-market setting of politics. More recent general entrepreneurship theorists have noticed and corrected this rational-actor conceptualization of entrepreneurship. Morris (1998), for example, characterizes the entrepreneurial decision as realizing 'a pattern – a trend, a possibility, an incongruity, an unmet need – when it is still taking shape'. Shane and Venkataraman (2000) purposefully use 'conjecture' to distinguish entrepreneurial decisions from rational economic decisions. Citing Casson (1982), Shane and Venkataraman write:

> An entrepreneurial discovery occurs when someone makes the conjecture that a set of resources is not put to its 'best use'. . . If the conjecture is acted upon and is correct, the individual will earn an entrepreneurial profit. If the conjecture is acted upon and incorrect, the individual will incur an entrepreneurial loss.

The early conceptions of entrepreneurship in public affairs, however, maintained the *homo economicus* model of economic behavior characteristic of public choice theory (see Engelen, 2007). Indeed, one could call these public sector entrepreneurs, *homo economicus politicus* (Shockley *et al.*, 2006).

Schumpeter and Kirzner separately make the fundamental point that rational economic decisions of *homo economicus politicus* and truly entrepreneurial decisions are distinct and not at all synonymous. For example, although he allows some room for rational calculation (Kirzner, 1979: 170), Kirzner places entrepreneurial discovery, or 'alertness to hitherto unnoticed opportunities' (Kirzner, 1973: 39), at the heart of his theory of entrepreneurship and as something altogether different from the rational, maximizing behavior of economic actors (Vaughn, 1994). 'Entrepreneurial discovery represents the alert becoming aware of what has been overlooked. The essence of entrepreneurship consists in seeing through the fog created by the uncertainty of the future' (Kirzner, 1997b). Moreover, entrepreneurial discovery is a creative act, not an instrumental one. Kirzner (1982) writes, 'Alertness must, importantly, embrace the awareness of the ways in which the human agent can, by imaginative, bold leaps of faith, and determination, in fact *create* the future for which his present acts are designed'. Thus, Kirzner implicitly locates entrepreneurship not only in economic behavior but also in all human action. The key is the uncertainty inherent to all human action: 'the aspect responsible for rendering human action unpredictable and incompletely explainable in terms of rationality, arises from the inherent uncertainty of [the] human predicament' (Kirzner, 1982). In Knightian terms (Knight, 1921/2006), entrepreneurial discovery is invoked in situations of uncertainty, not in situations of risk when economic rationality is most appropriate.

Schumpeter is no less careful than Kirzner in distinguishing entrepreneurial decisions from rational economic calculation. Schumpeter identifies entrepreneurial decisions with novel intuitions that defy instrumental rationality. He writes in *The Theory of Economic Development*:

> Here the success of everything depends upon the intuition and the capacity of seeing things in a way which afterwards proves to be true, even though it cannot be established at the moment, and of grasping the essential fact, discarding the unessential, even though one can give no account of the principles by which it is done. (p. 85)

In other words, far from the rational calculation of business planning and strategy, insight from 'gut' feelings drives the Schumpeterian entrepreneur. As Gloria-Palermo (2002) contends, Schumpeterian entrepreneurs operate not by instrumental rationality but by an 'energetic' rationality, one which originates in 'novel intuitions about future developments' (pp. 25–6). In fact, Yu (2001) uses Kirznerian entrepreneurial discovery to encompass both Schumpeterian and Kirznerian theories entrepreneurship, leaving no room at all for rational calculation in either theory.

Table 8.1   Theories of entrepreneurship in public affairs that over-emphasize rational calculation

Citation	Short description, summary, or extract
(Wilson, 1974/1995)	*Entrepreneurship as cost-benefit analysis I*: 'The role of the policy entrepreneur in modifying programs varies with the kind of issue' in terms of his or her costs-benefits calculations (p. 336)
(Riker, 1986)	*Entrepreneurship as 'heresthetics'*: 'managing and manipulating and maneuvering' (p. ix)
(Baumgartner and Jones, 1993)	*Entrepreneurship as probabilities and expectations*: Entrepreneurship as 'The willingness of a political actor to invest resources in a given lobbying struggle is likely to be related to two things: The probability of success . . . and the expected benefits' (p. 22)
(Schiller, 1995)	*Entrepreneurship as cost-benefit analysis II*: 'Political entrepreneurs' in Congress engage in cost-benefit analysis before sponsoring a bill
(Wawro, 2000)	*Entrepreneurship as rational resource allocation*: '[Legislative entrepreneurship] is a set of activities that a legislator engages in . . . for the purpose of passing legislation by combining various legislative inputs and issues in order to affect legislative outcomes' (p. 4)
(MacLeod, 2002)	*Entrepreneurship as preferences and expectations*: Policy entrepreneurship, which is here defined as challenging the status quo, 'can be thought of as a function of preferences and expectations of success' (p. 59)

The first requirement of a theory of entrepreneurship in public affairs is that 'the theory emphasizes something like Kirznerian entrepreneurial discovery or Schumpeterian novel intuitions, not instrumental rational calculation'. Table 8.1 catalogues existing theories of entrepreneurship in public affairs that over-emphasize rational calculation and neglect the essential mechanisms of entrepreneurship in the classical theories of Kirzner (entrepreneurial discovery) and Schumpeter (novel intuitions).

Entrepreneurs, Leaders, Capitalists, and Managers

Another popular misconception is that entrepreneurs are simply leaders by another name or some sort of generic economic actor in capitalism, namely, managers or even the fabled capitalist him- or herself. While

Kirzner says very little if anything about leadership, Schumpeter might possibly be to blame for confusing entrepreneurs with leaders because leadership does play an important role in Schumpeterian entrepreneurship. Leadership is specifically required in order to overcome resistance to the large-scale change that Schumpeterian entrepreneurship entails. According to Schumpeter, leadership is 'necessary in order to wrest, amidst the work and care of the daily round, scope and time for conceiving and working out the new combination and to bring oneself to look upon it as a real possibility as a day-dream'. In other words, leadership ushers in the changes that entrepreneurship produces. 'He (the leader) "leads" the means of production into new channels.' Therefore, to Schumpeter, leadership is 'a new and another kind of effort of will' distinct from entrepreneurship.

Both Schumpeter and Kirzner make considerable effort to distinguish the role of entrepreneurs from those of other economic actors. In fact, Kirzner and Schumpeter specifically contrast the entrepreneur from the capitalist. In Schumpeterian entrepreneurship, the assumption of risk divides the entrepreneur from the capitalist as the provider of financial capital. The entrepreneur does not assume the risk; rather, the capitalist does (see Hebert and Link, 1988; High, 2002). As Schumpeter (1934/2002) himself unequivocally asserts, 'The entrepreneur is never the risk bearer' (p. 137). Although the two may coincide on occasion, risk is not required for entrepreneurship. 'Contrary to popular opinion concerning entrepreneurs,' McKee (1991) asserts, 'the Schumpeterian variety are not risk takers' (p. 3). (Also see Gloria-Palermo, 2002; Kanbur, 1980.) Similarly, Kirznerian entrepreneurial discovery does not require any sort of capitalistic investment. As Kirzner (1973) puts it, 'The discovery of a profit opportunity *means the discovery of something obtainable for nothing at all.* No investment at all is required; the free ten-dollar bill is discovered to be already within one's grasp' (p. 48, emphasis in the original). Indeed, Kirzner argues even more strongly that capitalistic investment is separate from entrepreneurship: '*Pure* entrepreneurship,' Kirzner (1973) declares, 'is exercised only in the *absence* of an initially owned asset' (p. 16, emphasis in the original). Thus, both Schumpeter and Kirzner insist that entrepreneurs generally are not capitalists because, in both of their theories, each serves a different and distinct role in an economic system.

Schumpeter also argues that entrepreneurship must also be differentiated from management. Schumpeter maintains that entrepreneur's role occurs only at the very beginning of the organizational lifecycle of a business, that is, when the entrepreneur uses novel intuitions to innovate and start a business. Once the business is operational, however, the entrepreneur ceases to be an entrepreneur and at that point becomes a manager, using his or her instrumental rationality to run the business. Schumpeter (1934/2002) explains, 'Everyone is an entrepreneur only when he actually "carries out new combinations," and loses that character as soon as he builds up his business, when he settles down to running it as other people run their businesses' (p. 78). In other words, the entrepreneur seizes the entrepreneurial opportunity to 'carry out a new combination' while the manager takes over once the opportunity has been realized. Bull and Willard (1993) assert that the Schumpeterian entrepreneur is not a manager by definition. 'Schumpeter's definition is acceptably precise,' they write. 'An entrepreneur is the person who carries out new combinations, causing discontinuity . . . A manager who operates an existing business, perhaps even with continuous adjustment in small steps, does not cause discontinuity, and thus, by definition, is not an entrepreneur'. Therefore, according to the classical theorists, the entrepreneur is altogether different from the leader, capitalist (i.e., bearer of the financial risk), and manager.

The second requirement of a theory of entrepreneurship in public affairs is that 'the theory must recognize that entrepreneurship is a distinct and self-reflexive activity unto itself'. Table 8.2 catalogues recent theories of entrepreneurship in public affairs that either do not distinguish between entrepreneurship and management or simply conflate them.

Ubiquity of Entrepreneurship

As explained above, one of the two fundamental insights of the classical conception of entrepreneurship is the ubiquity of entrepreneurship in all human endeavors. A theory of entrepreneurship in public affairs must therefore also recognize that entrepreneurship, far from being a rare occurrence, pervades public affairs. As Morris (1998) proclaims, 'Entrepreneurship is a universal construct that is applicable to any person, organization (private or public, large or small), or nation' (also see Morris and Jones, 1999). Remarkably, Schumpeter, Kirzner, and many well-known theorists of presumably private sector entrepreneurship astonishingly make little or no mention of the private sector in their theoretical work. For example, Schumpeter in his later work *Capitalism, Socialism, and Democracy* (1950) explicitly argues that 'the entrepreneurial alertness takes place in the mind of the politician and the consequences can be compared with those of a technological innovation, namely to reform or revolutionize the pattern of production by exploiting an invention' (Albrecht, 2002: 651). Kirzner deliberately constructs his theory of entrepreneurship on the work of Ludwig von Mises, particularly on Mises' magnum opus *Human Action* (1949/1996). In *Human Action*, Mises insists that entrepreneurship is universally present in human action: 'This function [of entrepreneurship] is not the particular feature of a special group or class of men; it is inherent

Table 8.2   *Theories of entrepreneurship in public affairs that confuse entrepreneurs with leaders, capitalists, and managers*

Citation	Short Description, Summary, or Extract
(Dahl, 1961)	*'The gifted political entrepreneur'*: 'A leader who knows how to use his resources to the maximum is not so much the agent of others as others are his agents' (Dahl, 1961)
(Hood, 1991; Massey,1993; Pollitt, 1993)	*New Public Management (NPM)*: A key assumption is that 'private-sector methods for managing activities (regardless of what they are) are almost inherently superior to the methods of the traditional public sector' (Peters, 1996, p. 21)
(Kingdon, 1995, 2nd edition)	*Policy entrepreneurship as the investment of resources*: '[The defining characteristic of policy entrepreneurs], much as in the case of a business entrepreneur, is their willingness to invest their resources – time, energy, reputation, and sometimes money – in the hope of future return' (p. 122)
(Moore, 1995)	*'Entrepreneurial advocacy'*: Comprised of 'diagnostic skills' and 'tactics' (p. 151)
(M. Schneider and Teske, 1992; M. Schneider et al., 1995)	*Public entrepreneurs as risk-taking managers*: Two of the three defining characteristics of public entrepreneurs as 'agents of change' are 'their willingness to take risky action in the pursuit of opportunities they see, and their ability to coordinate the actions of other people to fulfill their goals' (M. Schneider *et al.*, 1995: 8)
(Moon, 1999)	*'Managerial entrepreneurship'* is simply entrepreneurship in the public sector
(Morris and Jones, 1999)	*Public sector entrepreneurship as business process reengineering*: 'Entrepreneurship implies an innovative, proactive role for government in steering society toward improved quality of life [for example, generating alternative revenues, improving internal processes]' (p. 87)
(Baez and Abolafia, 2002)	*Bureaucratic entrepreneurs as business strategists*: 'Extraordinary interruptions . . . may lead [bureaucratic entrepreneurs] to think strategically about whether and how to alter current routines to accommodate new environmental expectations' (p. 526)
(Feeley, 2002)	*Policy entrepreneur as managerial tactician*: 'A successful policy entrepreneur is able to correctly assess which goals will be most attractive to the constituency groups she is targeting and will adjust her tactics accordingly to maximize her chances for success' (p. 126)

Table 8.3   Specialized theories of entrepreneurship in public affairs

Citation	Short Description, Summary, or Extract
(Roberts, 1992)	Political entrepreneurs vs. policy entrepreneur vs. bureaucratic entrepreneur vs. executive entrepreneur
(Schiller, 1995)	*Senators as political entrepreneurs*: 'The senator's decision calculus rests on a number of factors: the receptiveness of the political and policy environment, institutional position, potential administration support, financial cost, another senator's role in the issue and opportunities for publicity' (p. 190)
(Boyett, 1997)	*Unit-level public managers*: 'Entrepreneurship occurs in the public sector where there is an uncertain environment, a devolution of power, and at the same time re-allocation of resource ownership, to unit management level. It is driven by those individuals, particularly susceptible to the "manipulation" of their stakeholders and with a desire for a high level of social "self-satisfaction", who have the ability to spot market opportunities and who are able through follower "manipulation" to act on them' (p. 90)
(Wawro, 2000)	*Legislative entrepreneurship*: 'A set of activities that a legislator engages in . . . for the purpose of passing legislation by combining various legislative inputs and issues in order to affect legislative outcomes' (p. 4)
(Carpenter, 2001)	*Bureaucratic entrepreneurship*: 'The incremental selling of new program ideas through experimentation and piecemeal coalition building' (p. 30)

in every action and burdens every actor' (pp. 252–3). Further, two contemporary and foundational articles on presumably private sector entrepreneurship – Bull and Willard's 'Towards a theory of entrepreneurship' (1993) and Bygrave and Hofer's 'Theorizing about entrepreneurship' (1991) – make no mention of the private sector at all. As Koppl (2006) reiterates, 'entrepreneurs are not a class of people distinct from other persons, and entrepreneurial behavior is not a class of actions distinct from other actions. Entrepreneurship is a human universal' (also see Koppl and Minniti in this volume).

The following theories of entrepreneurship in public affairs in Table 8.3 are particular instances of entrepreneurship in public affairs. They are more accurately characterized as specialized theories of entrepreneurial activity in the public sector rather than as general theories of entrepreneurship in

public affairs, as I am attempting to do in this chapter. The third requirement of a theory of entrepreneurship in public affairs is that 'the theory
indeed be a *general* theory, that is, capable of encompassing most, if not all,
instances of entrepreneurship in the public sector'.

THE CAUSAL FUNCTIONALITY OF
ENTREPRENEURSHIP

In the classical conception, entrepreneurship produces important effects in
a market economy. In Kirznerian entrepreneurship, 'the entrepreneurial
role drives the ever-changing process of the market' (Kirzner, 1997a). The
primary effect of entrepreneurship is equilibration, that is, the movement
of a market toward an equilibrium state. 'For me,' Kirzner (1973) writes,
'the changes the entrepreneur initiates are always toward the hypothetical
state of equilibrium' (p. 73). Entrepreneurship and equilibration are central
to the market process because they facilitate profit opportunities.
According to Kirzner (1973), entrepreneurial opportunities for profit occur
only in disequilibrium resulting from human error,[7] usually taking the form
of arbitrage opportunities arising from price discrepancies (p. 26). In economics terms, the market is in a state of disequilibrium because a given
product or service can be purchased in one place cheaper than it can be sold
in another. When the entrepreneur's alertness identifies the potentially
profitable arbitrage opportunity in disequilibrium and acts entrepreneurially by buying cheap and selling dear, the equilibration process is triggered
(Kirzner, 1979: 116). Once the entrepreneurial transaction has been con-
summated, the entrepreneurial opportunity begins to deteriorate and the
disequilibrium begins to lessen as the system moves toward equilibrium
(Kirzner, 1999). 'The dynamic competitive process of entrepreneurial discovery,' Kirzner (1997a) writes, 'is one which is seen as *tending systematically toward* . . . the path to equilibrium' (p. 62, emphasis in the original).
Thus, the major effect of Kirznerian entrepreneurship is to move the
market toward equilibrium. 'Scope for market entrepreneurship, in the
context of the passage of time,' Kirzner (1982) concludes, 'arises then from
the need to coordinate markets also across time.'

Like Kirznerian entrepreneurship, Schumpeterian entrepreneurship also
produces important effects in a market economy. In fact, Schumpeter places
the effects of entrepreneurship at the center of his theory of economic
change and development. 'Development,' Schumpeter argues in *The Theory
of Economic Development* (1934/2002), 'is spontaneous and discontinuous
change in the channels of flow, disturbance of equilibrium, which forever
alters and displaces the equilibrium state previously existing' (p. 64). In

other words, entrepreneurship in the form of the carrying out of new combinations is the main cause of economic development (see Bull and Willard, 1993). In Schumpeterian entrepreneurship, 'introducing a new good or method of production, opening of a new market, identifying a new source of supply of raw materials or half-manufactured goods, or carrying out of the new organisation of any industry' (p. 66) all individually or in combination have the potential to cause 'spontaneous and discontinuous change' in an economy and spur economic development (also see Schumpeter, 1926, 2003; Sweezy, 1943.) 'By introducing innovations,' McKee (1991) observes, 'the [Schumpeterian] entrepreneurs jump-start the system from the range of equilibrium . . . The overall impact regenerates the system, causing it to expand' (p. 8).[8] Thus, as in Kirzner's theory, Schumpeter's theory of entrepreneurship is a functional one that emphasizes the effects of entrepreneurship, namely, to drive positive economic growth and development.

The fourth requirement of a theory of entrepreneurship in public affairs is that, like Schumpeterian and Kirznerian entrepreneurship, 'the theory features the larger, systemic effects directly and observably produced by entrepreneurship in public affairs'. The following theories of entrepreneurship in public affairs in Table 8.4 either neglect the effects of entrepreneurship in public affairs altogether, or if they include some sort of effects, they are relatively minimal and circumscribed.

Another essential component common to both Schumpeterian and Kirznerian entrepreneurship and the classical conception – and one that is

Table 8.4   Theories of entrepreneurship in public affairs either neglecting or minimizing the effects of entrepreneurship

Citation	Short description, summary, or extract
(Lewis, 1977)	The public entrepreneur is an agency or director that/who 'creates or profoundly elaborates a public organization' (p. 9)
(Kanter, 1983)	'Quiet entrepreneurs' in the private or public sectors 'test limits and create new possibilities for organizational action by pushing and directing the innovation process' (p. 210)
(Polsby, 1984)	Policy entrepreneurs 'interface' or convey alternatives to policymakers (p. 167)
(Ramamurti, 1986)	'The term "public entrepreneur" is used here to mean "an individual who undertakes purposeful activity"' (p. 143)
(Holcombe, 2002)	'Political entrepreneurship occurs when an individual observes and acts on a political profit opportunity' (p. 143)
(Kobrak, 2002)	A public entrepreneur is a 'public manager as a proactive, entrepreneurial type' (p. xv)

a logical extension to the above discussion on the effects of entrepreneurship – is that the function of entrepreneurship takes priority over the
description of entrepreneurs or mere identification of entrepreneurial
activity.[9] Both Kirzner's and Schumpeter's theories of entrepreneurship
can be understood as causal, functional theories of how entrepreneurship
produces equilibrative effects in the market (Kirzner) or economic growth
and development (Schumpeter). In *The Theory of Economic Development*
(1934/2002), Schumpeter clearly distinguishes between entrepreneurship
and entrepreneurs when he defines enterprise, or entrepreneurial activity,
as 'the carrying out of new combinations' and entrepreneurs as 'the individuals whose function it is to carry them out'. 'The "entrepreneur",'
Schumpeter writes, 'is merely the bearer of the mechanism of change', thus
leaving the more substantive role of causing the change to the process of
entrepreneurship. It is thus entrepreneurship, and not the entrepreneur,
that drives economic growth and development. In Schumpeter's theory,
entrepreneurs are subordinate to the function of entrepreneurship in the
economy.

The priority of entrepreneurship over the entrepreneur is even more
apparent in Kirznerian entrepreneurship. Kirzner is not concerned with the
identification of individual entrepreneurs. Since, according to Kirzner, any
individual has the potential to be an entrepreneur because uncertainty is an
unavoidable element of all human action, whosoever turns out to be an
entrepreneur is at most of secondary importance. Of primary importance,
rather, are the effects of entrepreneurship. Similarly, Kirzner (1999)
prioritizes the function of entrepreneurship over instrumentality of the
entrepreneur:

> While psychological and personal qualities of boldness and creativity, and self-
> confidence will doubtless be helpful or even necessary in order for a person to
> 'see' such price differentials in the open-ended, uncertain world in which we live
> (with 'seeing' defined as necessarily implying the grasping of the opportunity
> one has seen), the *analytical essence* of the pure entrepreneurial role is itself inde-
> pendent of these specific qualities.

Like Schumpeter, Kirzner places entrepreneurship and its effects as the
cornerstones in explaining the market process. 'The market process . . .,'
Kirzner (1992) writes, 'consists of those changes that express the sequence
of discoveries that follow the initial ignorance that constituted the disequilibrium state' (p. 44). In other words, according to Kirzner, entrepreneurship – not the individual entrepreneur – plays the vital function in the
market. As Vaughn (1994) puts it, 'Kirzner is clear that he is describing a
function rather than a kind of person, just as labor and capital are themselves functions in economic theory' (p. 142). Or, as Gloria Palermo (2002)

Table 8.5   Theories that under-emphasize the function of entrepreneurship in the public sector

Citation	Short Description, Summary, or Extract
(Doig and Hargrove, 1987)	Entrepreneurship conflated with the leadership of certain political appointees, high-level civil servants or military officers, or other actors in the policy process
(Lipsky, 1980; Scholz *et al.*, 1991	Street-level bureaucrats are identified as the source of entrepreneurship in the public sector
(Osborne and Gaebler, 1992)	Entrepreneurship in reinventing government stems from empowering public sector managers and staff

puts it, 'Kirzner's theory of entrepreneurship focuses on the equilibrium *function* of the entrepreneur' (p. 36, emphasis added).

Therefore, it is entrepreneurial activity, not individual entrepreneurs, that is paramount in both Schumpeterian and Kirznerian entrepreneurship. The function of Schumpeterian and Kirznerian entrepreneurship takes precedence over its instruments, namely, mere entrepreneurs. Unlike the theories of entrepreneurship in public affairs listed in Table 8.5 emphasizing the identification of individual entrepreneurs over entrepreneurial activity, the fifth requirement of a theory of entrepreneurship in public affairs is that, like both Schumpeterian and Kirznerian entrepreneurship, it gives priority to the function of entrepreneurship over the mere instrumentality of individual entrepreneurs.

POLICY ENTREPRENEURSHIP

This chapter thus far has been dedicated to critiquing a wide variety of existing theories of entrepreneurship in public affairs through the lenses of Schumpeter's and Kirzner's classical theories of entrepreneurship. The critique has also yielded the requirements for a theory of entrepreneurship in public affairs that would render such a theory consistent with Schumpeterian and Kirznerian entrepreneurship. The requirements for reconceptualizing entrepreneurship in public affairs in a way that is consistent with Schumpeter's and Kirzner's classical theories are encapsulated in Box 8.1. The five requirements in Box 8.1, however, necessitate considerable explication, which I do below as I also discuss many of the most prominent theories of entrepreneurship in public affairs generally and policy entrepreneurship specifically.

BOX 8.1   REQUIREMENTS FOR RECONCEPTUALIZING ENTREPRENEURSHIP IN PUBLIC AFFAIRS

1. Emphasis on something like Kirznerian entrepreneurial discovery or Schumpeterian novel intuitions, not instrumental rational calculation.
2. Recognition that entrepreneurship is a distinct and self-reflexive activity unto itself.
3. A general theory capable of encompassing most, if not all, instances of entrepreneurship in the public sector.
4. Featuring the larger effects of entrepreneurship in public affairs.
5. Priority given to the function of entrepreneurship over the instrumentality of individual entrepreneurs.

Policy Entrepreneurship: Explicating Requirements 1, 2, and 3

The first requirement – that something like Kirznerian entrepreneurial discovery or Schumpeterian novel intuitions be emphasized – is the key to reconceptualizing policy entrepreneurship. It must first be acknowledged this is not the first scholarly work to call for ideas from Schumpeterian and Kirznerian entrepreneurship to be carried over to the public sector.[10] As far as I can tell, this important distinction belongs to the research of Schneider, Teske and Mintrom (Mintrom, 2000; Schneider and Teske, 1992; Schneider *et al.*, 1995). In their 1992 article in the *American Political Science Review*, Schneider and Teske divide entrepreneurship theory into the Kirznerian and Schumpeterian varieties: 'Kirzner's entrepreneur is defined by an "alertness to disequilibrium" and independently injects new elements into markets . . . For Schumpeter, entrepreneurial activity is most likely to emerge when a market approaching equilibrium'. Then, in their 1995 book, Schneider, Teske, and Mintrom ally themselves to Kirzner by making alertness to opportunity the 'central feature' of their definition of the public entrepreneur.[11] And there is evidence that their distinction between Kirznerian and Schumpeterian entrepreneurship has influenced subsequent scholarship (for example, Sheingate, 2003). One immediate problem is that their otherwise solid scholarship seems to rely more on secondary commentary on Kirzner's and Schumpeter's primary works rather than their own close reading. Consequently, their use of Kirznerian and Schumpeterian entrepreneurship can be vulnerable to inaccuracy or the wrong emphases. One example quoted above is that their definition of Schumpeterian entrepreneurship as 'most likely to emerge when a market approaching equilibrium' not only is inconsistent with Schumpeterian theory but also is somewhat contrary. Even more of a difficulty, however, comes from their work ceasing at the invocation of Schumpeter and Kirzner and not incorporating any of the requirements of their theories of entrepreneurship beyond the first requirement. In this reconceptualization of entrepreneurship in public affairs, by contrast, the inclusion of Kirznerian entrepreneurial discovery and Schumpeterian novel intuitions (the first requirement of Box 8.1) is the beginning of a proper theory, not the end.

A fair question arising from this first requirement is: What precisely is an entrepreneurial opportunity in public affairs? Again, Kirzner argues that entrepreneurial opportunities in markets occur only in disequilibrium resulting from human error, usually taking the form of arbitrage opportunities. Although strictly speaking there are no price discrepancies in the public sector, there certainly are opportunities in the public sector that can be linked to human error. For example, Lipsky (1980) suggests that the human inability to design machine-like government organizations that can perfectly control 'street-level bureaucrats' or to implement operational procedures that might constrain their activities give these front-line public sector employees opportunities every day to utilize their own judgment and discretion in delivering government services and, essentially, making agency policy. Behn (1998) asserts that the seven 'failures of governance' – organizational, analytical, executive, legislative, political, civic and judiciary – provide many opportunities for public managers to exercise their 'obligation to lead'. And Doig and Hargrove (1987), among many others (for example Ingram and Ullery, 1980; Polsby, 1984; Sheingate, 2003), argue that the fragmentation of American federalism and constitutionally shared federal powers, which most likely the Framers devised not out of their own human error but because of the ineradicable tendency to err in all humans, provides many opportunities for policy innovation. The theme that links these examples is that Kirznerian entrepreneurial opportunities occur in the public sector from human error.

The second requirement in Box 8.1 can be seen as a logical extension of the first. Entrepreneurial opportunities in the public sector are not metaphorical; rather, they are real occurrences that are homologous to entrepreneurial opportunities in markets. If entrepreneurial opportunities arising in the public sector are real (objectively or subjectively), so must be the mental processes enabling their discovery (for example, Schumpeterian novel intuitions), the physical activities involved in acting on their discovery, and the effects that follow entrepreneurial activity. Moreover, entrepreneurship is not the product of rational calculation, strategizing, risk-taking, or effective management. Rather, entrepreneurship works through another, altogether distinct faculty, such as 'carrying out new combinations' (Schumpeter, 1934/2002: 60), 'seeing through the fog' (Kirzner, 1997b: 51), or the 'anticipation of uncertain events' (Mises, 1949/1996: 290). As Mises (1949/1996) puts it, 'Economics, in speaking of entrepreneurs, has in view not men, but a *definite action*' (p. 252, emphasis added). Thus, entrepreneurship is a definable and observable action, a distinct and self-reflexive activity unto itself, as the second requirement in Box 8.1 requirement maintains.

The third requirement in Box 8.1 is largely a semantic one. The requirement that the reconceptualization is not simply another narrow or specialized theory, that it is general enough to encompass most if not all instances of entrepreneurship in public affairs, is essentially a request that the most appropriate general conceptual term for the entrepreneurial phenomena in public affairs is chosen. Hitherto in this study the phenomena of interest have been referred to as 'entrepreneurship in public affairs'; however, another conceptual term might be more appropriate if it conveys more qualitative or quantitative meaning.

I argue that 'policy entrepreneurship' is the best-available term to encompass almost all of entrepreneurial phenomena in public affairs. Unlike the term 'entrepreneurship in public affairs', which might imply that entrepreneurship in the public sector is the province of only governmental actors, policy entrepreneurship better accommodates the reality that governance today typically involves private, nonprofit, or other non-governmental actors (Skelcher, 2000). As was argued above, it is important to acknowledge that entrepreneurial activity occurs in the public sector; entrepreneurship, as the classical theorists argue, is ubiquitous in human action. While entrepreneurship in public affairs adequately connotes the locus of entrepreneurial activity occurring in the public sphere, policy entrepreneurship not only retains the locational connotation but also conveys additional meaning by denoting the universal object of any activity in public affairs, that is, to influence policy.

Expressed in the crudest and most simplistic terms, the actions (and inactions) of legislatures, bureaucracies, executives, judiciaries, interest groups, citizens, the media, and any other player in public affairs all directly or indirectly influence policy. Schneider and Ingram give a sense of this when they point out in the preface to their book *Policy Design for Democracy* (1997) that policy content is not only found in legislation but also in 'statutes, guidelines, court rulings, and practices of case workers' (p. ix). If policy content is found in all forms of government output, as Schneider and

Ingram imply, then all government processes producing such output affect 'policy' writ large. And, if all government processes affect policies, then inputs into government processes must also affect policies. Of course, the magnitude of the influence varies, but the essential point is that one would be hard-pressed to identify any activity in public affairs is not in some way directed towards influencing a policy domain.

Entrepreneurship in public affairs is no different from any other activity in public affairs in that the object towards which it is directed is influencing policy. The narrow or specialized theories of entrepreneurship in public affairs catalogued in Table 8.3 offer instructive examples that illustrate this fact. Schiller's (1995) 'senators as political entrepreneurs' and Wawro's (2000) 'legislative entrepreneurship' are theories that are clearly meant to capture entrepreneurial activity affecting the policy content embodied in legislation. Similarly, Carpenter's (2001) 'bureaucratic entrepreneurship', which he defines as 'the incremental selling of new program ideas' (p. 30), is directed towards policy because, according to Carpenter, such entrepreneurial activity in the late nineteenth and early twentieth centuries enabled the US Department of Agriculture, Post Office, Interior Department to gain considerable autonomy not only in managing existing policies but also in expanding their policy influence in new areas (see below for more discussion of Carpenter's work). The theories of entrepreneurship in public affairs listed in Table 8.3 are best described as particular instances of entrepreneurial behavior in the public sector, as was argued above, but also are unnecessarily confined to small slivers of the policy domain. Some forms of entrepreneurship in public affairs directly or indirectly influence policy; the term 'policy entrepreneurship' conveys this central insight better than does the entrepreneurship in public affairs. Therefore, I urge that the most appropriate term for entrepreneurship in public affairs is policy entrepreneurship and will exclusively employ that term henceforth.

Interlude: Acknowledged Debt to (and Critique of) Riker, Kingdon, and Baumgartner and Jones

Several very prominent, excellent theories of policy entrepreneurship precede the one being developed here. Both William Riker and John Kingdon have developed a functional conception of policy entrepreneurship. Riker endowed his conceptualization of policy entrepreneurship with the primary function of destabilizing previously stable voting situations (see Riker, 1980, 1982), culminating in *The Art of Political Manipulation* (1986) and its notion of 'heresthetics' as the art of 'managing and manipulating and maneuvering' (p. ix) a voting situation in order to accomplish a desired policy outcome. And Kingdon in *Agendas, Alternatives, and Public*

Policies (1995, first edition published in 1986), also introduced into policy analysis an influential functional conception of policy entrepreneurship, the main function of which is the 'coupling', or joining problems, policies, and politics either by promoting preferred policy alternatives or by '[lying] in wait for a [policy] window to open' (p. 181). Conceiving of the term 'policy entrepreneurship' and deploying their theories in the 1980s, Riker and Kingdon deserve all the credit for being the originators of the powerful idea of policy entrepreneurship for political and policy studies.

The problem common to both Riker and Kingdon's conceptions, however, is that they in no way conform to the essence of entrepreneurship theory as developed by Schumpeter and Kirzner, the originators of general, classical entrepreneurship theory. There is nothing 'entrepreneurial' about their theories of policy entrepreneurship. Again, the first requirement in Box 8.1 – that something like Kirznerian entrepreneurial discovery or Schumpeterian novel intuitions be emphasized – is intended primarily to link a theoretically sufficient theory of entrepreneurship in public affairs to the classical theories. Neither Riker's nor Kingdon's theories of policy entrepreneurship conform to this requirement because neither includes, much less emphasizes, anything like Kirznerian entrepreneurial discovery or Schumpeterian novel intuitions. For policy entrepreneurship to be eventually robust enough for empirical work based on it in policy research to advance, it must be grounded in the classical theories. Although Riker insists that heresthetics is 'an art, not a science' (Riker, 1986: ix), his elaboration of the heresthetics is based on agenda control, strategic voting, and clever manipulation, all of which more closely approximate variations of rational calculation than of entrepreneurial discovery, novel intuitions, or, for that matter, even any true form of art, though surely he meant the term metaphorically. And Kingdon mistakenly conflates entrepreneurship and management when he writes, '[Policy entrepreneurs'] defining characteristic, much as in the case of a business entrepreneur, is their willingness to invest their resources – time, energy, reputation, and sometimes money – in the hope of future return' (Kingdon, 1995: 122). Nothing differentiates Kingdon's policy 'entrepreneur' from a manager deciding how to allocate resources. More technically, Kingdon's policy entrepreneur operates in the realm of Knightian risk, not uncertainty. The absence of anything like Kirznerian entrepreneurial discovery or Schumpeterian novel intuitions generally renders Riker's and Kingdon's theories of policy entrepreneurship incompatible with the classical Schumpeterian and Kirznerian theories of entrepreneurship[12] and, therefore, improperly specified.

The absence of Kirznerian entrepreneurial discovery or Schumpeterian novel intuitions in Riker's and Kingdon's early theories of policy entrepreneurship is also evident in two more recent versions of entrepreneurship in public affairs: Carpenter's (2001) bureaucratic entrepreneurship and Baumgartner and Jones' more recent versions of policy entrepreneurship (Baumgartner and Jones, 1993, 2002; Jones and Baumgartner, 2005). Carpenter creates his own (that is, not based on prior theories of entrepreneurship in public affairs) theory of 'bureaucratic entrepreneurship', which he defines as 'the incremental selling of new program ideas through experimentation and piecemeal coalition building', in order to account for the forging of bureaucratic autonomy. 'Bureaucratic entrepreneurship,' he writes, 'is the process by which agency leaders experiment with new programs and gradually convince diverse coalitions of organized interests, the media, politicians of the value of their ideas and their bureaus.' In a recent article in The *Journal of Politics*, Crowe (2007) extends Carpenter's conception of political entrepreneurship as 'the building of organizational reputations, the cultivation of multiple networks, and the pursuit of change through measured action'. Although Carpenter's theory does not explicitly draw on Riker or Kingdon, the same problem arises. There is certainly little that the classical theorists would recognize as entrepreneurial.

Baumgartner and Jones explicitly build their theory of policy entrepreneurship on Riker's and Kingdon's theories (see Baumgartner and Jones, 1993: Chapter 1). In *Agendas and Instability in American Politics* (1993), Baumgartner and Jones characterize policy entrepreneurship as investing resources operating in a realm of risk, not uncertainty, much like Kingdon does: 'The willingness of a political actor to invest resources in a given lobbying struggle is likely to be related to two things: The probability of success . . . and the expected benefits' (p. 22). As they say themselves, this policy entrepreneur is simply a generic policy actor. They leave this theory mostly undeveloped and untested in this early work, presumably relying on the strength of Kingdon's theory. In their subsequent, edited work *Policy Dynamics* (2002), Baumgartner and Jones let their contributors struggle with the notion of policy entrepreneurship. MacLeod (2002), the contributor confronting the issue of policy entrepreneurship most diligently in *Policy Dynamics*, went so far as to provide a probabilistic formula for policy entrepreneurship that apparently is deeply indebted to Riker's. 'Decisions by groups or members of government institutions to challenge the status quo,' MacLeod writes, 'can be thought of as a function of preferences and expectations of success' (p. 59).[13] Based on Riker and Kingdon, the theory of policy entrepreneurship devised by Baumgartner and Jones and their collaborators propagates their fatal flaws, such as over-emphasizing rational calculation with a statistical formula, conflating strategic management with entrepreneurship, and failing to include anything like Kirznerian entrepreneurial discovery or Schumpeterian novel intuitions. Thus, not only are these prior theories of policy entrepreneurship generally incompatible with the classical conceptions of Kirznerian or Schumpeterian entrepreneurship, but they are also specifically insufficient to satisfy the third requirement in Box 8.1 that I have extensively argued above is met by using the term 'policy entrepreneurship'. For these reasons, the theory of policy entrepreneurship being reconceptualized herein acknowledges considerable debt to Riker's, Kingdon's, and Baumgartner and Jones' work but depart from these prior theories.

Policy Entrepreneurship: Explicating Requirements 4 and 5

The fourth and fifth requirements in Box 8.1 – that the effects of entrepreneurship in public affairs be incorporated and that the function of entrepreneurship be given priority over the instrumentality of individual entrepreneurs – comprise the joint requirement that policy entrepreneurship incorporate *causal functionality*, the second insight of the classical theorists. Riker's, Kingdon's, and Baumgartner and Jones' theories of policy entrepreneurship do indeed recognize this requirement that entrepreneurial activity both serves a function and is capable of producing effects in the policy process.

- The function of Riker's policy entrepreneurship is to upset voter situations with the primary effect of creating a type of disequilibrium in the vote.
- The function of Kingdon's policy entrepreneurship is to merge the different policy streams by introducing policy alternatives when the political environment is most receptive with the primary effect of garnering attention for the preferred policy alternative.
- The function of Baumgartner and Jones' policy entrepreneurship is to 'alter other people's understandings of the issues in which they deal' through the manipulation of 'policy images' and changing 'policy venues' (Baumgartner and Jones, 1993: 42) with the primary effect of securing the most favorable conditions for the sought-after policy change.

Therefore, Riker's, Kingdon's, and Baumgartner and Jones' prior theories of policy entrepreneurship do indeed feature causal functionality in the policy process and recognize that policy entrepreneurship is capable of producing effects.

Yet, the causal functionality in Riker's, Kingdon's, and Baumgartner and Jones' versions of policy entrepreneurship is not equal to the causal functionality in Schumpeterian and Kirznerian entrepreneurship. The effects that follow from Riker's (creating disequilibrium in voting situations), Kingdon's (merging policy streams for the preferred policy alternative), and Baumgartner and Jones' (securing the most favorable conditions for the sought-after policy change) are narrowly circumscribed effects and thus rather weak forms of causal functionality. By contrast, both Kirzner and Schumpeter entrepreneurship incorporate strong forms of causal functionality in which entrepreneurship is the primary determinant of market states. For instance, Kirznerian entrepreneurship produces the macro-effect of stabilizing the market for a commodity or service. As discussed above, the primary effect of Kirznerian entrepreneurship is equilibration, or moving the market back toward an equilibrium state by correcting the price discrepancies resulting from human error that produce arbitrage opportunities in the market. As Vaughn (1994) puts it, Kirznerian entrepreneurs are 'guarantors of coordination' in the market (p. 144) as they are responsible for removing the source of market disequilibrium and returning the market to a state of greater stability, if not equilibrium.[14]

There is, however, an even stronger statement of the causal functionality of political entrepreneurship provided by Sheingate's (2003) extremely powerful rendering of political entrepreneurship as a source of endogenous institutional change in *Studies in American Political Development*. Sheingate robustly specifies political entrepreneurship by emphasizing the causal, 'transformative effects' of entrepreneurship 'on politics, policies, or institutions', though the latter are the exclusive focus of the article. This strong causal functionality of political entrepreneurs is enabled by the complexity inherent to political institutions. Institutional complexity provides 'the opportunities for speculation, the resources for creative recombination, and the assets entrepreneurs use to consolidate innovation into institutional change'. Even Sheingate's policy entrepreneurship, however, is limited by the now-predictable weakness of not including the other components of the conceptual apparatus that a proper theory of entrepreneurship in public affairs requires, including something like Kirznerian entrepreneurial discovery or Schumpeterian novel intuitions. Indeed, Miroff's (2003) insightful critique of Sheingate in which Miroff discards Sheingate's political entrepreneurship in favor of leadership is most likely the consequence of incompletely grounding his theory in the classical theorists Kirzner and Schumpeter or other available entrepreneurship theorists in Sheingate's otherwise superior rendering.

BOX 8.2   POLICY ENTREPRENEURSHIP: A
RECONCEPTUALIZATION OF
ENTREPRENEURSHIP IN PUBLIC
AFFAIRS

Policy entrepreneurship [3] serves the equilibrative function [5] of returning stability to a policy domain [4] when an empirically observable entrepreneurial opportunity is discovered [1] and exploited [2].

CONCLUSION

It is the argument of this chapter that a proper theory of entrepreneurship in public affairs (that is, policy entrepreneurship) must satisfy all five requirements of the classical Kirznerian and Schumpeterian conceptions of entrepreneurship in order for the promise of policy entrepreneurship as a theoretically robust and empirically useful concept can be realized. Founded on the five requirements for reconceptualizing entrepreneurship in public affairs listed in Box 8.1, a theory of policy entrepreneurship is presented in Box 8.2. The location of each requirement in the theory is indicated by the corresponding number in brackets.

Now the theory of policy entrepreneurship reconceptualized in this chapter must be used and tested to see just how robust it really is . . .

NOTES

1. The phrase 'classical view' is not meant to denote a unitary theory of entrepreneurship underlying the thought of Mises, Kirzner, and Schumpeter, although there are distinct similarities and complementarities between all three that are explored below. Instead, 'classical view' connotes a *general perspective or a set of similar premises* on which all three economists base their theories of entrepreneurship as well as the recognition that these three were the last of the great entrepreneurship theorists As the term the entrepreneurship increased, the theorists confronting it dropped off. The last great theorists of entrepreneurship (see Formaini, 2001).
2. 'Economics, in speaking of entrepreneurs, has in view not men, but a definite action' (Mises, 1949/1996: 252–3).
3. 'Kirzner is clear that he is describing a function rather than a kind of person, just as labor and capital are themselves functions in economic theory' (Vaughn, 1994: 142).
4. Many scholars maintain that Kirznerian and Schumpeterian entrepreneurship are complementary. Bifurcating Kirznerian entrepreneurial discovery into 'ordinary' vs. 'extraordinary' discovery, Yu (2001) unifies Schumpeterian and Kirznerian

entrepreneurship by assigning the former to Kirzner and the latter to Schumpeter. Hebert and Link (1988) find complementarity in Schumpeterian and Kirznerian entrepreneurship as Schumpeter's entrepreneur creates disequilibrium, which then stimulates Kirznerian entrepreneurial discovery. Boudreaux (1994) and Choi (1995) separately argue that both Schumpeterian and Kirznerian entrepreneurship are equilibrating. Perhaps most importantly, Kirzner (1999) himself acknowledges the complementarity of Kirznerian and Schumpeterian entrepreneurship: 'Schumpeter is concerned to enable us to see, *from the outside*, as it were, what constitutes the essence of capitalism . . . My own focus on the entrepreneur was inspired by the objective of enabling us to see the *inside* workings of the capitalist system' (p. 16, emphasis in the original).

5. Much of the review of prior theories of public sector entrepreneurship is adapted from Shockley *et al.*, (2006).

6. 'Public sector' entrepreneurship is meant to be a broad category encompassing all available theories of entrepreneurship said to be occurring in the public sector. At least initially, 'policy' entrepreneurship is a particular kind of entrepreneurship in public affairs. In the end, it will be argued that public sector and policy entrepreneurship are conceptually synonymous.

7. I interpret 'human error' to be synonymous with the suboptimal decisions and actions resulting from bounded rationality (see Simon, 1945/1976, 1982), imperfect information (for example, Hayek, 1945), incomplete knowledge (for example, Hayek, 1952), and other limitations from cognitive processing or the human condition.

8. Similarly, Schumpeter in *Capitalism, Socialism, and Democracy* (1950) contends that political entrepreneurs spark revolutionary change, much like technological innovation 'reform[s] or revolutionize[s] the pattern of production by exploiting an invention' (Albrecht, 2002: 651).

9. In a contemporary assessment, Bygrave and Hofer (1991) not only insist on separating the process of entrepreneurship from the entrepreneur but they also give priority of importance to the former.

10. For general entrepreneurship research, Gartner's (1990) 'two viewpoints on entrepreneurship' might have been the first to introduce the distinction between Kirznerian and Schumpeterian entrepreneurship.

11. Mintrom in *Policy Entrepreneurs and School Choice* (2000) seems to depart from his collaborators Schneider and Teske's preference for the classical entrepreneurship theory of Schumpeter an Kirzner by defining policy entrepreneurs are 'individuals with well-developed social skills [who] are able to engineer major changes in how policy communities come to think about issues'.

12. It is hard to resist the thought, however, that at least Kingdon would have revised his theory if he were more conversant with theories of private sector entrepreneurship. Lying in wait for policy windows to open seems much more compatible with something like Kirznerian entrepreneurial discovery than with rational calculation.

13. The specific formula offered is (MacLeod, 2002: 59):

Probability (decision to challenge the status quo) = (actor preference) * (perception of chances of success) + *e*

14. It is important to emphasize that Kirzner in *Competition and Entrepreneurship* (1973) only argues that 'the changes the entrepreneur initiates are *always toward* the hypothetical state of equilibrium' (p. 73, emphasis added), not necessarily reaching equilibrium. Kirzner may have modified his position in subsequent work.

REFERENCES

Albrecht, J. (2002), 'Environmental issue entrepreneurship: a Schumpeterian perspective', *Futures*, **34**, 649–61.

Baez, B. and M.Y. Abolafia (2002), 'Bureaucratic entrepreneurship and institutional change: a sense-making approach', *Journal of Public Administration Research and Theory*, **12**(4), 525–52.

Baumgartner, F.R. and B.D. Jones (1993), *Agendas and Instability in American Politics*. Chicago, IL: The University of Chicago Press.

Baumgartner, F.R. and B.D. Jones (2002), *Policy Dynamics*, Chicago, IL: The University of Chicago Press.

Behn, R.D. (1998), 'What right do public managers have to lead?', *Public Administration Review*, **58**(3), 209–24.

Boudreaux, D. (1994), 'Schumpeter and Kirzner on competition and equilibrium', in P.J. Boettke and D.L. Prychitko (eds), *The Market Process: Essays in Contemporary Austrian Economics*, Aldershot, UK and Brookfield, US: Edward Elgar.

Boyett, I. (1997), 'The public sector entrepreneur – a definition', *International Journal of Entrepreneurial Behavior & Research*, **3**(2), 77–92.

Bull, I. and G.E. Willard (1993), 'Towards a theory of entrepreneurship', *Journal of Business Venturing*, **8**, 183–95.

Bygrave, W.D. and C.W. Hofer (1991), 'Theorizing about entrepreneurship', *Entrepreneurship Theory and Practice*, **16**(2), 13–22.

Carpenter, D.P. (2001), *The Forging of Bureaucratic Autonomy: Reputation, Networks, and Policy Innovation in Executive Agencies, 1862–1928*. Princeton, NJ: Princeton University Press.

Casson, M. (1982), *The Entrepreneur: An Economic Theory*, Totowa, NJ: Barnes & Noble Books.

Choi, Y.B. (1995), 'The entrepreneur: Schumpeter vs. Kirzner', in P.J. Boettke and M.J. Rizzo (eds), *Advances in Austrian Economics (Volume 2, Part A)*, London: JAI Press.

Crowe, J. (2007), 'The forging of judicial autonomy: political entrepreneurship and the reforms of William Howard Taft', *Journal of Politics*, **69**(1), 73–87.

Curry Jr., R.L. and L.L. Wade (1968), *A Theory of Political Exchange: Economic Reasoning in Political Analysis*, Englewood Cliffs, NJ: Prentice-Hall.

Dahl, R.A. (1961), *Who Governs? Democracy and Power in an American City*, New Haven, CT: Yale University Press.

Doig, J.W. and E.C. Hargrove (eds) (1987), *Leadership and Innovation: A Biographical Perspective on Entrepreneurs in Government*, Baltimore, MD: The Johns Hopkins University Press.

Engelen, B. (2007), 'Thinking things through: the value and limitations of James Buchanan's public choice theory', *Review of Political Economy*, **19**(2), 165–79.

Feeley, T.J. (2002), 'The multiple goals of science and technology policy', in F.R. Baumgartner and B.D. Jones (eds), *Policy Dynamics*, Chicago, IL: The University of Chicago Press, pp. 125–54.

Formaini, R.L. (2001), 'The engine of capitalist process: entrepreneurs in economic theory', *Economic and Financial Review (Federal Reserve Bank of Dallas)* **Q IV**, 2–11.

Frohlich, N. and J.A. Oppenheimer (1972), 'Entrepreneurial politics and foreign policy', *World Politics*, **24**(Supplement: Theory and Policy in International Relations), 151–78.

Frohlich, N., J.A. Oppenheimer and O.A. Young (1971), *Political Leadership and Collective Goods*, Princeton, NJ: Princeton University Press.

Gartner, W.B. (1990), 'What are we talking about when we talk about entrepreneurship?', *Journal of Business Venturing*, **5**(1), 15–28.

Gloria-Palermo, S. (2002), 'Schumpeter and the Old Austrian School: interpretations and influences', in R. Arena and C. Dangel-Hagnauer (eds), *The Contribution of Joseph Schumpeter to Economics: Economic Development and Institutional Development* New York: Routledge, pp. 21–39.

Hayek, F.A. (1945), 'The use of knowledge in society', *American Economic Review*, **35**(4), 519–30.

Hayek, F.A. (1952), *The Counter-Revolution of Science: Studies on the Abuse of Reason*, Glencoe: Liberty Press.

Hebert, R.F. and A.N. Link (1988), *The Entrepreneur: Mainstream Views and Radical Critiques* (2nd edn), New York: Praeger.

High, J. (2002), 'The roles of entrepreneurship in economic growth', paper presented at the Entrepreneurship and the Modern Space-Economy: Evolutionary and Policy Perspectives, Tinbergen Institute, Amsterdam, The Netherlands, 10-11 June.

Holcombe, R.G. (2002), 'Political entrepreneurship and the democratic allocation of resources', *Review of Austrian Economics*, **15**(2/3), 143–60.

Hood, C. (1991), 'A public management for all seasons?', *Public Administration*, **69**, 3–19.

Ingram, H.M. and S.J. Ullery (1980), 'Policy innovation and institutional fragmentation', *Policy Studies Journal* **8**, 664–82.

Jones, B.D. and F.R. Baumgartner (2005), *The Politics of Attention: How Government Prioritizes Problems*. Chicago, IL: The University of Chicago Press.

Jones, P. (1978), 'The appeal of the political entrepreneur', *British Journal of Political Science*, **8**(4), 498–504.

Kanbur, S.M. (1980), 'A note on risk taking, entrepreneurship, and Schumpeter', *History of Political Economy*, **12**(4), 489–98.

Kanter, R.M. (1983), *The Change Masters: Innovation and Entrepreneurship in the American Corporation*. New York: Simon and Schuster.

Kingdon, J. (1995), *Agendas, Alternatives, and Public Policies* (2nd edn), New York: Addison-Wesley.

Kirzner, I.M. (1973), *Competition and Entrepreneurship*, Chicago, IL: The University of Chicago Press.

Kirzner, I.M. (1979), *Perception, Opportunity, and Profit: Studies in the Theory of Entrepreneurship*, Chicago, IL: The University of Chicago Press.

Kirzner, I.M. (1982), 'Uncertainty, discovery, and human action: a study of the entrepreneurial profile in the Misesian system', in I.M. Kirzner (ed.), *Method, Process, and Austrian Economics: Essays in Honor of Ludwig von Mises* Lexington, MA: Lexington Books, pp. 139–59.

Kirzner, I.M. (1992), 'The meaning of market process', in I.M. Kirzner, *The Meaning of Market Process: Essays on the Development of Modern Austrian Economics* New York: Routledge, pp. 38–54.

Kirzner, I.M. (1997a), 'Entrepreneurial discovery and the competitive market process: an Austrian approach', *Journal of Economic Literature*, **35**(1), 60–85.

Kirzner, I.M. (1997b), *How Markets Work: Disequilibrium, Entrepreneurship and Discovery*, London: The Institute of Economic Affairs.

Kirzner, I.M. (1999), 'Creativity and/or alertness: a reconsideration of the Schumpeterian entrepreneur', *Review of Austrian Economics*, **11**, 5–17.

Knight, F.H. (1921/2006), *Risk, Uncertainty, and Profit*, Mineola, NY: Dover Publications, Inc.

Kobrak, P. (2002), Introduction, in P. Kobrak (ed.), *The Political Environment of Public Management*, New York: Longman, pp xiii–xx.

Koppl, R. (2006), 'Entrepreneurial behavior as a human universal', in M. Minniti (ed.), *Entrepreneurship: The Engine of Growth (Volume 1: People)* Westport, CT: Praeger, pp. 1–19.

Lewis, E. (1977), *American Politics in a Bureaucratic Age*, Cambridge, MA: Winthrop Publishers.

Lipsky, M. (1980), *Street-Level Bureaucracy: Dilemmas of the Individual in Public Services*, New York: Russell Sage Foundation.

MacLeod, M.C. (2002), 'The logic of policy feedback: telecommunications policy through the creation, maintenance, and destruction of a regulated monopoly', in F.R. Baumgartner and B.D. Jones (eds), *Policy Dynamics*, Chicago, IL: The University of Chicago Press, pp. 51–72.

Massey, A. (1993), *Managing the Public Sector: A Comparative Analysis of the United Kingdom and the United States*, Aldershot, UK and Brookfield, US: Edward Elgar.

McKee, D.L. (1991), *Schumpeter and the Political Economy of Change*. New York: Praeger.

Mintrom, M. (2000), *Policy Entrepreneurs and School Choice*, Washington, DC: Georgetown University Press.

Miroff, B. (2003), 'Entrepreneurship and leadership', *Studies in American Political Development*, **17**, 204–11.

Mises, L. (1949/1996), *Human Action: A Treatise on Economics* (4th edn), San Francisco, CA: Fox & Wilkes.

Moon, M.J. (1999), 'The pursuit of managerial entrepreneurship: does organization matter?', *Public Administration Review*, **59**(1), 31–43.

Moore, M.H. (1995), *Creating Public Value: Strategic Management in Government*. Cambridge, MA: Harvard University Press.

Morris, M.H. (1998), *Entrepreneurial Intensity: Sustainable Advantages for Individuals, Organizations, and Societies*. Westport, CT: Quorum Books.

Morris, M.H. and F.F. Jones (1999), 'Entrepreneurship in established organizations: the case of the public sector', *Entrepreneurship Theory and Practice*, **24**(1), 71–91.

Olson, M. (1965), *The Logic of Collective Action: Public Goods and the Theory of Groups*, Cambridge, MA: Harvard University Press.

Osborne, D. and T. Gaebler (1992), *Reinventing Government: How the Entrepreneurial Spirit is Transforming the Public Sector*, Reading, MA: Addison-Wesley.

Peters, B.G. (1996), *The Future of Governing: Four Emerging Models*, Lawrence, KS: University Press of Kansas.

Pollitt, C. (1993), *Managerialism and the Public Services: Cuts or Cultural Change in the 1980s?* (2nd edn), Cambridge, UK: Blackwell Publishers.

Polsby, N.W. (1984), *Political Innovation in America: The Politics of Initiation*. New Haven, CT: Yale University Press.

Ramamurti, R. (1986), 'Public entrepreneurs: who they are and how they operate', *California Management Review*, **28**(3), 142–58.

Riker, W.H. (1980), 'Implications from disequilibrium of majority rule for the study of institutions', *American Political Science Review*, **74**(2), 432–46.

Riker, W.H. (1982), *Liberalism Against Populism: A Confrontation Between the Theory of Democracy and the Theory of Social Choice*, San Francisco, CA: W.H. Freeman and Co.

Riker, W.H. (1986), *The Art of Political Manipulation*, New Haven, CT: Yale University Press.

Roberts, N.C. (1992), 'Public entrepreneurship and innovation', *Public Productivity & Management Review*, **16**(2), 137–8.

Schiller, W.J. (1995), 'Senators as political entrepreneurs: using bill sponsorship to shape legislative agendas', *American Journal of Political Science*, **39**(1), 186–203.

Schneider, A.L. and H. Ingram (1997), *Policy Design for Democracy*, Lawrence, KS: University Press of Kansas.

Schneider, M. and P. Teske (1992), 'Toward a theory of the political entrepreneur: evidence from local government', *American Political Science Review*, **86**(3), 737–47.

Schneider, M., P. Teske, and M. Mintrom, (1995), *Public Entrepreneurs: Agents for Change in American Government*, Princeton, NJ: Princeton University Press.

Scholz, J.T., J. Twombly and B. Headrick (1991), 'Street-level political controls over federal bureaucracy', *American Political Science Review*, **85**(3), 829–50.

Schumpeter, J.A. (1926/2003), 'Entrepreneur' (M.C. Becker and T. Knudsen, trans.), in *Advances in Austrian Economics: Austrian Economics and Entrepreneurial Studies* Oxford, UK: Elsevier, pp. 235–65.

Schumpeter, J.A. (1934/1961), *The Theory of Economic Development: An Inquiry into Profits, Capital, Credit, Interest, and the Business Cycle*, Cambridge, MA: Harvard University Press.

Schumpeter, J.A. (1934/2002), *The Theory of Economic Development: An Inquiry into Profits, Capital, Credit, Interest, and the Business Cycle*, New Brunswick, NJ: Transaction Publishers.

Schumpeter, J.A. (1950), *Capitalism, Socialism, and Democracy*, New York: Harper & Row.

Shane, S. and S. Venkataraman (2000), 'The promise of entrepreneurship as a field of research', *Academy of Management Review*, **25**(1), 217–26.

Sheingate, A.D. (2003), 'Political entrepreneurship, institutional change, and American political development', *Studies in American Political Development*, **17**, 185–203.

Shockley, G.E., P.F. Frank, R.R. Stough and K.E. Haynes (2006), 'Toward a theory of public sector entrepreneurship', *International Journal of Entrepreneurship and Innovation Management*, **6**(3), 205–23.

Simon, H.A. (1945/1976), *Administrative Behavior: A Study of Decision-Making Processes in Administrative Organization* (3rd edn), New York: The Free Press.

Simon, H.A. (1982), *Models of Bounded Rationality*, Cambridge, MA: The MIT Press.

Skelcher, C. (2000), 'Changing images of the state: overloaded, hollowed-out, congested', *Public Policy and Administration*, **15**(3), 3–19.

Sweezy, P.M. (1943), 'Professor Schumpeter's theory of innovation', *The Review of Economic Statistics*, **25**(1), 93–6.

Vaughn, K.I. (1994), *Austrian Economics in America: The Migration of a Tradition*, Cambridge, UK: Cambridge University Press.

Wagner, R.E. (1966), 'Pressure groups and political entrepreneurs: a review article', *Public Choice*, **1**, 161–70.

Walker, J.L. (1975), 'Performance gaps, policy research, and political entrepreneurs', *Policy Studies Journal*, **3**, 112–16.

Walker, J.L. (1977), 'Setting the agenda in the US Senate: a theory of problem selection', *British Journal of Political Science*, **7**, 423–45.

Wawro, G. (2000), *Legislative Entrepreneurship in the US House of Representatives*, Ann Arbor, MI: The University of Michigan Press.

Wilson, J.Q. (1974/1995), *Political Organizations*, Princeton, NJ: Princeton University Press.

Yu, T.F.-L. (2001), 'Entrepreneurial alertness and discovery', *Review of Austrian Economics*, **14**, 47–63.

PART 4

Only a semantic difference? Social entrepreneurship, nonprofit entrepreneurship and social enterprise

9. A unified theory of social enterprise

Dennis R. Young

INTRODUCTION

The term 'social enterprise' is interpreted in a variety of ways by scholars, policymakers, leaders in the business, nonprofit and public sectors, and by interested parties in different parts of the world (Nyssens and Kerlin, 2006). In Europe, for example, social enterprise tends to connote the engagement of various non-governmental forms of enterprise, including nonprofit organizations and cooperatives, in public service activity to address the employment issues and other needs of marginalized groups (Kerlin, 2006). In the US, by contrast, social enterprise has come to describe the under-taking of commercial ventures and engagement with business corporations by nonprofit organizations across a broad spectrum of public service-related activity (Young and Salamon, 2002). In addition, some scholars think about social enterprise along a public/private continuum of organizational forms and arrangements, where the emphasis is on achieving social innovation (Dees and Anderson, 2006). And, there is a growing group of practitioners and policymakers who see social enterprise as a new institutional form in itself – a kind of hybrid economic enterprise which combines profit-making with the achievement of social goals. Indeed, several countries in Europe, including Belgium, Italy and the United Kingdom, have enacted legislation to create new forms of social purpose organizations (Kerlin, 2006).

The diverse conceptions of social enterprise do center, however, around a common notion that social enterprise involves the engagement of private sector forms of enterprise and market-based activity in the achievement of social purposes. The variety of understandings derives in part from the fact that social enterprise takes place in different economic and political contexts, giving rise to alternative manifestations of the common underlying thrust. A related reason is that interests in social enterprise arise from several different segments in society – each of which twists the concept in a particular way. While considerable attention has been focused on so-called 'social entrepreneurs' as the genesis of social enterprise activity (Light, 2006), this chapter will argue that the phenomenon is much more complex than that. Governments, nonprofits, corporations, consumers, workers, investors, donors, volunteers as well as entrepreneurs per se, play a variety of important roles both in the consumption and production of social enterprise activity. Only by sorting through the diverse interests of these various groups can the phenomenon of social enterprise be clarified and fully understood.

A UNIFIED THEORY

The phenomenon of social enterprise has various theoretical underpinnings. However, given the current state of theory development, social enterprise can only be understood in a piecemeal way – different strands of theory applying to different manifestations of social enterprise. To date, no overall conceptual framework ties it all together in a comprehensive way. The purpose here is to offer the general outlines of such a framework. What we suggest is very simple – the basic economics paradigm of supply and demand as applied to social enterprise.

Specifically, there are various sources of demand for services produced through social enterprise forms. These include individuals who purchase services and goods, corporations that embrace such activity as an element in their corporate strategies, and governments that seek more efficient or effective ways of addressing social problems and delivering services. Similarly, there are alternative sources of supply, each with its own sets of motivations and incentives. Social entrepreneurs are driven by public and personal goals and nonprofit organizations seek to sustain themselves financially while addressing their social missions. Investors, donors and volunteers all seek both personal and social satisfactions from the resources they offer to the production of social enterprise.

The 'market' for social enterprise activity which equilibrates these sources of demand and supply is of course very complex and hardly reducible to simple graphs or equations. However, an overall picture can be built up through the piecemeal process of synthesizing the theoretical fragments underlying each element of supply or demand for social enterprise.

DEMAND FOR SOCIAL ENTERPRISE

A common form of social enterprise is the sale of commercial goods and services by nonprofit organizations, presumably products that could as well be produced by for-profit organizations. Examples include gift shop items in museum stores, tourist packages offered by university alumni associations, bakeries or restaurants operated by nonprofit social service organizations, second hand merchandise shops operated by agencies such as Goodwill or the American Cancer Society, and parking garages operated by universities or performing arts centers. A distinguishing feature of these commercial offerings is that they could as well be sold by for-profit businesses. They are, in economists' terms, private goods – fully rival and excludable and without any significant externalities or issues of contract failure (James and Young, 2006). A parallel category of social enterprise outputs are products marketed by for-profit corporations with the intent of contributing (all) profits to charity – such as *Newman's Own* salad dressing.

The question at hand is why consumers demand these particular products, as opposed to their purely commercial counterparts. Clearly there is a base level of demand regardless of source of supply – people will purchase tee shirts, go on trips or park in garages whether or not they are provided by a nonprofit organization or a charity-minded corporation. However, a demand for social enterprise requires that consumers prefer to purchase these goods from favored (socially-oriented) suppliers and/or decide to consume more of such goods if offered by those suppliers. Why might they do so? Several possibilities exist.

First, some of these goods are unique or 'differentiated products' in the sense that they carry the imprint of the sponsoring organization, and hence have added value. A tee shirt with a university logo or an art reproduction bought at a museum store carries with it the legitimacy or prestige of the institution from which it is purchased. Second, the consumer is likely to understand that the purchase represents a 'tie-in sale' wherein a portion of the profits go to supporting the charitable activities of the institution. This added 'warm glow' benefit makes these purchases more attractive – perhaps enough to convince a shopper to try *Newman's Own* salad dressing rather than stick with the usual brand, or to purchase baked goods from an alternative bakery whose sponsoring organization is helping to employ challenged workers.

Finally, some commercial goods provided through a social enterprise may offer the consumer greater assurance of quality. A tour of the Galapagos Islands conducted by a university alumni association with access to renowned faculty may promise greater insights and access to current thinking about evolution than a commercial tour, and even an art reproduction bought from a museum store may be thought to be more authentic than one purchased in an ordinary book or print store.

Furthermore, some manifestations of social enterprise may involve production of goods or services characterized by 'asymmetric information' between consumers and producers, wherein consumers in a market setting find themselves at some disadvantage in determining whether they are receiving a good bargain. Asymmetric information and 'contract failure' constitute basic theoretical justifications for the participation of nonprofit organizations in the marketplace (Hansmann, 1987). This argument may extend to various manifestations of social enterprise, such as new ventures undertaken by existing or new nonprofits, involving day care for children or the elderly, tutoring, employment training, credit counseling, or various other services where the consumer has difficulty judging quality, veracity or honest pricing.

For these various reasons, a distinct demand may exist for commercial goods produced in the context of social enterprise, even if such goods themselves are peripheral to the specific social missions of the producing organizations and even if alternative products are available in the commercial marketplace.

Another part of the demand for social enterprise comes from business corporations. Corporations can often achieve important strategic goals, such as positioning their products, motivating their employees and improving their public relations, by associating themselves with charitable causes (Louie and Brooks, 2006). They can do this by sponsoring events and programs and having their own goods and services co-branded with a respected charitable organization. For example, financial corporations sell some of their credit cards by stamping them with the logos of charitable institutions to which they pay a small percentage of revenues from consumer purchases. Alternatively, corporations will sponsor special exhibitions by museums, zoos or arboretums from which they receive considerable positive publicity and for which they offer substantial grant support.

A fine line separates mainstream nonprofit activity that happens to be supported in part by corporate philanthropy and 'social enterprise' activity that might not be otherwise undertaken without such support. When a museum puts on an exhibit on changing fashions which happens to be supported by a clothing designer, or where a health charity, supported by a corporate grant, promotes a particular medical device or pharmaceutical product for its constituents, the line is sometimes blurred. Nonetheless, it is clear that a demand for these forms of social enterprise exists in the corporate community, and it derives from the strategic goals of corporations as well as possible eleemosynary motives of corporate leaders (Burlingame and Young, 1996).

A parallel source of demand comes from government. Indeed, in many parts of the developed world, government is a prime mover in social enterprise development, through direct government grants and contracts for such ventures, or by subsidizing clients who would have been served by public programs or otherwise unserved. Here the issue is whether forms of social enterprise, such as the production of public services by nonprofit and business sector organizations can better, or more cheaply, accomplish social goals than direct service by government itself. For example, can nonprofit and for-profit organizations, with governmental financing and oversight, provide employment, education and training, vocational re-habilitation, substance abuse counseling, leadership and entrepreneurship education, and so on, more effectively than a public sector program admin-istered solely within governmental auspices?

There are a number of reasons to think that such enterprises can often do so. First, there is an efficiency argument which posits that smaller (or sometimes larger) scale, market-disciplined, more specialized private organizations that must compete for contracts are likely to have lower costs or better quality than government agencies. Such economies can derive from economies (or diseconomies) of scale to which private entities more easily adjust, or from competition itself. This argument may of course be counter-balanced by risks of corruption if the contracting process is not properly administered. In addition, there is the argument that the goals of many social enterprise activities are intrinsically better addressed in a market context because they involve market processes. For example, learn-ing how to become a reliable employee or how to run a small business may be better taught through actual involvement in a business enterprise than through a government training program.

More generally, one must consider the question of government's com-parative advantages and disadvantages. In particular, government may be quite efficient at collecting and distributing resources, through the tax system for example, but not so efficient in directly delivering services. Private contractors can be more efficient than government in the actual delivery of services. Regimes of contracting out versus direct service provis-ion by government entail different types and levels of 'transactions costs'. In particular, in-house production involves substantial supervisory and procedural costs while contracting out entails costs of search for, and over-sight of, prospective contractors. Thus, for each potential area of service provision government needs to determine when outsourcing is more efficient than in-house production, by weighing these different costs against one another. Over time, we have witnessed an evolution towards the 'hollow state', in both the US and abroad, where government concentrates on financing and oversight functions, leading increasingly to contracting out of service delivery to private parties (Skelcher, 2000). A demand for social enterprise on the part of government has arisen in those areas where out-sourcing has become the favored mode of public service delivery, including various mental health, community development and social services (Smith, 2002). An interesting case in point was the welfare reform initiative in the United States which led to increased contracting out to human service providers in areas such as child care, employment and training, emergency food services and overnight shelters (De Vita, 1999).

Overall, demand for social enterprise emerges from three main sources – consumers of commercial products who prefer purchasing from social enterprise providers, corporations seeking strategic benefits by association with social enterprise, and governments seeking more efficient or effective ways to address public goals through social enterprise contracting arrangements. These sources of demand provide the resources that help entice potential suppliers of social enterprise activity. And each is understood via different elements of economic theory – elements that underwrite consumer preferences, corporate profit-enhancement and governmental efficiency-seeking, respectively.

SUPPLY OF SOCIAL ENTERPRISE

The supply of social enterprise depends substantially on the activity of so-called 'social entrepreneurs' willing to respond, as individuals or via host organizations, to the abovementioned demands for the products of social enterprise. Alternatively, social entrepreneurs proactively create a supply of social enterprise activity for which they hope to actualize latent demand. The supply of social enterprise also depends on the providers of investment capital and volunteer resources who are willing to support the social objectives involved, or who, in some cases, may benefit from the social and economic returns to their investments.

Three main theoretical constructs help us understand the supply side of social enterprise. The first is the market for social entrepreneurs, specifically the notion that social ventures compete for entrepreneurial talent in a marketplace that offers a variety of material and intangible rewards. The second is an understanding of nonprofit organizations as multi-product firms. A third is an understanding of volunteering and giving behavior, including the willingness to supply capital or labor at below market rates, in order to support the benefits of a social enterprise. Consider each of these sources in turn.

Social entrepreneurship is now recognized as a subject of serious scholarly attention (Light, 2006). A key insight of the literature on social entrepreneurship is that entrepreneurship is a generic phenomenon required to catalyze change and create new forms of activity in all parts of the economy (Dees and Anderson, 2006; Hisrich *et al.*, 1997; Young, 1983). Moreover, entrepreneurs are driven by a variety of motivations, not just profit-seeking (Young, 1983). Hence, they seek opportunities in a variety of venues to achieve their goals, which may vary from material reward, to achieving autonomy, to pursuing particular beliefs or artistic or professional satisfactions.

The choice of pursuing social enterprise activity within the framework of a nonprofit organization or indeed in a private sector business venue will depend on the opportunities that present themselves and the resources made available in particular instances. In this view, social enterprises can provide good matches between the motivations of certain varieties of entrepreneurs and the social and material goals of particular ventures. For example, an entrepreneur seeking to make both a good living and a contribution to society may prefer a social enterprise venture that offers both. A longstanding question in the entrepreneurship and economics literature is whether nonmaterial motives are dominated by profit-seeking motives. The pursuit of social enterprise in areas where straight business alternatives seem to be available suggests that nonmaterial entrepreneurial motivations can have a significant impact on supply.

Similar arguments can be made for suppliers of capital and labor for social enterprise ventures. Clearly, for example, volunteer labor is motivated by factors other than material reward (Preston, 2006). Here too, the possibilities are manifold, ranging from pure altruism and intrinsic satisfaction associated with addressing a social cause, to receipt of private benefits such as status, recognition and on-the-job-training, or in the case of *pro bono* volunteering, the satisfaction of professional obligations and values (Brudney, 2006). The same applies to paid workers who contribute their efforts to social enterprise activity. There is evidence, for example, that many paid workers in nonprofit organizations make so-called 'labor donations' by accepting lower pay than they can command elsewhere in exchange for other (psychic and social) benefits associated with their work and venue (Preston, 2004). These potentialities apply to suppliers of capital as well. Social enterprises can offer opportunities for financial return which might be less generous or riskier than alternatives available in the commercial sector. Yet, investors with an interest in social as well as private returns may be willing to invest in them, just as many investors or consumers prefer to support corporations that they consider to be socially responsible. Certainly this would be true of the investment decisions of many foundations and other nonprofits that consider 'program related investments' to be part of their investment portfolios (Cantori, 2006). In all, there is no reason to believe that all entrepreneurs and investors who fuel the private economy are solely motivated by material benefits and financial returns. Social enterprises, which combine private and social benefits in various proportions, can successfully attract the investments of these suppliers of key resources. Indeed, corporations such as Timberland and Starbucks make a particular point of distinguishing themselves through their support of social ventures, in part to make themselves attractive as commercial investments (Austin, 2000).

Finally, many examples of social enterprise manifest themselves within the context of existing organizations – profit and nonprofit. Here again entrepreneurial motivations come into play. Rosabeth Kanter (1983) coined the phrase 'intrapreneurship' to recognize that entrepreneurs operate inside organizations as well as in the open marketplace. Indeed, many of the best examples of nonprofit entrepreneurship are found within organizational boundaries and involve individuals who want to change the directions of their organizations in important ways (Young, 1985). In addition, there are structural reasons why nonprofit organizations in particular become the source of their own supply of social enterprise. The theory of nonprofit organizations as multi-product firms, first introduced by Estelle James (1983) and further elaborated by Burton Weisbrod (1998) and others, provides a systematic rationale for such internal venturing.

This theory can be summarized as follows. Nonprofits are run by (entrepreneurial) managers who have certain preferences for producing the social goods associated with the nonprofit's mission. These managers seek to avoid 'non-preferred' activity such as commercial ventures that contribute only to the net financial support of the organization. However, they derive satisfaction from the additional social programming that they can provide with the extra revenue that non-preferred activity can offer. Thus, nonprofit managers make trade-offs, deciding to undertake a certain level of non-preferred activity in order to maximize their overall satisfaction from the combination of preferred and non-preferred programming.

Many ventures undertaken by nonprofits can be understood through this framework. Social enterprise initiatives that contribute to the organization in purely financial terms may be undertaken and tolerated if they are profitable and do not damage the organization in other ways. Other social enterprise ventures are more comfortably pursued because they combine elements of social mission achievement with financial return. And still other social enterprises are maintained even when they lose money, because they make important contributions to the social mission. In general, the finding that most social enterprise ventures are closely related to the organization's mission (Massarsky and Beinhacker, 2002; Young, 2005) is consistent with this model of social enterprise as an important element in the supply of a multi-product nonprofit firm.

THEORY AND THE NATURE OF SOCIAL ENTERPRISE

The supply and demand framework helps to explain the varying concepts of social enterprise in different parts of the world. In particular, in Europe the growth of social enterprise appears to be demand-driven (Borzaga and Defourny, 2001; Borzaga and Santuari, 1998). Governments seeking ways to cope with high unemployment and the welfare of marginalized populations needed a new approach outside the traditional welfare state model. The private sector needed to be engaged, with entrepreneurial energies to find new and creative solutions to intransigent problems. In this milieu, the solution moved towards the kind of regime already common in the United States, governmental contracting out with private, largely nonprofit entities.

By contrast, social enterprise in the United States appears mostly to be supply-side driven (Kerlin, 2006). In particular, nonprofits facing increasing competition for funding, constrictions of governmental financing, and indeed competition with for-profit firms in traditionally nonprofit markets such as home health care or higher education, have sought ways to supplement their income with earned income ventures. As multi-product firms, these organizations found new combinations of preferred and non-preferred service offerings in order to survive and grow.

To be sure, both sides of the market needed to respond in each of these cases. In the European venue, new social entrepreneurial energies have been stoked by government policies, stimulating individuals and groups to set up new nonprofit organizations and those within existing charities to develop new contract offerings in response to governmental incentives. In the US case, the supply side initiative has found new pockets of demand among individual consumers interested in the new products and services offered, among philanthropic and governmental funders intrigued with creative market solutions to old problems, and among large corporations anxious to associate with socially worthy organizations and ventures. While the distinct origins of these two genres of social enterprise yield different forms and combinations in the short run, they can be viewed ultimately as manifestations of the same kinds of interactions of supply and demand for social enterprise activity. However, only a 'unified theory' of social enterprise which acknowledges both demand and supply side forces, allows us to recognize social enterprise as a coherent phenomenon and understand its variations from one venue to another.

THE EQUILIBRIUM FOR SOCIAL ENTERPRISE

The foregoing framework for social enterprise posits that forces of demand and supply come into balance in order to determine the level and type of social enterprise activity observed in the marketplace. An interesting question is why we seem to observe an increasing level of such activity in recent years. Another question is whether the character of social enterprise is changing, for example, becoming 'too commercial' as argued by Weisbrod (2004), and hence presenting dangers to society at large or to the host organizations which sponsor them. A review of influences on both the demand and supply sides of our theory helps to sort out these issues. Indeed, this analysis is an extension of that in the previous section which illuminates why social enterprise takes predominantly different forms in the US and Europe.

On the demand side much of the growth of social enterprise seems explainable by governmental retrenchment and withdrawal from direct service provision, on both sides of the Atlantic and elsewhere in the world. In European venues, such 'privatization' required the creation of new private (nonprofit) forms as well as movement from a regime of grants and gifts to a system of government contracting with existing charities. In the American context, privatization took the form of both governmental retrenchment in some areas such as the arts and social services, and greater reliance on demand-side financing, such as vouchers and tax credits in health care, economic development and education (Gronbjerg and Salamon, 2002). While the forms of response to these changes were different, both sets of developments encouraged growth in various manifestations of social enterprise. For example, in Europe much of social enterprise has been connected to the creation of new organizations to employ marginalized populations at government expense, while in the US social enterprise initiatives in the form of businesses employing disadvantaged workers have been created by nonprofit organizations and foundations partly to generate additional income to compensate for diminished government funding and partly to gain access to new (demand-side) forms of government support such as vouchers, tax credits and Medicaid payments.

On the supply side, the growth of social enterprise and its increasingly commercial flavor seem explainable by the engagement of commercially oriented, entrepreneurial energies unleashed by new opportunities for creativity, financial rewards and emphasis on a more business-like culture. Indeed, great concerns have been raised about 'mission-drift' wherein changes in personnel, the pressure of competition for resources, and the rewarding of market success, actually transform the internal logic of nonprofit organizations towards revenue maximization and away from maximum mission impact (James, 1998). In fact, contemporary demands for social enterprise do indeed appear to intensify the mission/market tensions inherent in nonprofit operations (Young, 2006). Whether nonprofits can successfully manage these tensions by continuing to subordinate market incentives to mission achievement remains an open question (Weisbrod, 1998), especially as nonprofits and for-profits become increasingly intertwined and distinctions between them continue to blur (Dees and Anderson, 2006).

Incidentally, while the mission-drift phenomenon now seems especially worrisome in the US context of supply-driven social enterprise, it is really an old wine in a new bottle. In the 1970s and 1980s, analysts in the US worried about undue influence of increased government funding on the integrity of nonprofit organizations (Kramer, 1981). This form of mission-drift has become more of an issue now in countries of Europe such as the United Kingdom, where the financing of nonprofit organizations has shifted from grants to contracts (Knapp and Kendall, 1993).

Another equilibrium-related issue suggested by the supply/demand framework is whether supply or demand for social enterprise can be influenced by specific organizational strategies or public policies. On the demand side, of course, public policies that favor private over public forms of public service delivery seem bound to encourage social enterprise of one kind or another. There are reasons to believe that policies can affect the supply of social enterprise as well. Light (2006), for example, suggests that the supply of social entrepreneurs may be elastic (presumably with respect to various kinds of incentives) rather than fixed or severely limited in supply as some previous observers have argued. Certainly a number of private sector strategies have been developed to support the pool of entrepreneurial talent and to encourage the supply of social enterprise, including the emergence of networks and associations of support for social entrepreneurs such as the Social Enterprise Alliance, Community Wealth Ventures, and Ashoka. An interesting question for research is whether these developments have indeed had an impact on the supply of social enterprise or have merely identified and shaped efforts that would have taken place anyway.

Finally, the demand-supply framework for understanding social enterprise suggests the value of analyzing the impact of various kinds of public policies on the magnitude and character of social enterprise activity. For example, the framework suggests that governmental outsourcing and privatization policies can be expected to encourage social enterprise activity, while regulatory and tax policies can be expected to influence the shape of those enterprises – for example, whether they take place in nonprofit or for-profit form.

CASES IN POINT

The influences of the forces of supply and demand on the development of social enterprise activity can be further appreciated through inspection of selected case studies. A few such cases are cited here to illustrate different forms of social enterprise and alternative circumstances under which it comes about.

The Georgia Justice Project (GJP) is a nonprofit organization in Atlanta devoted to providing legal assistance and other forms of support to indigent individuals involved in the criminal justice system, including incarcerated individuals, ex-convicts and those facing criminal charges (www.gjp.org). It was founded by John Pickens, a lawyer who, as a volunteer for his church's night shelter, learned that many poor families required legal advice.

As described by Executive Director, Doug Ammar, the GJP is an 'unlikely mix of lawyers, social workers and a landscaping company'. The latter company is called *New Horizon*, a venture started to enable GJP to hire men and women who have been in prison. The idea is not only to provide economic assistance to such individuals and their families but to build job skills and work experience that will enable future employment.

New Horizon can be understood as a supply-driven enterprise, conceived by an entrepreneurial director and staff who were motivated by a desire to address an important social problem. In the words of Mr Ammar: 'We did not have any dedicated funds. We were not responding to an RFP. We were not responding to any known demand – only the needs of our clients for employment . . . We have never had nor sought government support for this . . . We believed that the business could pay for itself. We were not aware of the potential this business would create in the funding world. . . . Over the next [first] few years, the business created a great financial drain on our operation – we lost tens of thousands of dollars for years . . . But at the same time we created an opportunity for our donors' (e-mail message; 18 September 2006).

Currently, the company succeeds not only in providing critical employment experience to clients but also generates substantial revenues to help support the landscaping business and the rest of GJP's operations. Overall, *New Horizon's* direct earnings contribute almost 27 percent of GJP's total revenue. The largest proportion of GJP's revenues, approximately 72 percent, comes from gifts and grants, much of that driven by support of *New Horizon*. A small remaining component of income derives from interest on savings accounts and court fees. Aside from such fees, GJP receives no government funding.

Demand for *New Horizon* stems from the marketplace itself – businesses and residential customers who require landscaping services and who are attracted both by its competitive prices and service quality and the special benefit of knowing that the company is helping to address an important social problem. Additional components of 'demand' take the form of donor support – particularly conservative lawyers and Southern donors who are attracted to *New* Horizon's 'bootstrapping' philosophy wherein at-risk clients are trained and employed in a bottom-line business and expected to show up every day and work to get their lives on track.

It seems clear that *New Horizon* was not primarily demand-driven. No government funds were designated to create special employment services of this kind, nor were households, philanthropic foundations or businesses clamoring for a new landscaping service manned by ex-convicts. No doubt, however, there was a latent demand on the part of sympathetic users, es-pecially other nonprofits with grounds that required tending, as well as segments of the local donor community including attorneys, churches, foundations and corporations.

Another especially visible case in point is the recent establishment of *Google.org* by *Google, Inc.* (Hafner, 2006). *Google.org* is described as a for-profit philanthropy seeded by *Google, Inc.* with $1 billion to address poverty, disease and global warming. One of its first initiatives is to develop an ultra-fuel efficient hybrid car engine in order to reduce global depen-dence on oil. The unusual for-profit format for *Google.org* provides the company with substantial flexibility to invest its funds in various kinds of promising technological and social ventures, and avoid various regulations that constrain conventional nonprofits or foundations. As such, *Google.org* ignores some sources of potential demand for its projects, such as tra-ditional donations or government contracts that might require nonprofit status. However, given its origin and source of capital, these may be of little consequence to the success of *Google.org*.

That is not to say, however, that *Google.org* is entirely supply-driven. In particular, *Google.org* clearly serves the needs of its parent corporation, helping the latter to fulfill its promise to investors to devote 1 percent of its stock and 1 percent of its profits to philanthropy. This intent may be viewed in both demand and supply terms. Clearly the founders of *Google, Inc.* have incorporated some of their own social objectives into their plans for using the new wealth that the company has created. And indeed they have engaged an executive director for the company whose career encompasses substantial experience in public health, and who can thus be expected to push new ventures on the basis of their potential social benefits. However, *Google.org* is also an important strategic initiative of the parent corpora-tion that will contribute to its commercial success in the marketplace by bolstering its benevolent public image. Hence, the advent of *Google.org* can as well be reasonably described as partly demand-driven, stemming in large measure from the strategic needs of its successful parent corporation.

Other cases of social enterprise are more clearly demand-driven, stemming from public sector policy and resource allocation. For example, under the Social Labour Provision Act in the Netherlands, local authorities are responsible for establishing so-called sheltered or social workshops in order to employ individuals with physical and mental handicaps. According to Renooy (2001) these units have been set up as public corporations and foundations, and have engaged in subsidized work in manufacturing, horticulture and other areas of economic activity. Similarly, in the United Kingdom, the Health Services and Care in the Community Act of 1993 was the impetus for new voluntary and cooperative enterprises providing community and home-based services for the elderly, the mentally ill, or the physically disabled, in place of large government institutions (Spear, 2001). In Germany, the so-called Work Integration Social Enterprises (WISE) also stem in large measure from policies that require government partnerships with private suppliers in order to employ jobless workers (Bode *et al.*, 2004). In the United States, the establishment of nonprofit Community Development Corporations followed a similar scenario, where government initiative provided the resources and mandate for the establishment of locally-based social enterprises to address the needs of low income communities (Vidal, 2002). In all these cases, demand in the form of government programs and resources was explicit, although the emergence of social enterprise also depended on the response of latent sources of supply – for example, potential social entrepreneurs who exploited new opportunities created by government.

THE FUTURE OF SOCIAL ENTERPRISE STUDY

The supply/demand framework for understanding social enterprise has the potential for integrating heretofore disparate subject matter into a more coherent whole. At the root of social enterprise is the notion that governments cannot address all important social needs by themselves, and that other vehicles and sources of support are available, and indeed will emerge, to address those needs. Indeed, governments' realization of their limitations is growing, leading to increasing levels of social enterprise development in various forms. Nor do traditional private forms of enterprise such as conventional nonprofit organizations exhaust the set of possibilities through which social enterprises can develop. Commercial ventures by nonprofits, cooperative forms, public/private partnerships, corporate initiatives and indeed hybrid organizations with mixed financial and social goals, are all possible under various circumstances.

The supply/demand framework suggests that if there is a latent demand for addressing a particular social need, then social enterprise may come about in one of two ways – by making the latent demand explicit through government funding programs or initiatives by private sources of funds, and then working to develop or attract potential sources of supply; or through social entrepreneurship, undertaken by individuals and teams within or outside existing organizations, that formulate social projects and then cobble together support from latent sources of demand.

Viewed in total, this perspective on social enterprise brings together several streams of existing study and scholarship from a number of different disciplines, including the study of traditional nonprofits in a variety of academic settings including schools of public administration, social work, interdisciplinary centers, and schools of business, the study of corporate philanthropy and social enterprise in schools of management and business, and research on welfare state policies in schools of policy studies, social work and departments of political science. A full understanding of social enterprise will therefore require crossing these disciplinary boundaries and perhaps even redefining the study of privately-based, socially directed economic activity in a manner that transcends the old labels of nonprofit organization, social entrepreneurship or corporate philanthropy.

ACKNOWLEDGMENTS

The author wishes to thank Lewis Faulk for his help with sources for this chapter, Janelle Kerlin for her suggestions and comments on a first draft, and Doug Ammar for his insights about the Georgia Justice Project.

REFERENCES

Austin, James E. (2000), *The Collaboration Challenge*, San Francisco, CA: Jossey-Bass.
Bode, Ingo, Adalbert Evers and Andreas Schulz (2004), 'Facing new challenges, work integration social enterprises in Germany', paper presented to the International Society for Third-Sector Research, Toronto, July.
Borzaga, Carlo and Jacques Defourny (eds) (2001), *The Emergence of Social Enterprise*, London: Routledge.
Borzaga, Carlo and Alceste Santuari (eds) (1998), *Social Enterprises and New Employment in Europe*, Trento Italy: Regione Autonoma Trentino-Alto Adige

and Autonome Region Trentino-Sudtirol in cooperation with the European Commission – D.G.-V CGM- 'Consorzio Nazionale della Cooperazione Sociale'.

Brudney, Jeffrey L. (2006), 'The distinctiveness and efficiency of *pro bono* volunteering', in Dennis R. Young (ed.), *Wise Decision-Making in Uncertain Times*, New York: The Foundation Center, pp. 205–23.

Burlingame, Dwight and Dennis R.Young (eds) (1996), *Corporate Philanthropy at the Crossroads*, Bloomington, IN: Indiana University Press.

Cantori, Greg (2006), 'Holistic grantmaking', in Dennis R. Young (ed.), *Wise Decision-Making in Uncertain Times*, New York: The Foundation Center, pp. 171–89.

Dees, J. Gregory and Beth Battle Anderson (2006), 'Framing a theory of social entrepreneurship: building on two schools of practice and thought', in Rachel Mosher-Williams (ed.), *Research on Social Entrepreneurship*, ARNOVA Occasional Paper Series, **1** (3), 39–66.

De Vita, Carol J. (1999), 'Nonprofits and devolution: what do we know?' in Elizabeth T. Boris and C. Eugene Steuerle (eds), *Nonprofits & Government: Collaboration and Conflict*, Washington, DC: The Urban Institute, pp. 213–33.

Gronbjerg, Kirsten A. and Lester M. Salamon (2002), 'Devolution, marketization, and the changing shape of government-nonprofit relations', in Lester M. Salamon (ed.), *The State of Nonprofit America*, Washington, DC: Brookings Institution Press, pp. 447–70.

Hafner, Katie (2006), 'Philanthropy Google's way: not the usual', *The New York Times*, 14 September, pp. 1, C4.

Hansmann, Henry (1987), 'Economic theories of nonprofit organization', in Walter W. Powell (ed.), *The Nonprofit Sector: A Research Handbook*, New Haven, CT: Yale University Press, pp. 27–42.

Hisrich, Robert D., Everette Freeman, Anne P. Standley, John A. Yankey and Dennis R. Young (1997), 'Entrepreneurship in the not-for-profit sector: the state of the art', in Raymond W. Smilor and Donald L. Sexton (eds), *Entrepreneurship 2000*, Chicago, IL:Upstart Publishing Co., pp. 321–35.

James, Estelle (1983), 'How nonprofits grow: a model', *Journal of Policy Analysis and Management*, **2**, 350–65.

James, Estelle (1998), 'Commercialism among nonprofits: objectives, opportunities, and constraints', in Burton A. Weisbrod (ed.), *To Profit or Not to Profit*, New York: Cambridge University Press, pp. 271–85.

James, Estelle and Dennis R. Young (2006), 'Fee income and commercial ventures', in Dennis R. Young (ed.), *Financing Nonprofits*, New York: AltaMira Press, pp. 93–119.

Kanter, Rosabeth (1983), *The Change Masters: Innovation and Entrepreneurship in the American Corporation*, New York: Simon & Schuster.

Kerlin, Janelle (2006), 'Social enterprise in the United States and abroad: learning from our differences', in Rachel Mosher-Williams (ed.), *Research on Social Entrepreneurship*, ARNOVA Occasional Paper Series, **1** (3), 105–25.

Knapp, Martin and Jeremy Kendall (1993), 'Policy issues for the UK Voluntary Sector in the 1990s' in Avner Ben-Ner and Benedetto Gui (eds), *The Nonprofit Sector in the Mixed Economy*, Ann Arbor, MI: The University of Michigan Press, pp. 221–41.

Kramer, Ralph M. (1981), *Voluntary Agencies in the Welfare State*, Berkeley, CA: University of California Press.

Light, Paul C. (2006), 'Searching for social entrepreneurs: who they might be, where they might be found, what they do', in Rachel Mosher-Williams (ed.), *Research on Social Entrepreneurship*, ARNOVA Occasional Paper Series, **1** (3), pp. 13–37.

Louie, Alison and Arthur C. Brooks (2006), 'Engaging business with nonprofits', in Dennis R. Young (ed.), *Wise Decision-Making in Uncertain Times*, New York: The Foundation Center, pp. 191–204.

Massarsky, Cynthia W. and Semantha L. Beinhacker (2002). 'Enterprising non-profits: revenue generation in the nonprofit sector', Yale School of Management-Goldman Sachs Foundation Partnership on Non-profit Ventures, (http://www.ventures.yale.edu/docs/Enterprising_Nonprofits.pdf).

Nyssens, Marthe and Janelle Kerlin (2006), 'Social enterprise in Europe', working paper presented to the International Society for Third Sector Research, Bangkok Thailand, July, 14 pp.

Preston, Anne E. (2004), 'Compensation in nonprofit organizations', in Dennis R. Young (ed.), *Effective Economic Decision-Making by Nonprofit Organizations*, New York: The Foundation Center, pp. 47–66.

Preston, Anne E. (2006), 'Volunteer resources', in Dennis R. Young (ed.), *Financing Nonprofits*, New York: AltaMira Press, pp. 183–204.

Renooy, Piet H. (2001), 'The Netherlands: neighborhood development enterprises', in Carlo Borzaga and Jacques Defourny (eds) *The Emergence of Social Enterprise*, London: Routledge, pp. 236–51.

Skelcher, C. (2000), 'Changing images of the state: overloaded, hollowed-out, congested', *Public Policy and Administration*, **15**(3), 3–19.

Smith, Steven R. (2002), 'Social services', in Lester M. Salamon (ed.), *The State of Nonprofit America*, Washington, DC: Brookings Institution Press, pp. 149–86.

Spear, Roger (2001), 'United Kingdom: a wide range of social enterprises', in Carlo Borzaga and Jacques Defourny (eds), *The Emergence of Social Enterprise*, London: Routledge.

Vidal, Avis C. (2002), 'Housing and community development', in Lester M. Salamon (ed.), *The State of Nonprofit America*, Washington, DC: Brookings Institution Press, pp. 219–39.

Weisbrod, Burton A. (ed.) (1998), *To Profit or Not to Profit*, New York: Cambridge University Press.

Weisbrod, Burton A. (2004), 'The Pitfalls of Profits', *Stanford Social Innovation Review*, Winter, 40–7.

Young, Dennis R. (1983), *If Not For Profit, For What?*, Lexington, MA: Lexington Books.

Young, Dennis R. (1985), *Casebook of Management for Nonprofit Organizations: Entrepreneurship and Organizational Change in the Human Services*, New York: Haworth Press.

Young, Dennis R. (2005), 'Mission-market tension in managing nonprofit organizations', Working Paper NP 05-02, Nonprofit Studies Program, Andrew Young School of Policy Studies, Georgia State University.

Young, Dennis R. and Lester M. Salamon (2002), 'Commercialization, social ventures, and for-profit competition', in Lester M. Salamon (ed.), *The State of Nonprofit America*, Washington, DC: Brookings Institution Press, pp. 423–46.

Young, Dennis R. (2006), 'Social enterprise in community and economic Development in the USA', *International Journal of Innovation and Entrepreneurship Management*, **6** (3), 241–55.

10. A model of nonprofit and socially motivated entrepreneurial behavior

Peter M. Frank

INTRODUCTION

Entrepreneurship theory has evolved considerably in recent years with extensive research from scholars representing various disciplines.[1] With this growing body of research, the entrepreneur has been re-conceptualized to mean a diverse set of individuals engaged in various forms of entrepreneurship. While this lack of consensus for whom and what is entrepreneurship permeates the market focused literature, an increasing body of entrepreneurship research has arisen to explain similar behavior in the nonprofit sector. As with entrepreneurship theory, significant ambiguity exists on what is meant by the term 'nonprofit entrepreneur'. Researchers and practitioners alike use multiple terms and descriptions to explain entrepreneurial activity that lies outside traditional market-orientated and motivated bounds.

The purpose of this research is to develop a conceptual model to explain the scope of entrepreneurial phenomena that is currently observed in the nonprofit, philanthropic, and social sector; and, other entrepreneurial activities considered in the public interest. In particular, the model presented here describes and differentiates the various forms of entrepreneurship occurring in both the nonprofit and market sectors that is considered, at least in part, to be socially motivated. This research is important for several reasons, but the primary application is to aid in the ability to study entrepreneurial activity empirically, and to aid in encouraging broad-based entrepreneurial solutions to social problems or 'extra-market' provision of goods and services.

It is clear that researchers and practitioners alike are calling entrepreneurial activity in the nonprofit sector, that appears identical, different things. Nonprofit entrepreneurship, social entrepreneurship, social enterprise, and socially motivated ventures, are all terms used to describe in some cases the same entrepreneurial activity and in other cases different phenomena all together. The distinction, or lack thereof, between nonprofit and social enterprise/entrepreneurship is highlighted by the fact that almost all organizations that educate, promote, or support these entrepreneurs first define who they are talking about before they proceed to explain the purpose for why they exist. This is a fundamental reality when dealing with a discipline such as entrepreneurship where the term is defined in whatever manner the practitioner or researcher finds most useful. Thus, the aim of this chapter is to provide a conceptual model to explain the various forms of entrepreneurship that result from socially motivated discovery and creativity.

The first section of this chapter briefly explains what entrepreneurship is according to economic theory and applies this foundational understanding of entrepreneurial behavior to the nonprofit sector. Then, the various forms of entrepreneurial activity being observed in the nonprofit/social sector are reviewed, which leads to the final section where a conceptual model for understanding entrepreneurship in the nonprofit sector, as well as socially motivated entrepreneurship, is proposed. A concluding section follows.

ENTREPRENEURIAL BEHAVIOR

Historically the entrepreneur is used to explain the action of business creation or innovation in a market context, but theorists have grappled with developing a cohesive theory of entrepreneurship for decades and new theoretical contributions continually emerge (Shane, 2003). Yet, it is clear that in the writings of economists Joseph Schumpeter and Israel Kirzner the foundational theory of entrepreneurship has existed since the early 1970s. Schumpeter wrote in the early part of the twentieth century, and Kirzner's classic work was written in 1973. Thus, the essential explanations of what entrepreneurship is and who entrepreneurs are was established by these two economists, and their contributions toward a broad understanding of entrepreneurial behavior are critical to this day.[2]

The fundamental principles of entrepreneurship elucidated in the writings of Schumpeter and Kirzner are synthesized by the following (Kirzner, 1973; Schumpeter, 1950 [1942], 1961 [1911]):

- Opportunity Recognition – Discovery
- Creation
- Innovation
- Equilibration

Entrepreneurship is a function or a process that involves these characteristics and is embodied in individuals who carry out such acts regardless of economic sector. Entrepreneurship and entrepreneurial behavior are embodied in 'what' is accomplished and not 'where' or within a specific context. There are certainly varying institutional preconditions and catalysts for entrepreneurs to act in a market versus a non-market (nonprofit) setting (Shockley and Frank, 2006), yet the entrepreneurial act is universal within the private, nonprofit, or public sector.[3]

Kirzner explains this first principle of entrepreneurial behavior as alertness to opportunities. 'Entrepreneurial discovery represents the alert becoming aware of what has been overlooked. The essence of entrepreneurship consists in seeing through the fog created by the uncertainty of the future' (Kirzner, 1997: 51). This opportunity recognition is a defining feature of entrepreneurial behavior, which, as indicated previously, is ubiquitous in all economic sectors. It is often easy to see ex post how entrepreneurs are alert and subsequently discover opportunities to create and innovate. In markets the signal for innovation can be seen in new products or ideas resulting in profits, and in the nonprofit sector the signal might be seen in a new method to deliver social services to the poor, for example. These next two characteristics of entrepreneurship are embodied in the theoretical contributions of both Kirzner and Schumpeter. Entrepreneurship consists of creative acts that move the economic system forward or acts that 'reform or revolutionize the pattern of production' (Schumpeter, 1950 [1942]: 132). The entrepreneur is involved in discovering an opportunity and thus takes on the process of creating and/or innovating, and this role is the action of fulfilling a function that is not limited to market-based 'production'.

The final principle that defines entrepreneurial behavior in any context is equilibration. For Kirzner equilibration is crucial because any economic system is in a constant state of disequilibrium, and thus profit opportunities exist waiting to be discovered and exploited. The entrepreneurial role is to discover opportunities existing in a state of disequilibrium moving the system toward equilibrium. Just as markets never reach a perfectly competitive equilibrium, there are always opportunities for moving the macro system toward equilibrium in a non-market context as well.[4] Previous contributions to the field of nonprofit entrepreneurship (Bilodeau and Slivinski, 1998; Glaeser and Shleifer, 2001; Young, 1986) focus on either the Schumpeterian model or, in the case of Bilodeau and Slivinski, the rational maximizing economic agent of mainstream economic theory.[5] The decision to be an entrepreneur, narrowly defined, might necessitate adherence to a particular model of human behavior, yet entrepreneurship in any institutional context is more than rational economic maximization. As Kirzner explains, an entrepreneur cannot know with certainty the means and ends of his or her decision to act (Kirzner, 1973). Entrepreneurial action in a nonprofit context is catalyzed by a perceived need or gap in the provision of a good or service, but the framework of exploiting this gap is never known with certainty. The Glaeser and Shleifer (2001) article explains the entrepreneurial decision in the nonprofit sector as a decision based on signaling quality to the potential customer (that is nonprofit hospitals), but this still forces nonprofit entrepreneurial theory into a very narrowly defined class of decisions.

Thus, the general theoretical description of entrepreneurship in the market context, the Schumpeterian and Kirznerian entrepreneur, clearly applies to all economic sectors.[6] The characteristics of entrepreneurial behavior described previously are observed in the nonprofit sector, and any general theory of entrepreneurship should not confine this decision to a for-profit, market context.[7] When using this theoretical foundation of entrepreneurship and applying it to the nonprofit sector, it is clear that entrepreneurship is a function defined by the characteristics listed previously and not necessarily a specific person or a specific outcome. Quite often entrepreneurship results in the creation of organizations (Gartner, 1989), yet it is not limited to such activities. What follows is a review of the various forms of entrepreneurial behavior, as observed and defined by researchers and practitioners alike, in the nonprofit sector, as well as a review of entrepreneurial decisions that are said to be socially motivated. Multiple forms of nonprofit and/or social entrepreneurship benefit multiple constituents throughout the world, yet there is confusion in research and practice as to what this phenomenon should be called and subsequently how it should be analyzed.

WHAT IS NONPROFIT AND/OR SOCIAL ENTREPRENEURSHIP?

Nonprofit/social entrepreneurship is a field of practice and research that has been growing rapidly over the past two decades. For a field of inquiry that is relatively new, the attention given to these entrepreneurs is quite remarkable. It is obvious that these entrepreneurs are making a significant difference throughout the world in helping to lessen social problems, while providing resources, goods and services to many marginalized populations. One of the problems in researching this field is that there is no consensus on what is nonprofit and/or social entrepreneurship. Various definitions exist, and each organization that supports these entrepreneurs (re)defines whom they are talking about. In their new edited volume on the subject, Mair *et al.* (2006) present an extensive table dedicated to listing how social entrepreneurship is defined by each author within the book. A book titled

Social Entrepreneurship thus must provide multiple definitions for the 'concepts' therein.

In another recent paper, Light (2006) (contained in an additional edited volume on the subject) sets out to define these terms and does a nice review of the early literature on the subject. He explains how social entrepreneurs are identified and found, and he puts forth a research methodology to find and analyze the 'pattern-breaking' ideas they develop. Yet, ambiguity remains as social entrepreneurs are defined in extremely broad terms and can operate in, and cut across, multiple sectors where they can be found 'almost anywhere'. Other researchers around the world are taking advantage of both the benefits of nonprofit/social entrepreneurship and the opportunities to research this field; however, a great deal of attention is paid to defining what exactly these entrepreneurs do (Mair and Marti, 2005; Parkinson, 2005).

Consequently, this entrepreneurial behavior that is outside of purely market-driven purposes is called social enterprise, social entrepreneurship, social innovation or nonprofit entrepreneurship. It is argued that these phenomena combine elements that may cut across the varying 'schools of thought' that make up the universe of entrepreneurial behavior that is more than simply profit motivated (Dees and Anderson, 2006). Yet, continuity does exist when looking at how these terms are used and practiced especially if research begins from a common starting point; that is, a theoretically grounded explanation for entrepreneurial behavior as conceived previously. Reviewing then what researchers and practitioners alike call and name social or nonprofit entrepreneurship can lead to a unified understanding of what these functional roles actually consist of and what they create.

Social Enterprise

Often the term for social entrepreneurship is interchanged with the concept of social enterprise, or they are considered sister terms (Gentile, 2002). Yet, social enterprise is a unique strategy for resource acquisition and growth within a nonprofit organization (Massaraky, 2006). As Young points out in this volume, the term social enterprise is used to explain different actions depending on the context where it is used. In the US, social enterprise is often defined as 'any earned-income business or strategy undertaken by a nonprofit to generate revenue in support of its charitable mission'.[8] In other contexts, social enterprise includes public service functions and other arrangements involving the public, nonprofit, and private sectors.

The Harvard Business School promotes social enterprise through an initiative designed to generate knowledge that 'helps individuals and organizations create social value'.[9] Thus, the broad approach to social enterprise at Harvard leaves the door open for a wide variety of activities. This approach to social enterprise includes 'contributions any individual or organization can make toward social improvement, regardless of its legal form (nonprofit, private, or public-sector)'. Again, here social enterprise is potentially a universe of ideas that help to meet the needs of marginalized populations around the world, yet this expansive conception of the term makes it very difficult to isolate and analyze what is or is not a social enterprise initiative. Additionally, these activities at times look very much like the actions of social entrepreneurs. Is there an important distinction to be made?

Social Entrepreneurship

A useful distinction should be made separating the activities of social entrepreneurship and social enterprise, yet the former encompasses an even broader array of actions. Often social entrepreneurship and social enterprise are conflated but it is important to conceptually separate these actions. Again, the focus here is on what is social entrepreneurship and not who are social entrepreneurs (this 'who' question is dealt with by Parker, Chapter 11, this volume). Organizations that promote social entrepreneurship and researchers who analyze what these entrepreneurs must define whom or what they are promoting or researching. One of the leading promoters of social entrepreneurship around the world is William Drayton, and the organization he founded, Ashoka, which defines social entrepreneurship in the equilibrating terms described previously. According to Ashoka, 'the job of a social entrepreneur is to recognize when a part of society is stuck and to provide new ways to get it unstuck. He or she finds what is not working and solves the problem by changing the system'.[10] While this conception of social entrepreneurship aligns well with the notion of equilibration described previously, the function of the social entrepreneur as conceptualized by Ashoka is so broad that it is difficult to say specifically what it is short of 'solving large-scale social problem[s]'.

Gregory Dees, another leader in the field, operates a center out of Duke University focused on teaching a promoting social entrepreneurship. At the Center for the Advancement of Social Entrepreneurship (CASE) these entrepreneurs create social value in any sector (private, public, or nonprofit) using not a specific method but an 'approach . . . that embraces the fundamental principles of entrepreneurship'.[11] Again, this conception of social entrepreneurship becomes so broad that it is difficult to isolate what activities create social value and therefore should be fostered and developed.

The multiple sector approach to defining social entrepreneurship is prevalent in other recent research, yet it is also noted that this broad approach highlights the need for theoretical grounding within the field. While these entrepreneurs are defined as innovative agents for social change in any sector, the nonprofit and private (business) sectors is where most research is conducted (Austin *et al.*, 2006). In addition, several organizations that promote social entrepreneurship emphasize that sector is unimportant. 'Social entrepreneurs are not bound by sector norms or traditions and they emerge as leaders in all three sectors' states a leading supporter of social entrepreneurship in Canada.[12]

Further organizations and researchers attempt to define social entrepreneurship as a much more specific act of engaging in market-oriented activity yet for a social purpose. The social entrepreneur is someone who 'brings to life new business opportunities but who is motivated by public and social good rather than the need for personal profit'.[13] Or, social entrepreneurs seek 'the art of simultaneously pursuing both a financial and a social return on investment' that is, essentially innovating in a market-driven context motivated by more than monetary profit.[14] Still others call social entrepreneurs those who otherwise act like business entrepreneurs but they operate in the nonprofit sector.[15]

Finally, some organizations use the term social entrepreneurship to mean any act that can be deemed in the public good or for the benefit of society. Any innovative method of solving a social problem is the result of social entrepreneurship. Social entrepreneurs are 'transforming today's society and working to educate our youth, protect our environment, defend human rights, and alleviate hunger and homelessness, among other issues'.[16] Again, these entrepreneurs are creating solutions that bridge the pure profit motive of business entrepreneurs by innovating in a for-profit context yet seeking a dual return (social impact and profitability). At times the term socially motivated venture is used here to emphasize this dual return. For-profit social ventures has also been used to classify those market based entrepreneurial decisions that also have social motives (Dees and Anderson, 2003).

Nonprofit Entrepreneurship

The previous contributions that attempt to establish a theoretical model for understanding the function of nonprofit entrepreneurship typically articulate an economic argument analogous to the theory for understanding business entrepreneurship. That is, nonprofit entrepreneurs operate in the nonprofit sector for rational reasons in order to provide appropriate signals to potential customers, or donors, regarding either the quality of the product or service or the assurance of the proper use of funds (Bilodeau and Slivinski, 1998; Glaeser and Shleifer, 2001). Thus, these entrepreneurs always operate (by definition) in the nonprofit sector and, regardless of their motives, they choose this sector for economic (incentives and signaling) reasons. Customers feel better going to a nonprofit hospital; for example, because profit will not interfere with service quality.

The distinction here between these entrepreneurs and social entrepreneurs is quite clear, where social entrepreneurs are often (yet not always) defined broadly to operate in multiple sectors, nonprofit entrepreneurs are those that function exclusively in the nonprofit sector. Nonprofit entrepreneurs do not have to create an organization within the nonprofit sector, yet their innovation or creativity often leads to this outcome. A further distinction between these entrepreneurs is also important to point out. The current theoretical contributions explaining nonprofit entrepreneurship, while incomplete, are much closer to a well defined model than the lack of theory many researchers point out in the social entrepreneurship literature. Researchers and practitioners use these concepts interchangeably, yet the need for theoretical clarity is, as one group of scholars state, 'pressing' (Austin *et al.*, 2006).

Consequently, what follows is a model that attempts to define this field of entrepreneurship in a manner that will allow for consistent usage of the various terms for nonprofit/social entrepreneurial activity. This model is a simple typology that has been adapted from earlier research on the nature of entrepreneurial behavior in the private, nonprofit, and public sectors. By starting with the robust economic theory of entrepreneurial behavior, one can more easily establish some theoretical underpinnings for this behavior in the nonprofit sector as well as when motivated by more than pure monetary profit.

A MODEL OF NONPROFIT ENTREPRENEURIAL BEHAVIOR

Clearly entrepreneurial behavior exists in all sectors. As evidenced previously, this behavior is demonstrated outside of purely market-driven conditions within the nonprofit sector. This entrepreneurial behavior is also observed within the market, yet the motives are different from those of business entrepreneurs seeking to attain at least a market rate of return. In order to explain the universe of entrepreneurship in the nonprofit sector or for socially motivated reasons, a typology of entrepreneurship has been adapted from previous research on the institutional conditions necessary for entrepreneurial behavior in the private, public, and nonprofit sectors (Shockley and Frank, 2006).

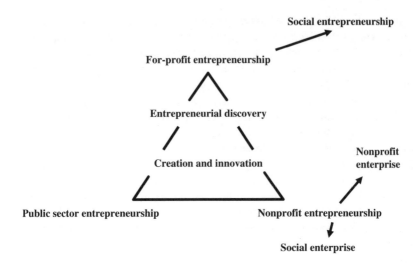

Figure 10.1 Typology of entrepreneurial behavior

Figure 10.1 represents a typology of entrepreneurial behavior, which provides a framework for understanding and defining the various forms of entrepreneurship described previously. By using this typology researchers can speak a common language regarding the myriad actions often lumped together as nonprofit or social entrepreneurship. This typology is intended to provide clarity and a basic framework that can be used to classify these unique entrepreneurs who respond to a different set of incentives than the for-profit business entrepreneur (Frank, 2006).

The first component of the model in Figure 10.1 is the top portion of this tripartite framework: social entrepreneurship as an extension of for-profit entrepreneurship. Social entrepreneurship, as it is often defined, is a form of for-profit entrepreneurship in that the signals evidenced in the marketplace for a social entrepreneur to act are like those for a for-profit entrepreneur. Social entrepreneurship is embodied in an innovative action that is catalyzed by discovering an unmet need in the marketplace and capitalizing on that need. The reason social entrepreneurs are necessary is because insufficient incentives exist for market provision alone. The initial investment is too significant and the potential return is too minimal to encourage the market or business entrepreneur to act. Any entrepreneur may discover the opportunity, but the social entrepreneur, concerned with the dual bottom line, will initiate a means to bring the social system into equilibrium without requiring at least a market rate of return on the initial investment. Thus, the social entrepreneur is sometimes more involved than the business entrepreneur in securing funding for his or her project often through donors instead of venture capitalists. Just as in for-profit entrepreneurship, the entrepreneur does not have to be the risk taker (in terms of monetary risk), yet the social entrepreneur often risks capital knowing the return will be below the market rate because there is a social return sought as well.

The social entrepreneur is motivated to act because of the existence of a profit opportunity, yet unlike the for-profit entrepreneur this profit opportunity does not just signal the need (the area of disequilibrium) it also signals a chance to make a difference and create social value. Social entrepreneurship is defined as the establishment of a for-profit entity, providing an unmet need in the existing marketplace, while simultaneously seeking both a financial and social return on investment. This definition is similar to one used currently in the literature, yet it narrowly defines this type of entrepreneurial behavior in order to provide a consistent basis from which research can be conduced going forward.

The next part of Figure 10.1 provides the basis for understanding entrepreneurial behavior in the nonprofit sector. As indicated earlier, there are two primary types of nonprofit entrepreneurship: nonprofit enterprise and social enterprise. The unifying aspect of this entrepreneurial behavior is that it is fully embedded in the nonprofit sector. In contrast to social entrepreneurs, nonprofit entrepreneurs operate outside traditional market structures where any profit is used for operational purposes alone and is not returned to the stakeholders (Hansmann, 1980). These entrepreneurs are not focused on the dual bottom line, for very often nonprofit entrepreneurs require no fees for service and thus have no potential for profit.

The two distinct forms of nonprofit entrepreneurship reflect an important difference in the type of innovative and creation activity taking place. The nonprofit entrepreneur may establish a nonprofit organization, thus engaging in nonprofit enterprise, or may establish a social enterprise in order to provide revenue for the ongoing operation of a nonprofit. A social enterprise begins from a nonprofit and may turn into a for-profit form, yet it seeks both to resource and carry out the mission of the nonprofit from which it came. Thus, in defining these terms a nonprofit enterprise is the entrepreneurial act of discovering or creating innovative approaches to non-market solutions to social problems by establishing a nonprofit organization. A social enterprise is the entrepreneurial act of discovering or creating an earned income strategy by a nonprofit or the creation of a separate income generating entity by a nonprofit.

This definition of social enterprise is more narrowly defined than the framework expressed by Young in this volume, yet his unified theory is not incompatible with the typology developed here. The distinction here between social entrepreneurship and social enterprise is more in form than substance. A social enterprise draws on resources from a nonprofit, and subsequently provides resources to a nonprofit, while social entrepreneurs establish organizations that provide a return to the stakeholders involved in the social venture. Beyond making a semantic argument, this difference is important because it helps to distinguish entrepreneurial activity that is the result of innovation based in the market versus the nonprofit sector. The famous Grameen Bank started by Muhammad Yunus is a for-profit micro-lending organization that is a prominent example of social entrepreneurship; on the other hand, The Pittsburgh Project (TPP) a community development nonprofit established a social enterprise. In order to provide job skills and training for those in its leadership development program, TPP started a coffee shop to teach and train those in the program as well as generate some earned income for the overall nonprofit. Similar entrepreneurial behavior was necessary to establish both the ventures in the aforementioned examples, but one is set up to provide returns to investors (who are the borrowers of the Grameen Bank) and the other is set up to support the mission of the nonprofit.

This model of entrepreneurial behavior distinguishes between the commonly conflated terms nonprofit entrepreneurship, social entrepreneurship, social enterprise, and nonprofit enterprise. The theory used to ground the typology in Figure 10.1 is rooted in the entrepreneurship theory established by economists Schumpeter and Kirzner. This is important because it is much easier to build theory from a solid base than to tread on shaky ground. By defining these non-market entrepreneurial actions as the model presented here suggests, researchers and practitioners alike can understand the incentives and catalysts for these actions.

CONCLUSION

While the universe of non-market entrepreneurial behavior is not explained here, the typology presented in Figure 10.1 is intended to provide some theoretical grounding to this ever expanding field. Social entrepreneurship and the various forms of nonprofit entrepreneurship are functions that yield specific outcomes that are much more easily analyzed, and subsequently promoted, when they are not defined so broadly. Additionally, it is important to define social entrepreneurs as those who discover an opportunity to add social value, meeting a need or fulfilling a gap in the market, specifically targeted toward marginalized people. Yet the need for social change may be the primary catalyst for these entrepreneurs, even though the incentives for market provision are weak.

As the fields of nonprofit and social entrepreneurship continue to grow, further theory development may be necessary to expand the typology presented here. While the theory of entrepreneurial behavior grounded in a for-profit context is quite robust, new organizational forms may arise creating the need for an expanded model of non-market behavior. It might also be prudent to focus theoretical attention on mixed-form organizations, those that receive capital from private and public sources, due to the different incentives created by a wide variety of constituents. Also, there is an important literature on organizations that operate in markets where for-profit, nonprofit and government providers all coexist (Marwell and McInerney, 2005). Further theoretical development, within the context of the entrepreneurial behavior typology, might help explain the incentives that drive provision from these three sectors. Social and nonprofit entrepreneurship are burgeoning fields of research and practice, and a framework to define and explain these crucial functions in terms of economic entrepreneurial behavior should provide a starting point for a unifying dialogue going forward.

NOTES

1. There are several reviews of this literature see (Bates, 1993; Baumol, 1993; Casson, 1982; Hebert and Link, 1988).
2. See Koppl and Minniti (Chapter 2 this volume) for an excellent analysis of Kirzner's contribution.
3. See Shockley (Chapter 8 this volume) for entrepreneurial behavior in the public sector.
4. Equilibrium in the market often refers to price equilibrium, and the entrepreneur finds the gaps in the market where price disparities exist and exploits them (thus discovering a profit opportunity). In a non-market context equilibration may entail price gaps or it might consist of equilibrating the macro system in terms of provision of goods and services where market incentives to produce are weak. See Hansmann, (1987) for some, yet not an exhaustive list, of the theoretical explanations for nonprofit provision.
5. A review of these theories can be found in (Frank, 2006).
6. For a nice review of the synthesis between the Schumpeterian and Kirznerian entrepreneur see (Shockley *et al.*, 2006).
7. Again, see Koppl and Minniti (Chapter 2 this volume).
8. See the Social Enterprise Alliance at www.se-alliance.org.
9. See Harvard Business School at www.hbs.edu/socialenterprise.
10. See Ashoka at www.ashoka.org.
11. See Duke University and CASE at www.fuqua.duke.edu/centers/case.
12. See Canadian Centre for Social Entrepreneurship at www.bus.ualberta.ca/ccse.
13. See the Social Enterprise Coalition at www.socialenterprise.org.uk.
14. See Institute for Social Entrepreneurs at www.socialent.org.
15. See Social Enterprise Magazine Online at www.socialenterprisemagazine.org, and the Community Action Network at www.can-online.org.uk.
16. See the program information on social entrepreneurship at New York University's Stern School of Business at stern.nyu.edu.

REFERENCES

Austin, J., H. Stevenson and J. Wei-Skillern (2006), 'Social and commercial entrepreneurship: same, different, or both?', *Entrepreneurship Thoery and Practice*, **30**(1), 1–22.

Bates, T. (1993), 'Theories of entrepreneurship', in R.D. Bingham and R. Mier (eds), *Theories of Local Economic Development: Perspectives From Across the Disciplines*, Newbury Park, CA: Sage Publications.

Baumol, W.J. (1993), 'Formal entrepreneurship theory in economics: existence and bounds', *Journal of Business Venturing*, **8**, 197–210.

Bilodeau, M. and A. Slivinski (1998), 'Rational nonprofit entrepreneurship', *Journal of Economics and Management Strategy*, **7**(4), 551–71.

Casson, M. (1982), *The Entrepreneur: An Economic Theory*, Totowa, NJ: Barnes & Noble Books.

Dees, J.G., and B.B. Anderson (2003), 'For-profit social ventures', *International Journal of Entrepreneurship Education*, **2**, 1–26.

Dees, J.G. and B.B. Anderson (2006), 'Framing a theory of social entrepreneurship: building on two schools of practice and thought', in R. Mosher-Williams (ed.), *Research on Social Entrepreneurship: Understanding and Contributing to an Emerging Field* Vol. 1, No. 3, Indianapolis, IN: ARNOVA occasional paper series, pp. 39–66.

Frank, P.M. (2006), 'Non-profit entrepreneurship: extending the concept of profit opportunities', *International Journal of Entrepreneurship and Innovation Management*, **6**(3), 224–40.

Gartner, W.B. (1989), '"Who is an Entrepreneur?" Is the wrong question', *Entrepreneurship Thoery and Practice*, **13**(4), 47–68.

Gentile, M.C. (2002), 'Social impact management and social enterprise: two sides of the same coin or a totally different currency?', The Aspen Institute working paper, New York.

Glaeser, E.L. and A. Shleifer (2001), 'Not-For-Profit Entrepreneurs', *Journal of Public Economics*, **81**, 99–115.

Hansmann, H.B. (1980), 'The Role of Nonprofit Enterprise', *The Yale Law Journal*, **89**(5), 835–901.

Hansmann, H.B. (1987), Economic theories of nonprofit organization, in W.W. Powell (ed.), *The Nonprofit Sector: A Research Handbook* New Haven, CT: Yale University Press, pp. 27–42.

Hebert, R.F., and A.N. Link. (1988), *The Entrepreneur: Mainstream Views and Radical Critiques*, 2nd edn, New York: Praeger.

Kirzner, I.M. (1973), *Competition and Entrepreneurship*, Chicago, IL: The University of Chicago Press.

Kirzner, I.M. (1997), *How Markets Work: Disequilibrium, Entrepreneurship and Discovery*, London: The Institute of Economic Affairs.

Light, P.C. (2006), 'Searching for social entrepreneurs: who they might be, where they might be found, what they do', in R. Mosher-Williams (ed.), *Research on Social Entrepreneurship: Understanding and Contributing to an Emerging Field*, Vol. 1, No. 3, Indianapolis, IN: ARNOVA occasional paper series, pp. 13–37.

Mair, J. and I. Marti (2005), 'Social entrepreneurship research: a source of explanation, prediction, and delight', University of Navarra IESE Business School working paper, Barcelona, Spain.

Mair, J., J. Robinson and K. Hockerts (eds.) (2006), *Social Entrepreneurship*, London: Palgrave.

Marwell, N.P., and P.-B. McInerney (2005), 'The nonprofit/for-profit continuum: theorizing the dynamics of mixed-form markets', *Nonprofit and Voluntary Sector Quarterly*, **34**(1), 7–28.

Massaraky, C.W. (2006), 'Coming of age: social enterprise reaches its tipping point', in R. Mosher-Williams (ed.), *Research on Social Entrepreneurship: Understanding and Contributing to an Emerging Field*, vol. 1, no. 3, Indianapolis, IN: ARNOVA occasional paper series, pp. 67–87.

Parkinson, C. (2005), 'Meanings behind the language of social entrepreneurship', Lancaster University Management School working paper 072, Lancaster.

Schumpeter, J.A. (1950 [1942]), *Capitalism, Socialism, and Democracy*, 3rd edn, New York: Harper & Brothers.

Schumpeter, J.A. (1961 [1911]), *Theory of Economic Development*, Oxford: Galaxy Books.

Shane, S.A. (2003), *A General Theory of Entrepreneurship: The Individual-Opportunity Nexus*, Cheltenham, UK and Northampton, MA, USA: Edward Elgar.

Shockley, G.E. and P.M. Frank (2006), 'An institutional typology of entrepreneurship: entrepreneurial discovery in the for-profit, nonprofit, and public sector', Arizona State University working paper, Phoenix, AZ.

Shockley, G.E., R.R. Stough, K.E. Haynes and P.M. Frank (2006), 'Toward a theory of public sector entrepreneurship', *International Journal of Entrepreneurship and Innovation Management*, **6**(3), 205–23.

Young, D.R. (1986), 'Entrepreneurship and the behavior of nonprofit organizations: elements of a theory', in S. Rose-Ackerman (ed.), *The Economics of Nonprofit Institutions: Studies in Structure and Policy*, New York: Oxford University Press, pp. 161–84.

11. Social entrepreneurs: a neoclassical theory

Simon C. Parker

INTRODUCTION

A growing body of research highlights the scale and importance of non-market entrepreneurship. A central premise of this book is that despite growing interest in this phenomenon, serious gaps in our knowledge remain. The present chapter explores one gap in particular, relating to the people who create and operate non-market enterprises – people I shall call 'social entrepreneurs' in this chapter. I ask the following questions: What kinds of people become social entrepreneurs? Why do they choose to participate in non-market rather than market activities? Are people more likely to become social entrepreneurs at particular points in their lives? And if so when?

The present chapter contains a novel theoretical framework designed to answer these questions. The extant literature on social and not-for-profit entrepreneurship contains little by way of theory on these issues, so I believe that such a contribution may be timely. In an excellent recent survey, Haugh (2006) draws attention to various motives of people driven to become social entrepreneurs. These motives include the articulation of one's beliefs; making a contribution to society; and realizing a dream or vision. There are also various claims that social entrepreneurs possess particular character traits (Drucker, 1989; Leadbeater, 1997; Bornstein, 1998; Prabhu, 1999; Thompson et al., 2000). However, there is little agreement about what exactly those traits might be. Weisbrod (1988: 32–33) cites some evidence that managers of non-profit enterprises may attach greater importance to being cheerful, forgiving, and helpful than managers of for-profits – who are more likely to value financial prosperity, ambition and power. Weisbrod also referred to findings showing that employees of not-for-profit law firms earn less than their counterparts in commercial law firms, but declare themselves to be more satisfied with their careers. However, these tentative findings do not get to the heart of the questions posed above. And, in line with criticisms of the psychological 'traits approach' in mainstream entrepreneurship research (Gartner, 1988) it is unclear how successful research will be that simply applies that approach to the specific context of non-market entrepreneurship.

This chapter follows a different direction, analysing the behaviour of social entrepreneurs in terms of a rational neoclassical occupational choice approach developed in the economics of entrepreneurship literature (Parker, 2004, 2005). Numerous studies in this literature analyse the decision to become an entrepreneur in terms of occupational choice in the labour market. A key insight from this work is that individuals only become entrepreneurs if they obtain greater expected utility from entrepreneurship than from paid employment; otherwise they become employees. I propose applying a dynamic variant of this framework to analyse the decision to become a social entrepreneur. This variant can be regarded as an extension of the well-known life cycle consumption model of Modigliani and Brumberg (1954), in which rational forward-looking individuals choose optimal trajectories of consumption and effort over their remaining lifetimes. I extend this model by allowing individuals to divide their time between relatively low-paying non-market activities, which nonetheless confer a non-market benefit to those engaged in it; and relatively well paying market work, which includes paid employment and conventional market entrepreneurship. The aim of the chapter is to identify which individuals are the most likely to engage in non-market entrepreneurship, and when in their life cycle they do so. Although the basis of the model is somewhat technical, the reader should easily be able to follow the logic by skipping the mathematics and reading only the words.

The next section states the assumptions and structure of the model. The two that follow present the key results and implications of extending the model in several ways. The results are discussed in the light of the available evidence, including recent findings from the UK Social Entrepreneurship Monitor (Harding, 2006). The final section concludes.

THEORY

Consider an individual with given ability and wealth, who is thinking about engaging in social entrepreneurship. In each period, the individual has to choose (a) how to divide her available time of one unit between work h and leisure $(1-h)$, and (b) what fraction of her work time $0 \leq \alpha \leq 1$ should be spent in non-market entrepreneurship (denoted by NME hereafter) and what fraction should be spent in some outside option (PE hereafter). PE could be either 'traditional' market entrepreneurship or paid employment; it makes no difference for the purposes of the present chapter precisely what activities PE includes.[1] The individual's choices of leisure and work time spent in NME need not be the same in each period. Indeed, it will be shown below that in general individuals will do best by making systematically different choices at different stages of their lives. Note that the individual can mix time between NME and PE, reflecting a mix of social and private objectives.

The individual obtains utility at each t from three sources: consuming goods $c(t)$, leisure $1h(t)$, and participation in NME. In principle, satisfaction from NME could be obtained for at least two different reasons. For example, individuals could derive satisfaction from work itself, e.g., enjoyment from taking part in the activities of a non-market venture. This satisfaction is additional to the utility obtainable from consuming out of income that is derived from such venturing (see below). Alternatively, individuals might altruistically value the flow of benefits that non-market enterprise yields to others.[2] For maximum generality, we write the satisfaction from working in NME as $\psi(\alpha h)$, where αh is the work input into a non-market venture. Thus if ψ is the identity function (that is, $\psi(\alpha h) = \alpha h$), then work input is deemed to be the source of satisfaction. If instead ψ is a 'production function' that is increasing in its input, then output is deemed to be the source of satisfaction. An advantage of proceeding in this manner is that the key results can be derived for general ψ without restricting our interpretation to a particular source of satisfaction.

Letting U denote a utility function which is increasing and concave in its three arguments, individuals obtain utility:

$$U(t) = U\{c(t), 1 - h(t), \psi[\alpha(t)h(t)]\} \tag{11.1}$$

in period t, where the time dependence of consumption, leisure and benefits from NME is made explicit in Equation 1.1.

Note that both interpretations of $\psi(\cdot)$ discussed above differ from philanthropy, because working for an NME differs from transferring wealth to outside institutions. The latter is more properly regarded as a consumption activity, which can be subsumed into $c(t)$. To see this point more clearly, suppose that individuals receive $\gamma\omega$ pounds per hour from working in NME, where ω is the financial return available in PE, and $0 < \gamma < 1$ is a parameter. Philanthropy implies a negative value of γ, something we do not consider here as we are primarily interested in non-market enterprises that can still provide a living for the social entrepreneur. With $0 < \gamma < 1$, the non-market enterprise generates some income but not as much as in market activities.[3]

With initial assets of $\alpha_0 \geq 0$, the individual's budget constraint can be written as:

$$\frac{\partial a(t)}{\partial t} = ra(t) + w[1 - \alpha(t)]h(t) + \gamma w\alpha(t)h(t) - c(t) \qquad (11.2)$$

That is, assets accumulate period-to-period at the rate of return (interest rate) r, as well as from savings. Savings are represented in Equation 11.2 as the difference between income (from market and non-market activities) and consumption. Finally, suppose that the individual remains economically active for T periods, and that they discount future utility at the rate ρ $>0.$[4] Values of ρ can differ from person to person, a key feature of the model explored below. High values of ρ are associated with impatient people, who give a greater weight to enjoying resources now compared with the future; whereas low values of ρ are associated with more patient people who give greater weight to enjoyment in the future relative to the present.

Denote terminal assets at time T by $a(T)$, and the utility from bequeathing this to offspring by $\upsilon[a(T)]$, where υ is a general increasing and concave function. The individual's objective is to choose the *set* of values of $c(t)$, $h(t)$ and $\alpha(t)$ for every time period $t \in [0,T]$ to maximize:

$$\int_0^T U\{c(t), 1 - h(t), \psi[\alpha(t)h(t)]\} \, e^{-\rho t}dt + \upsilon[a(T)]e^{-\rho T} \qquad (11.3)$$

subject to Equation 11.2. The integral is simply the discounted sum (present value) of all present and future utilities, including from bequests. The discount factor is $e^{-\rho t}$. The final term is the discounted utility of the bequest. The maximization of Equation 11.3 subject to Equation 11.2 and $a(0) = a_0$ is a standard optimal control problem, whose solution sheds light on social entrepreneur's behaviour, as we now discuss.

WHO ARE THE SOCIAL ENTREPRENEURS?

Our key results follow from the following pair of relations which solve the social entrepreneur's decision problem stated in the previous section:

$$\frac{\partial U}{\partial c} \propto e^{(\rho - r)t} \qquad (11.4)$$

$$\frac{\partial U}{\partial \alpha} = \frac{\partial U}{\partial \psi}\frac{\partial \psi}{\partial \alpha} = w(1 - \gamma) \cdot \frac{\partial U}{\partial c} \qquad (11.5)$$

Equation 11.4 describes the optimal trajectory of individuals' consumption paths over time, while Equation 11.5 describes the optimal trajectory of their participation in non-market entrepreneurship. The partial derivative $\partial U/\partial c$ is the marginal utility that the individual receives from an additional unit of consumption, while $\partial U/\partial c$ is the marginal utility that the individual receives from devoting an extra unit of time to non-market entrepreneurship. Marginal utility is taken to diminish as greater amounts of a good are enjoyed.

To understand these solutions, it is helpful to consider two different types of individual. A 'Type A' person is relatively 'patient' and discounts their utility less than the interest rate (that is, $\rho < r$), whereas a 'Type B' person is relatively 'impatient' and discounts their utility more than the interest rate ($\rho > r$). By inspection of Equation 11.4 and taking account of diminishing marginal utility, the consumption streams of A (*resp.*, B) individuals steadily increase (*resp.*, decrease) with age. This turns out to have key implications for who engages in non-market entrepreneurship and at what stages in their lives, as well as which social entrepreneurs contribute the most to this sector.

To see the effects on the individual's decision to participate in non-market entrepreneurship, observe from Equaion 11.5 that the marginal utility from being a social entrepreneur is directly proportional to marginal utility from c (by the RHS of (5)). Therefore, the arguments of the preceding paragraph apply equally to participation in non-market entrepreneurship. That is, Type A individuals have non-market participation paths α^* (t) that increase with age, whereas Type B individuals have $\alpha^*(t)$ paths that decrease with age. It can also be shown that leisure $l^*(t)$ follows the same paths as $\alpha^*(t)$ and c^* (t) by individual type.

It is important to note that the two types of individual that have been identified are distinguished from each other by their willingness to work and save early in their working lives, instead of consuming leisure and goods. When young, Type A individuals take relatively little consumption or leisure. They work hard and save to build up their assets, which they achieve most efficiently by working predominantly in PE. Type As remain wealthy throughout their lives, accumulating sufficient assets to bequeath and to finance growing consumption, leisure and non-market entrepreneurship engagement as they age.

Type B individuals follow the opposite pattern. When young, Type B individuals do not build up their assets, indulging instead in consumption, leisure, and their taste for working in non-market entrepreneurship. But these choices have implications for future decisions, because to satisfy their resource constraints they must eventually start to reduce their consumption, leisure and time spent in NME in order to pay for their earlier consumption and to satisfy their bequest motive. Hence Type B individuals optimally choose consumption, leisure and non-market entrepreneurship participation paths that all decrease continuously over their lifetimes. It can also be shown that Type Bs are never as wealthy as Type As.[5]

One might even choose to depict Type A individuals as 'wealthy do-gooders', who 'give something back to society' in later life; and Type B individuals as 'jaded idealists' who eventually 'join the real world'. However, we would not insist on such an interpretation.

Notice that the theoretical insights about non-market entrepreneurship do not change if entrepreneurs and managers in NME are distinct. Suppose the former start new non-market enterprises while the latter merely manage existing ones. The patterns of entrepreneurial *entry* into NME are exactly as described above for *participation* in NME; in an empirical context, however, one must now recognize that some participation in NME might be managerial rather than entrepreneurial. In other words, the implications for both entrepreneurial and managerial participation in NME over the life cycle are the same.

Some independent evidence bears on these theoretical predictions. Johnson (2003) observed the prevalence of prior private sector experience and wealth in her study of Canadian social entrepreneurs, though her study is based on a very small sample. This gives some support to the notion of Type A individuals, as does the qualitative study of BITC (2001), as summarized by Thompson (2000):

> The growth of Business in the Community and other initiatives has shown that some social entrepreneurs are clearly seasoned and successful business entrepreneurs and executives who wish to 'put something back' into society, both before and after they retire from, or reduce their commitment to, their main occupation. (Thompson, 2000: 414)

However, the most robust evidence that bears on the model comes from the Social Entrepreneurship Monitor (SEM), which in 2005 surveyed 27 296 18–64 year olds randomly stratified by UK region. In her summary report, Harding (2006) reported the following findings. Younger people are more likely to become social entrepreneurs than any other age group (for example, 3–9 per cent of 18–24 year olds, compared with 2.8 per cent of over-55s). These were often poorer individuals, who were found to become increasingly disillusioned with non-market entrepreneurship as they aged; most surviving social entrepreneurs were observed to be older. These findings are consistent with the presence of both Type A and B individuals in the population – as one might expect. That is, poorer individuals who enter NME primarily when they are young often drop out of it as they age (Type Bs), at the same time as older individuals enter NME after they have acquired assets which can help them survive running a non-market enterprise for longer (these are the Type As). Interestingly, Harding also noted that those in part-time employment are most likely to be running an established social enterprise (2006: 21); this is of course consistent with the model's structure, which fully allows part-time engagement in NME via the continuous choice variable $\alpha \in [0, 1]$.[6]

FURTHER IMPLICATIONS OF THE MODEL

It is possible to enrich the simple model outlined in the previous section in various ways. Below we consider heterogeneous tastes for non-market entrepreneurship; heterogeneous asset endowments and borrowing constraints; and heterogeneous abilities.

With regard to heterogeneous tastes, consider two individuals, D and E, who are identical in all respects (including intertemporal discount rate ρ), except that D has a greater appreciation of non-market entrepreneurship than E does. In which case $\partial U^D/\partial \psi > \partial U^E/\partial \psi$ (for all t), where a superscript denotes an individual. Hence to satisfy (Equation 11.5) as an equality, we must have $\alpha^D > \alpha^E$. Logically, if person D derives greater marginal utility from engaging in non-market entrepreneurship than E, then (unsurprisingly) D will optimally spend a greater amount of time in it than E will.

If individuals start their working lives with different amounts of wealth, an additional result can be derived. Consider two individuals F and G, who have different initial asset endowments but who are identical in all other respects. Suppose F is born wealthier than G. Then although γ may be high enough that both F and G are able to engage in NME and support themselves in this activity, F can indulge their taste for NME easier than G can because their budget constraint is more relaxed than G's. It then follows directly that F will spend a greater fraction of their working life engaged in NME than G, at all ages. This prediction remains if wealth-based borrowing constraints that restrict access to NME start-up are introduced into the model (Evans and Jovanovic, 1989). Evidently, such constraints are likely to reduce the number of Type B social entrepreneurs more than the number of Type A social entrepreneurs. According to Harding's (2006) evidence from the SEM, financing constraints do indeed appear to be binding for many social entrepreneurs.

This prediction might also help to explain intergenerational involvement in non-market entrepreneurship. Historically, wealthy dynasties have played a prominent role in initiating and perpetuating a tradition of non-market enterprise. Prominent examples of this in British history include nineteenth-century English aristocrats and merchants such as the seventh Earl of Shaftesbury and Robert Owen. The association between initial wealth holdings and participation in NME – which can be perpetuated over time given the bequest motive present in Equation 11.3, might therefore help to explain this interesting and historically important phenomenon.

Finally, consider differences in ability between individuals. Are more or less able individuals more or less likely to become social entrepreneurs? Consider innately talented individuals who can earn more in both NME and PE than others with less talent. For example, general talent might relate to the ability to recognize and exploit opportunities which could be equally valuable in market entrepreneurship (PE) and non-market entrepreneurship (NME). It then follows from the solution to our model that greater ability is associated with less leisure and a smaller fraction of work time devoted to non-market entrepreneurship. The reason is that the opportunity costs of spending time in NME rather than PE, and in leisure rather than in work, are now both higher. Thus abler individuals are predicted to spend a greater fraction of their time in market activities than the less able, who are likely to spend a greater fraction of their work time in non-market entrepreneurship, all else equal. Unsurprisingly, perhaps, the opposite result holds for any aspect of ability that is specific to NME. Greater ability that increases the returns in NME by more than in PE are predicted to promote NME as a rational occupational choice. To date, we know of no empirical work that tests this prediction. This may be because at present we know little about the dimensions of ability that is specific to NME. An example might be the ability to motivate volunteer labour which is more valuable in NME than PE because the latter tends to rely more on salaried employees who can be incentivized by monetary incentives. However, the ability to cajole and encourage might be equally valuable in some PE firms. Evidently, further research is needed to elucidate the essential aspects of ability in NME relative to PE, and to start the process of constructing useful empirical counterparts to the theoretical concepts. Researchers might also wish to consider the possibility that ability evolves over time, in such a way that serial NME entrepreneurship becomes possible; that would constitute a valuable theoretical extension of the model presented here.

CONCLUSION

This chapter has recognized the role of the social entrepreneur at the heart of non-market entrepreneurship, and has proposed a new neoclassical theory of social entrepreneurs. The theory isolates several characteristics of individuals who are likely to become social entrepreneurs at different times in their lives. A key role is ascribed to differences in rates of time preference. These give rise to endogenous optimal trajectories of wealth accumulation, which drive patterns of entry into and exit from non-market entrepreneurship. Rich and patient people with some predisposition to non-market activities are predicted to become social entrepreneurs later in their lives, while impatient but highly socially motivated people are also predicted to engage in this activity, albeit mainly at earlier stages of their lives. Individuals with high levels of general ability but below-average wealth are predicted to engage less in non-market entrepreneurship than their less able but wealthier counterparts.

By proposing systematic differences between individuals and the different circumstances and incentives they face as the key to understanding who becomes a social entrepreneur, the theory contributes to the literature a simple but theoretically grounded typology, which lends itself naturally to further extensions in future work. It also complements existing attempts to develop typologies based on traits (for example Fowler, 2000), though without the drawbacks of the latter identified by Gartner (1988). On the one hand, typologies may help to make sense of the diversity of non-market enterprises, which currently pose a severe challenge to researchers who wish to say something both general and substantive about these forms of entrepreneurship. On the other hand, typologies should be theoretically grounded and testable, in order to reduce the risk of proliferating arbitrary and competing taxonomies that at the end of the day obscure the subject more than they help to illuminate it. It is certainly to be hoped that future research will bring more data to bear on the chapter's predictions about individual differences and the decision to become a social entrepreneur – perhaps using large data samples along the lines of the SEM.

It is noteworthy in this respect that researchers in experimental economics have begun to make considerable progress in devising practical instruments to measure a key parameter of the theory proposed here, namely individuals' rates of time preference. These instruments may prove useful in efforts to measure the relative frequencies of the different types of social entrepreneur we have identified theoretically, and in a broader sense to test the theory outlined here.

More generally, the field of non-market entrepreneurship needs to develop a strong body of empirical work focused on social entrepreneurs. At present, with the notable exception of the SEM, the empirical literature in the area mainly contains case studies, which are interesting and helpful as far as they go, but which stop short of allowing researchers to draw generalizable conclusions about social entrepreneurs. The challenge for future research is to acquire large-scale evidence about social entrepreneurs without obscuring the individual-specific detail which is likely to be crucial for illuminating the identities of social entrepreneurs.

NOTES

1. Like Weisbrod (1988), managers of non-market enterprises are taken to be synonymous with entrepreneurs in NME. It makes no difference to the predictions of the model if they are distinct, as will be explained below.
2. Case study evidence from Shaw *et al.* (2001) points clearly to the satisfaction social entrepreneurs derive from involvement in NMEs. However, it does not indicate which of the two explanations is more pertinent to social entrepreneurs.
3. If $\gamma \geq 1$, it is easy to show that NME always dominates PE, and individuals will always choose to participate fully in NME. We do not discuss this (analytically uninteresting) case any further below. The most interesting, and arguably the most realistic, case is where individuals have to trade off financial benefits in PE for non-financial benefits in NME.
4. It makes no difference to our analysis whether the individual dies or retires at T, since we are only concerned in this chapter with decisions made over the working life. Parker and Rougier (2006) analyse the retirement decision of conventional for-profit entrepreneurs. We leave the intersection of retirement and *non-market* entrepreneurship as a topic for future research.
5. Type B individuals are not only poor because they run down their assets when young, but also because by working more in NME when young they receive lower financial returns and so accumulate fewer assets this way, too. However, it is also possible that the longer an individual stays in NME, the less valuable their human capital becomes in the market sector, PE. Then some Type Bs might remain in non-market entrepreneurship throughout their lives.
6. Harding also observed that education is associated with involvement in NME. Human capital theory predicts that individuals with lower rates of time preference ρ are more likely to be highly educated, while our model suggests that they are also more likely to be social entrepreneurs. However, we must accept that this is only indirect evidence of Type A behaviour.

REFERENCES

BITC (2001), *Business in the Community Annual Report*, London: BITC.

Bornstein, D. (1998), 'Changing the world on a shoestring: an ambitious foundation promotes social change by finding "social entrepreneurs"', *Atlantic Monthly*, **281**, 34–9.

Drucker, P.F. (1989), 'What businesses can learn from non-profits', *Harvard Business Review*, **67**(4), 88–93.

Evans, D.S. and B. Jovanovic (1989), 'An estimated model of entrepreneurial choice under liquidity constraints', *Journal of Political Economy*, **97**, 808–27.

Fowler, A. (2000), 'NGDOs as a moment in history: beyond aid to social entrepreneurship or civic innovation?', *Third World Quarterly*, **21**, 637–54.

Gartner, W. (1988), 'Who is an entrepreneur? is the wrong question', *Entrepreneurship Theory & Practice*, **13**, 47–68.

Harding, R. (2006), *The Social Entrepreneurship Monitor*, London Business School, http://www.london.edu/gem/socialentrepreneurshipmonitor.html.

Haugh, H. (2006), 'Non-profit social entrepreneurship', in S.C. Parker (ed.), *The Handbook of Entrepreneurship Research, Volume III*, New York: Springer.

Johnson, S. (2003), 'Young social entrepreneurs in Canada', *Mimeo*, Canadian Centre for Social Entrepreneurship, http://www.bus.ualberta.ca/ccse/Publications/.

Leadbeater, C. (1997), *The Rise of the Social Entrepreneur*, London: Demos.

Modiligiani, F. and R. Brumberg (1954), 'Utility analysis and the consumption function: An interpretation of cross-section data', in K. Kurihara (ed.) *Post-Keynesian Economics*, New Brunswick, NJ: Rutgers University Press.

Parker, S.C. (2004), *The Economics of Self-employment and Entrepreneurship*, Cambridge: Cambridge University Press.

Parker, S.C. (2005), 'The economics of entrepreneurship: what we know and what we don't', *Foundations & Trends in Entrepreneurship*, **1**(1), 1–55.

Parker, S.C. and J. Rougier (2006), 'Self-employment and the retirement decision', *Applied Economics*, **39**, 697–713.

Prabhu, G.N. (1999), 'Social entrepreneurial leadership', *Career Development International*, **4**, 140–5.

Shaw, E., J. Shaw and M. Wilson (2001), 'Unsung entrepreneurs: entrepreneurship for social gain', unpublished report, Barclays Centre for Entrepreneurship, Durham Business School.

Thompson, J. (2000), 'The world of the social entrepreneur', *International Journal of Public Sector Management*, **15**, 412–31.

Thompson, J., G. Alvy and A. Lees (2000), 'Social entrepreneurship – a new look at the people and the potential', *Management Decision*, **38,** 328–38.

Weisbrod, B.A. (1988), *The Nonprofit Economy*, Cambridge, MA: Harvard University Press.

12. What are social ventures? Toward a theoretical framework and empirical examination of successful social ventures

Ronit Yitshaki, Miri Lerner and Moshe Sharir

INTRODUCTION

Most of the literature pertaining to social entrepreneurship draws on the business entrepreneurship literature. The main difference between entrepreneurs operating in the business sector versus those in the not-for-profit sector is that social contribution, in the sense of mission and service, becomes the main goal of social entrepreneurs and not profitability or financial gains. Social entrepreneurship is based on opportunity recognition of social needs and is associated with innovativeness, proactiveness and risk taking (Sullivan Mort *et al.*, 2003).

Yet, given their vulnerability, there has been relatively little research into the aspects that influence the long-term survivability of social ventures, especially during their early years. The current chapter tries to identify the factors that may explain long-term survivability of social ventures. These factors are examined at two levels: external and internal explanations for survival. To explain long-term survivability, the chapter suggests a theoretical framework drawing on a combination of five theoretical perspectives: resource-dependent, institutional, social capital, resource-based and human capital.

We examine the factors contributing to survivability based on a large qualitative field-study of 33 social ventures that operated in various social arenas in Israel in 2000. A follow-up study conducted in 2005 revealed that 25 of these ventures had succeeded in surviving.

LITERATURE REVIEW

Social Entrepreneurship

Social entrepreneurs are 'People who realize where there is an opportunity to satisfy some unmet need that the state welfare system will not or cannot meet and who gather together the necessary resources and use these to "make a difference"' (Thompson *et al.*, 2000). As such, social entrepreneurs are perceived as change agents who create and sustain social value without being limited by the resources currently at hand (Stevenson and Jarrilo, 1991). Like business entrepreneurs, social entrepreneurs establish new organizations, develop and implement innovative programs, and organize or distribute new services. Even though they are differently motivated, the challenges and problems facing social entrepreneurs during the initiation, establishment and institutionalization of their ventures resemble those faced by business entrepreneurs (Edward, 1995; Piltz, 1995; Tropman, 1989; Young, 1986). However, their activity is valued by their ability to maximize social rather than economic returns (Sullivan Mort *et al.*, 2003). In addition, the norms effective in social markets do not parallel those governing economic markets (Emerson, 1998).

Social ventures that open up new areas of activity must often contend with an environment that does not recognize or appreciate their worth or inherent contribution. The social venture's over-dependence on external sources of funding is due to its inability to demand realistic fees for the services rendered to the majority of its clients (its direct customers), in addition to its reliance on volunteers and staff ready to accept below-market wages (Bygrave *et al.*, 1996; Emerson, 1998). Ventures promoting social change are also likely to face opposition from bodies that control existing policy and public resources (Sink, 1996).

In this chapter we propose a conceptual framework for social ventures' survivability based on external and internal explanations. We suggest an elaboration of the conceptual framework that combines five theoretical perspectives and develop a model for examining long-term survivability of social ventures.

CONCEPTUAL FRAMEWORK OF SOCIAL VENTURES' SURVIVABILITY

In order to identify factors that may explain long-term survivability of social ventures we draw on several theoretical perspectives. First, we address the issue of resource dependency – the dependence of organizations on resources within their environment. We claim that, owing to the dependence of social ventures on the external environment, including governmental agencies, foundations and NGOs, ensuring the needed resources is a requisite for their existence. Second, we address the issue of the need of organizations for legitimacy from the institutional perspective, claiming that this need is especially acute in social venturing. Third, we draw on social capital and network theory in addressing the aspects pertaining to network exploitation by social entrepreneurs. Fourth, we apply the resource-based view of firms to the internal resources of social ventures. Fifth and last, we focus on social entrepreneurs' human capital, such as their previous experience and education, skills and their total dedication.

The first three abovementioned perspectives: resource dependency, institutional and social capital theories, refer to the external environment, while the last two perspectives, the resource-based view of the firm and human capital, refer to the internal aspects of social ventures.

External Explanation of Survival of Social Ventures

As entrepreneurial firms, both business and social ventures are based on opportunity recognition and exploitation (Shane and Venkataraman, 2000); they are both exposed to 'liability of newness' (Stinchcombe, 1965) and a high rate of failure (Stinchcombe, 1965; Maidique, 1986; Shane and Venkataraman, 2000). In order to ensure higher survivability, a social venture needs to secure adequate resources, acquire legitimacy and develop social networks.

Resource Dependency of Social Ventures

When referring to external reasons, it appears that survival depends on the entrepreneurial firms' ability to ensure the needed resources and lower their dependence on the environment (Pfeffer, 1972; Pfeffer and Salancik, 1978; Astley and Van de Ven, 1983). Organizations can also lower their resource dependence by cooperating with other organizations (Pfeffer, 1987). Hrebiniak and Joyce (1985) suggested that lower resource dependence may increase the strategic choices available to firm managers.

Similar to business ventures, a low level of capitalization may influence social ventures' survivability (Bruno, *et al.*, 1992; Cooper, *et al.*, 1994). However, the adaptability of social ventures is more complicated relative to business ventures (Roper and Cheney, 2005). Social ventures are exposed to higher resource dependence in their environments because it might not be possible for them to provide their services and products to their clients at their commercial value. Thus, social ventures are heavily dependent on financial resources emanating from governmental grants and donations and on manpower resources provided by volunteers.

Social Ventures' Need for Legitimacy

The importance of obtaining legitimacy for the operation of organizations has been discussed in the institutional literature (Aldrich and Fiol, 1994; Aldrich and Martinez, 2001). Organizations compete not only for resources, clients and economic power, but also for political power and institutional legitimacy, as well as social adaptability. In particular, organizations that rely on the same sources of financing, personnel and legitimacy will be more dependent upon their suppliers (Dimaggio and Powell, 1983).

Social ventures depend on their ability to gain legitimacy in the sociopolitical arena to boost their chances of surviving (Jack and Anderson, 2002). As opposed to business ventures, a social venture's ability to create legitimacy and gain resources depends on its success in generating identification and empathy with its social values (Sullivan Mort *et al.*, 2003) and on the social entrepreneurs' ability to gain exposure in the public discourse (Sharir and Lerner, 2006).

In a recent study based on the life histories of founders of new ventures in Sweden, Delmar and Shane (2004) found the importance of three different foci for activities: the creation of social ties with external stakeholders, the establishment of external legitimacy, and the creation of routines to transform resources. They argued that new ventures would survive if the firm founders initially focused their efforts on legitimating activities because legitimacy enhances the ability of founders to create social ties with external stakeholders and initiate routines to transform resources.

The Social Capital and Networks of Social Entrepreneurs

Social capital refers to 'the actual and potential resources embedded within, available through and derived from the network relations possessed by an individual or social unit' (Nahapiet and Ghoshal, 1998: 243). Social capital refers to both distant and close connections in the social structure that facilitate a person's access to knowledge, resources and new opportunities (Adler and Kwon, 2002). Accordingly, social capital is a central source for understanding organizational dynamics, innovation and wealth creation (Nahapiet and Ghoshal, 1998; Baron and Markman, 2000; Johannisson, 1996; Burt, 1997; Aldrich and Zimmer, 1986; Davidsson and Honig, 2003; Jack and Anderson, 2002). The notion of the accumulation of social capital within the social network provides an insight into the way ventures are established and institutionalized and how they acquire their competitive capabilities and keep their market position (Wickham, 1998).

Social entrepreneurs, similar to business entrepreneurs, rely on their ability to create connections when initiating new ventures. However, since social entrepreneurship is more embedded in the social context, access to knowledge and resources is directly linked to the venture's ability to gain legitimacy and support. While raising funds in the business context is organized and formalized through venture capital, angels and banks, social initiatives' investments are less organized and depend on less formalized systems. As such, the social capital of social entrepreneurs is significantly more important as a factor in their ability to attract investments. In addition, the social entrepreneurs' ability to create strong relationships is of great importance for the creation of internal bonding and commitment among the venture's volunteers, employees as well as investors (Johannisson, 1987; Burt, 2000).

Another aspect that may impact the survivability of social ventures is related to the social entrepreneurs' ability to create collaborations. Entry into cooperative arrangements with other organizations is considered a complex process that requires emotional as well as organizational investments. The establishment of cooperation attests to the venture's operative capabilities (Huxham, 1996). Research on business entrepreneurship has emphasized that the ability to create strategic alliances can affect the venture's long-term survival (Wisnieski and Dowling, 2000), although it is unclear what kind of strategic alliances contribute to the survival of social ventures. In addition, little is known about how close relations between social ventures and their clients lead to developing distinctiveness and competitive advantage.

INTERNAL EXPLANATION OF SURVIVAL OF SOCIAL VENTURES

The Resource-Based View

According to the resource-based view of the firm, competitive advantage is created when firms maintain rare resources that enable them to create inimitable strategies and sustainable advantage (Barney, 1991; Dollinger, 1995). Dollinger (1995) argues that the resource-based view is the most appropriate for understanding new venture creation, because it best describes how entrepreneurs themselves build their businesses from the resources they currently possess or can realistically acquire. In addition, the resource-based view also focuses on the managerial role (Colbert, 2004).

Similar to business entrepreneurs, social entrepreneurs need to develop their internal intangible resources. These resources may be based on social entrepreneurs' human capital that is considered unique and idiosyncratic (Alvarez and Busenitz, 2001; Ireland *et al.*, 2003).

The Human Capital Approach

Previous studies of successful business ventures suggested that internal reasons for success have been associated with entrepreneurs' human capital, such as their education and previous experience (Gartner, 1985; Gimeno *et al.*, 1997) and with entrepreneurs' managerial abilities to make strategic decisions (Duchesneau and Gartner, 1990; Shane and Venkataraman, 2000; Aldrich and Martinez, 2001).

Entrepreneurs' human capital is important for the creation of competitive advantage (Ireland *et al.*, 2003). Firms' human capital may also be considered as a scarce resource that contributes to the creation of intellectual capital and differentiated competitive advantage (Porter, 1996; Ulrich, 1998; Wright and Snell, 1998; Bamberger and Meshoulam, 2000; Jackson and Schuler, 2000; Colbert, 2004). An entrepreneur's ability to acquire knowledge and experience is found to be a central aspect in explaining new ventures' business results (Becker *et al.*, 1997; Hitt *et al.*, 2001).

The acquisition and implementation of managerial skills in the initiation, planning and management of entrepreneurial ventures have been shown to be as valuable for the social sector as they are in the business sector (Brinckerhoff, 2000; Emerson and Twersky, 1996; Johnson, 2001; McLeod, 1997; Hisrich *et al.*, 1997; Piltz, 1995; Waddock and Post, 1991). Social entrepreneurs possess various leadership characteristics, significant personal credibility and the ability to generate a committed following for the project by framing it in terms of important social values, rather than in purely economic terms (Sullivan Mort *et al.*, 2003).

The application of business strategies may contribute to the success of nonprofit organizations in the following areas: strengthening the motivation of professional staff; efficient exploitation of volunteers; enhancement of competitive strengths when competing with profit-making organizations and with other non-profit organizations for funding, status, political influence, as well as service provision (Dees, 1998; Drucker, 1985; Eadie, 1997; Light, 1998; Skloot, 1988; Tuckman, 1998).

Figure 12.1 summarizes the conceptual framework we developed in a graphic model. This model relies on the resource dependence, institutional and social capital perspectives, which provide interrelated external explanations for the survivability of social ventures. In addition, this model relies on the resource-based and human capital perspectives that provide the

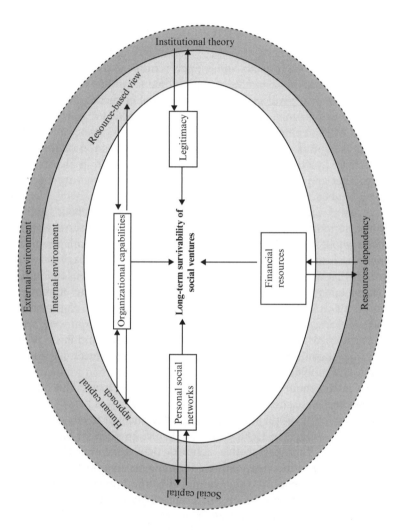

Figure 12.1: The conceptual model of external and internal explanations of social ventures long-term survivability

internal explanation of social ventures' survivability. This model suggests that survivability of social ventures depends on the combination of their abilities to acquire financial resources, gain legitimacy, develop organizational capabilities, and accumulate and use human and social capital.

EVALUATING SOCIAL VENTURE SURVIVABILITY

The challenges involved in establishing a new venture, especially the uncertainty and the lack of resources it must contend with, have led some researchers to view survival as the prime dimension of success (Van de Ven *et al.*, 1984). Furthermore, given the complexity of evaluating firm performance, it is often recommended to use multiple performance measures (Birley and Westhead, 1990; Kalleberg and Leicht, 1991; Westhead *et al.*, 2001), such as growth (for example, in revenues and/or in number of employees) that may indicate business strength, as well as ongoing survival (Merz and Sauber, 1995; McGee *et al.*, 1995).

The success of a new venture is dependent upon the entrepreneur's ability to mobilize support from others and the extent to which he/she is able to get others, whose knowledge, experience and management skills are complementary to his/her, to join him/her (Cooper, 1993). The odds of survival for ventures that were started with less than three employees are lower than the survival odds of ventures that started with five or more employees (Kirchhoff, 1997). Unclarified division of roles and parallel employment functions, which might be advantageous in the early stages of establishment, can endanger the venture's continued survival and the chances of its success in the transition stages from establishment to institutionalization (Chrisman *et al.*, 1998).

Usually, entrepreneurs are expected to plan their activities. This has led some researchers to assume that a new venture's success is heavily dependent on the quality of planning and on adherence to a business plan (Duchesneau and Gartner, 1990; Van De Ven and Joyce, 1981; Van de Ven *et al.*, 1984). Another perspective assumes that entrepreneurs do not operate based on routine. Generating and implementing innovative ideas requires unusual behavior and one cannot rely upon previous experience and routine actions (Baron, 2000). Furthermore, Sarasvathy (2001) maintained that entrepreneurs may operate in an open process in which the necessary resources are not pre-defined. Such a process necessitates the constant examination of attainable goals based on available resources, while analyzing the risks and being willing to bear losses. In the same vein, Bhide (1999) claimed that successful entrepreneurs are those who can recognize opportunities, focus on several important issues without waiting till they have all the answers and combine analysis with action. The main research question of this study is what are the determinants of survivability and success of social ventures.

Based upon the above considerations, the success criteria for social ventures can be defined as follows: (a) the degree to which the social venture achieves its declared goals; (b) the ability of the venture to ensure program/ service continuity and sustainability by acquiring the resources necessary to maintain ongoing operations; (c) the measure of resources available for the venture's growth and development; and (d) long-term survivability (Sharir and Lerner, 2006).

METHODOLOGY

This chapter is based on a large qualitative field study of 33 social ventures that was carried out during the period 1999–2001.[1] The ventures were all non-profit organizations, operating in various social areas in Israel.

The study was exploratory in nature. Case studies were first carried out on five social ventures, applying the method suggested by Eisenhardt (1989). Data were gathered from several sources: 57 interviews with entrepreneurs, team members, board members, clients and competitors, as well as participant observations. A comprehensive questionnaire was constructed on the basis of the pilot study, relating to the processes of initiation, establishment and institutionalization of social ventures. The questionnaire was then filled out by the founders of an additional 28 ventures, after in-depth interviews had been conducted with them.

Content analysis was carried out on publications and other documents of these 33 social ventures. The present study is based on a qualitative analysis of the data. In addition, a follow-up of the 33 ventures was conducted in 2005, five years after completing the processing and analysis of the data, for the purpose of examining the survivability status of all 33 social ventures that had been included in the original research. This follow up revealed that 25 ventures were still surviving.

Variables

Based on the literature review of factors that may explain the success of social ventures, we examined the following categories of variables:

- Resource dependence measures included budgets enabling the performance of ongoing operations, budgets enabling recruitment of salaried staff, and standing the market test (charging fees for the receipt of selected services or obtaining long-term contracts from public agencies).

- Legitimacy referred to gaining legitimacy in the public discourse and the ability to generate followers.
- Social networks included long-range cooperation with organizations in the voluntary or public sector, as well as personal social networks.
- Resource-based view and human capital approach measures included entrepreneurs' total dedication, previous managerial experience, management functioning, and preliminary planning.

Sample Description

The 33 social ventures examined operated in different fields of activity, in various geographic locations in Israel, and targeted a wide range of clients. The social entrepreneurs came from several sectors of Israeli society and included veteran Israelis, new immigrants, ultra-orthodox Jews and Israeli Arabs. Forty-eight percent of the founding entrepreneurs were women, 88 percent were over 40 years old and 51 percent of the ventures did not have substantive starting capital at their disposal at the initiation stage. The team members of the majority of the ventures had to work voluntarily or for below-market wages, even in the establishment stage.

MAIN RESULTS

Table 12.1 compares survivability between three groups of social ventures: those that met three success criteria in 2000 (Group A), those that met two success criteria (Group B) and those that met only one success criteria or none at all (Group C).

Table 12.1 shows that almost all of the social ventures that met three or two success criteria in 2000 had survived through 2005 (20 out of 21 ventures). In contrast, of the 12 social ventures that met only one criteria of success in 2000, only five ventures were still operating in 2005, while the other seven had discontinued their operations.

Table 12.1 also makes a comparison between the three groups in terms of their modes of operation in the national or local arena. This comparison shows that operation in the national arena is not a condition for the survival of a social venture. Thus, nine of the 13 ventures in Group A developed services at the national level (69 percent) while only two operated at the local level. In Group B, most of the ventures operated at the local level and only one of the eight ventures operated at the national level (12.5 percent). In

Table 12.1   Characteristics of the social ventures in 2000 versus 2005

| Social venture | Mode of operation in 2000 | | | Still |
Status in meeting success criteria in 2000	Self-help organization	Providing services at the national level	Providing services at the local level	operating in 2005
A **The 13 social ventures that met three success criteria**	2	9	2	13
B **The 8 social ventures that met two success criteria**	3	1	7	7
C **The 12 social ventures that had not yet succeeded**	5	3	4	5

Note: *Group B:* sub-categories of self-help organizations and organizations providing services at the local level sometimes overlap, and therefore the numbers of ventures sum up to 11 rather than to eight.

Group C, three of the 12 ventures (25 percent) operated at the national level. Interestingly, of the five social ventures in this last group that had survived, three operated in the mode of self-help organizations.

Next, we try to delineate the characteristics of the social ventures that may explain their differential long-term survivability. Table 12.2 presents the distribution of variable frequencies (in percentages) in 2000 among the three groups of social ventures.

Table 12.2 shows some differences between ventures in Groups A and B in terms of the frequencies of occurrence of each variable examined, although their survivability rates are almost the same (see Table 12.1). With regard to most of the variables, the occurrence rate is higher in Group A than in Group B and is higher in Group B than in Group C. The only exceptions pertain to management functioning (75 percent in Group B versus 61.5 percent in Group A) and the ability to generate followers (100 percent in Group B versus 92.3 percent in Group A).

Group C itself was found to be highly heterogeneous in terms of its survivability rates: only five of the 12 social ventures survived to 2005. To gain deeper insight, we looked at those variables that might explain why these five ventures had survived, while the other seven had failed. This further comparison between the two sub-groups (of Group C) indicated that,

Table 12.2 *Distribution of variable frequencies (in percentages) among the three groups of social ventures in 2000*

Theoretical perspectives	The social venture	The 13 social ventures that met the three success criteria (Group A)	The 8 social ventures that met two success criteria (Group B)	The 5 social ventures that survived even though they met only one success criteria (Group C1)	The 7 social ventures that have not survived (Group C2)
External					
Resource dependence	Budget enabling performance of ongoing operations	92.3	87.5	40.0	57.1
	Budget enabling recruitment of salaried staff	92.3	62.5	20.0	57.1
	Standing the market test	53.8	50.0	0.0	28.5
Legitimacy	Gaining legitimacy	76.9	50.0	60.0	0.0
	Ability to generate followers	92.3	100	80.0	28.5
Social networks	Long-range cooperation	53.8	37.5	20.0	42.8
	Personal social network	92.3	62.5	80.0	100.0
Internal					
Resource-based view and human capital approach	Previous managerial experience	53.8	50.0	60.0	28.5
	Management functioning	61.5	75.0	20.0	28.5
	Preliminary planning	69.2	62.5	80.0	85.7
	Total dedication	84.6	62.5	60.0	14.3

among the surviving ventures, the percentage of those ventures that gained legitimacy was higher than among the failing ones. In addition, the percentage of entrepreneurs who had had previous managerial experience was higher among the surviving ventures and they were also more dedicated to their ventures. Furthermore, the percentage of those ventures that exhibited an ability to generate followers was higher among the surviving ventures. Surprisingly, among the failing ventures, the percentage of ventures that had larger budgets for ongoing operations and for salaried staff was higher than among the surviving ones.

The findings pertaining to Group C may suggest that having budgets in the social arena does not guarantee long-term survivability. In addition the findings also suggest that having personal social networks does not necessarily secure long-term survivability.

Further comparison between the three groups revealed that long-term survivability was affected by the social ventures' ability to raise financial resources for ongoing operations, gain legitimacy, generate followers, develop personal social networks and develop internal capabilities. However, our findings show that the social ventures' ability to stand the market test and create long-term cooperation, as well as social entrepreneurs' previous managerial experience, are relatively less associated with the social ventures' survivability. Our findings also indicate that social ventures that operated in the national mode exhibited a higher ability regarding most of the examined variables than those ventures that operated in the local or self-help mode of operation.

Next, we provide various qualitative illustrations from our interviews with the social entrepreneurs to demonstrate the effects of the variables that may provide explanations for the long-term survivability of their social ventures.

EXPLAINING LONG-TERM SURVIVABILITY OF SOCIAL VENTURES – QUALITATIVE ANALYSIS

External Variables

The external aspects of our conceptual framework included gaining financial resources, gaining legitimacy, and creating and developing social networks and long-term cooperation (as shown in Table 12.2).

Obtaining budgets enabling the performance of ongoing operations
The following qualitative analyses provide two different examples that illustrate social ventures' ability – or lack thereof – to obtain financial resources and how this impacts their further operations. The case of the Jewish-Arab

Community Association in Acre (a surviving venture in Group B) serves as an example of the way in which an investment by a major foundation can generate investments by additional foundations. The Association succeeded in raising $350 000–$400 000 annually from ten foundations. The Association developed from a neighborhood committee established to handle water, sanitation and asset protection issues. A visit by a philanthropist to the neighborhood resulted in a $150 000 donation from the Clore Foundation that enabled a community center to be established in the neighborhood. This investment was followed by investments from other foundations.

Nonetheless, the majority of foundations invest in a venture's establishment stage, providing grants of various sizes for periods not exceeding three years. Entrepreneurs also mentioned that completing applications to foundations, writing proposals and submitting periodic progress reports demanded high-level skills and a significant investment of time and effort. This example serves to illustrate the pressures social ventures are likely to face when obtaining financial resources that cover only a limited period of operations, resulting in their need to be continuously mobilizing resources. The significance of the absence of a capital base for the venture was expressed by the couple who founded 'Good Circle' (a venture in Group C1, the sub-group for the surviving ventures from Group C):

> Tami: Menachem doesn't earn a living from *Ma'agal*. His income comes from other sources: he has a PhD in history. I pay myself a salary or don't, depending on circumstances. But, if you are talking only about money, ask my daughter, who is now 14 years old. Seeing how we worried, she once said: 'I feel like bringing someone to blow the place up. Who needs it?' The first computer used to administer Ma'agal was installed only in late December 1999 [note: the organization was founded in 1994]. Until then, we used our own personal computer. Our bedroom is so cramped, with the bed in one corner and the office equipment in the other. The telephone is our home phone. We received this room [the shelter where they hold classes] in September 1999. Everything, like the library, was put here only in January 2000.

Gaining legitimacy in the public discourse

Acquiring legitimacy in the socio-political arena determines the capital at the disposal of the social venture and increases its survivability odds (Aldrich and Fiol, 1994). Acceptance of the venture's vision in the public discourse indicates one of two conditions: the first assumes that public awareness of the issue is a permanent feature of the venture's environment; the second assumes that the issue's more prominent position on the public agenda is a response to the entrepreneur's media and lobbying activities. For example, investment in ventures, especially by foundations, has often been a consequence of the entrepreneurs campaigning to gain public acceptance of their vision and the position assigned to the target population's problem on the public agenda.

During an interview with Atty. Hasen Jabarin, founder and General Director of Adallah – the Legal Center for Arab Minority Rights in Israel (a venture in Group A), he made the following comments concerning the conditions that facilitated establishment of the venture:

> The timing of the venture's establishment, after the signing of the Oslo Agreements was crucial. During that same period, the subject of the Arab minority's civil rights began to be raised more forcibly, including its rights as stipulated in Israeli law. In addition, the opening of several new law schools, as well as passage of Basic Law: Human Dignity and Liberty (1992), prepared the groundwork for this kind of organization.

During Adallah's start-up period, the Ford Foundation had made a US$500 000 grant (covering a three-year period). When asked what would happen after the grant's termination, Jabarin replied: 'The truth is that donors compete among themselves. We're flooded with money, some of which I'd rather refuse.'

Ventures promoting social change are also likely to face opposition from bodies that control existing policy and public resources (Sink, 1996). Thus, the two failed ventures (Group C2), whose target population was youth at risk, were dependent on the National Probation Agency for gaining legitimacy and obtaining budgets for ongoing operations. At the time of the research, neither of these ventures had obtained the necessary budgeting.

Ability to generate followers
In most of the surviving social ventures, the staff received wages lower than they would have received as employees in regular organizations. The inability to pay personnel is manifest in the words of the entrepreneur behind the 'Organization of Lupus Patients in Israel' (Group B):

> I am aware of the great disadvantages stemming from the fact that we cannot pay wages to our employees. The burnout experienced by all activists is very high. Our activities demand continuing efforts – our endeavor differs from issuing stock on the stock exchange. It is difficult to recruit individuals for this type of activity. It is a thankless job. The target audience is very difficult and demanding, particularly when it feels at home. When we explain that our activities are voluntary and are not-for-profit, it does not make a difference to them.

Developing a social network
The process of mobilizing resources and expertise includes getting others to allocate capital, labor and effort to an enterprise with an, as yet, uncertain future. Indeed, the social capital incorporated in the entrepreneur's

social network is in itself one of the venture's most important resources, and serves to supplement the venture's human capital (Johannisson, 1996; Burt, 2000; Baron and Markman, 2000; Davidsson and Honig, 2003). Sometimes the entrepreneur starts out depending on the resources of the network to which he belongs. Consider the statement made by Ayalon Schwartz, founder of the Heschel Center for Environmental Leadership and Education (a venture in group A):

> When I ask myself why we succeeded, I think it was because of our ability to create ties with the 'elite'. In addition, when meeting the founders, we always came prepared with a list of products . . . one of the things I'm very good at is listening and discovering, in the course of a conversation, the point where what really matters to me touches upon what really matters to others.

Other times, the entrepreneur proactively creates the network and has to invest time and effort in its construction (Dubini and Aldrich, 1993; Roure and Keeley, 1990).

One in Nine (a venture in Group A) evolved out of the need of its founder to relieve her own severe distress as a single mother, without regular work and no family or economic support, who had undergone a mastectomy:

> It was terribly important for me to try to get women to do something about this disease . . .When I checked with the women's organizations in Israel on whether any of them were dealing with the issue of breast cancer, I found that none did so, though some focused on women's health. So I approached the editor of a women's magazine. I didn't know her, but she was eager to help . . . I was networking with all sorts of women active in all sorts of areas, on the radio and in the press. There was a time in 1994 that the Knesset (Israel's parliament) started to wake up to the issue of women . . . Then, one Knesset member was very helpful in distributing information and promoting the subject.

Developing long-term cooperation with other organizations

Cooperation is a process in which individuals and organizations exchange information, coordinate and share resources, work, risk, responsibility and rewards in a synergy that strengthens all participants (Himmelman, 1996). The achievement of cooperation is a complex process requiring the investment of emotional, as well as organizational, effort (Huxham, 1996; Wisnieski and Dowling, 2000). Many of the social ventures in Group A achieved long-term cooperation with other organizations. For instance, the success of Ofek Leyaldeinu can be explained by the ability of its founder to create a network of cooperation with other organizations in the public, as well as non-profit, sectors:

We began as partners in the development of community centers and programs for blind children. The A.D. Gordon Elementary School [located in Tel Aviv] is one of the main schools for blind children. During the day, the school operates as a regular school. In addition, it maintains a resource center that conducts afternoon activities, in which children from other areas also participate. Thanks to a contribution that we received from a private donor, we were able to set up a fantastic program. The Tel Aviv Municipality renovated six classrooms that were planned especially for our needs. The National Insurance Institute provided special equipment through the Fund for the Disabled . . . We don't operate the center but we have a say in everything that happens. . . . We also send our children to international summer camps. That's something that the government would never do . . . To acquire help, we affiliated ourselves to the Organization of Blind Students, which has all sorts of funds that distribute scholarships and grants to outstanding university students and recently began giving grants to exceptional high school pupils as well.

Internal Variables

The internal explanations of our conceptual framework (Table 12.2) included previous managerial experience, management functioning, an ability to generate followers, total dedication and standing the market test.

Previous managerial experience

The importance of knowledge and previous managerial experience for venture performance has been emphasized in the literature (see, for example, MacMillan *et al.*, 1987; Cooper *et al.*, 1994 ; Shane, 2003). Of the 13 successful entrepreneurs (Group A), seven had previous managerial experience, the salience of which is patently demonstrated in Etgarim, the Organization of Challenging Outdoor Sports and Active Recreation for the Disabled in Israel, founded by Yoel Sharon:

> I came from the world of film; the Israeli film world is an obstacle course where few survive . . . In Israel, you produce a million-dollar movie for one hundred thousand. I served in a paratroop unit in the Israeli army . . . there they teach you to be a survivor, to do everything necessary to endure. I applied all the techniques and everything else I learned in the industry when I founded Etgarim.

In the case of Natal – the Trauma Center for Victims of Terror and War in Israel, though its founder had no previous managerial experience, she well understood the need to invest in a strategic plan and to create a framework of paid professionals, working alongside volunteers.

Total dedication

Total dedication is one of the variables explaining the difference between successful and non-successful entrepreneurs (Bhide, 1999). It derives from

the resolve, determination and belief of the entrepreneurs in the importance and necessity of the vision they wish to realize.

Comparison between surviving and failing social ventures, in relation to
the entrepreneurs' personal dedication, elicited descriptions by their associates that could be reduced to a number of stock phrases: 'decisive and
resolved', 'willing to work hard', 'the ability to connect and recruit people
to support an idea', 'refusal to ignore difficulties, commitment, even at the
expense of family life, leisure time and other activities'. Entrepreneurs who
founded ventures that eventually failed were described by another set of
phrases: 'fear of taking action', 'fear of the implications of their actions',
'inability to focus'.

Standing the market test

The social entrepreneurship literature emphasizes the importance of
putting the service to the market test in order to reduce the dependency
upon grants and philanthropic contributions (Brinckerhoff, 2000; Emerson
and Twersky, 1996; Skloot, 1988; McLeod, 1997). In the case of Maala –
Business for Social Responsibility in Israel, standing the market test has
been discussed and explained in business terms:

> We are not an organization that brings non-profit organizations and business
> firms together. We help businesses to formulate a strategy in the area of social
> investment . . .We also try to work on the broad overall level, organizing confer-
> ences, seminars and workshops, and developing materials. Right now we are
> running a forum for community relations managers. The main objective is to
> create a market and professional awareness of the entire issue . . . I believe we have
> created a market . . . I want people to make a living from their work in this area.

DISCUSSION AND CONCLUSIONS

This study focuses on identifying factors affecting long-term survivability
of social ventures. Drawing on five theoretical perspectives, our model suggests that long-term survivability of social ventures depends on complex
dynamic variables that do not necessarily evolve linearly, but may interact
and therefore may be contingent on a specific context.

The findings revealed that survivability of social ventures is associated
with their ability to obtain financial resources, gain legitimacy and generate followers, as well as with the social entrepreneurs' personal social networks. Most of the entrepreneurs of the surviving ventures exhibited total
dedication, though only half of them possessed previous managerial experience and engaged in preliminary planning. On the other hand, the
findings indicated that standing the market test, long-term cooperation and

managerial functioning are relatively less crucial criteria for the long-term survivability of social ventures. Our findings also indicated that social ventures that operated in the national mode exhibited higher ability regarding most of the examined variables than those ventures that operated in the local or self-help mode of operation. These findings support our theoretical model, suggesting that survivability of social ventures depends on various internal and external reasons.

From the resource dependence view, it seems that social ventures can increase their survivability odds by lowering their resource dependency. Compared to business ventures, social ventures have fewer sources from which to raise financial capital. Furthermore, they have less option to stand the market test. Therefore, social ventures are highly dependent on governmental authorities, non-profit agencies and on the willingness of the public to provide financial support through donations. In addition, social ventures also depend on having a staff that is prepared to accept below-market wages, as well as on volunteers. Consistently, the findings indicated that long-term survivability was associated with social ventures' ability to raise financial resources for ongoing operations and having resources available for further initiation and development.

When we compared the ventures in Group C that had survived against those within that group that had ceased to operate, it was found that the percentage of ventures that had gained legitimacy was higher among the surviving ventures than among the failing ones. In addition, the percentage of entrepreneurs who had previous managerial experience was higher among the surviving ventures, and they were also more dedicated to their ventures. Furthermore, the percentage of ventures that exhibited an ability to generate followers was higher among the surviving ventures. Surprisingly, among the failing ventures, the percentage of ventures that had larger budgets for ongoing operations and for salaried staff was higher than among the surviving ones. These findings suggest that, while obtaining financial resources is a precondition for social ventures' establishment, it is not necessarily a guarantee ensuring long-term survivability.

From the institutional view, gaining legitimacy was found to be important to the long-term survivability of social ventures. Gaining legitimacy may impact their ability to promote their social values and influence the political discourse and social legislation. Legitimacy is therefore an important criterion, as it enables social ventures to compete over resources, create new connections within the social structure and generate followers, and also to manage committed volunteers, who are willing to activate the services without being paid.

These findings are supported by the fact that the survivability of ventures in Group C (sub-group C1) was found to be strongly associated with these ventures' ability to gain legitimacy and generate followers. One possible explanation for this finding might relate to the fact that all these ventures operated in the self-help mode of operation, which can be considered as a specific market niche requiring fewer financial resources.

From the social capital view, social ventures' survivability depends on social entrepreneurs' ability to accumulate social capital and gain access to knowledge and resources (Nahapiet and Ghoshal, 1998), in order to promote their values and goals. Consistently, the findings show that entrepreneurs' personal social networks are important for social ventures' survivability. The findings also indicated that social ventures tend to create long-range cooperation with other ventures, especially with those operating in the self-help mode. This cooperation enabled them to receive assistance in relation to management and infrastructure from other organizations in the public sector. However, while long-term cooperation was found to be an important criterion, it does not necessarily ensure long-term survivability.

According to the resource-based view, social ventures' survivability may be influenced by internal management's capabilities. Accordingly, our findings suggested that social entrepreneurs' total dedication as well as their previous experience and managerial planning are necessary criteria in ensuring survivability of social ventures. However, it seems that among these criteria, total dedication has relatively higher value as it enables social ventures to achieve their declared goals by providing stable and ongoing services.

This study examined the long-term survivability of social ventures based on data collected in 2000 *with a follow-up conducted in 2005*. It is suggested that further research will focus on more detailed follow-up research in order to provide robust causal explanation for the long-term survivability of social ventures. In addition, further research is recommended in order to understand the contingencies that impact the dynamic evolution and survivability of social ventures. This study also calls for further theoretical development regarding social ventures' strategic adaptation and survivability.

NOTE

1. The field study was carried out within the context of the third author's doctoral thesis at the School of Social Work, Ben-Gurion University of the Negev, Beer-Sheva, under the supervision of Prof. Benjamin Gidron.

REFERENCES

Adler P. and S. Kwon (2002), 'Social capital: Prospects for a new concept', *Academy of Management Review*, **27**(1), 17–40.

Aldrich, H. and C. Zimmer (1986), 'Entrepreneurship through social networks', in D.L. Sexton and R.W. Smilor (eds), *The Art and Science of Entrepreneurship*, Cambridge, MA: Ballinger, pp. 3–23.

Aldrich, H.E., and C.M. Fiol (1994), 'Fools rush in? The institutional context of industry creation', *Academy of Management Review*, **19**(4), 645–70.

Aldrich, H.E. and M.A. Martinez (2001), 'Many are called, but few are chosen: An evolutionary perspective for the study of entrepreneurship', *Entrepreneurship Theory and Practice*, **25**(4), 41–56.

Alvarez, S.A. and L.W. Busenitz (2001), 'The entrepreneurship of resource-based theory', *Journal of Management*, **27**, 755–75.

Astley, W.G., and A.H. Van de Ven (1983), 'Central perspectives and debates in organization theory', *Administrative Science Quarterly*, **28**, 245–73.

Bamberger, P. and I. Meshoulam (2000), *Human Resource Strategy: Formulation, Implementation, and Impact*, Thousand Oaks, CA: Sage.

Barney, J.B. (1991), 'Firm resources and sustained competitive advantage', *Journal of Management*, **17**, 99–120.

Baron, R.A. (2000), 'Psychological perspectives on entrepreneurship: Cognitive and social factors in entrepreneurs success', *Current Directions in Psychological Science*, **9**(1), 15–18.

Baron, R.A., and G.D. Markman (2000), 'Beyond social capital: How social skills can enhance entrepreneurs' success', *Academy of Management Executive*, **14**(1), 106–15.

Becker, B.E., P. Huselid, S. Pickus and M.F. Spratt (1997), 'HR as a source of share-holder value: Research and recommendations', *Human Resource Management*, **36**(1), 39–47.

Bhide, A. (1999), 'How entrepreneurs craft strategies that work', *Harvard Business Review on Entrepreneurship*, Harvard Business School Press.

Birley, S and P. Westhead (1990), 'Growth and performance contrasts between "Types" of small firms', *Strategic Management Journal*, **11**(7), 535–57.

Brinckerhoff, P.C. (2000), *Social Entrepreneurship: The Art of Mission-based Venture Development*. New York: Wiley & Sons.

Bruno, A.V., E.F. Mcquarrie and C.G. Torgrimson (1992), 'The evolution of new technology ventures over 20 years: Patterns of failure, merger, and survival', *Journal of Business Venturing*, **7**, 291–302.

Burt, R.S. (1997), 'The contingent value of social capital', *Administrative Science Quarterly*, **42**, 339–65.

Burt, R.S. (2000), 'The network entrepreneur', in R. Swedberg (ed.), *Entrepreneurship: The Social Science View*. Oxford: Oxford University Press.

Bygrave, D.W., D.D'Heilly, M. McMullen and N. Taylor (1996), 'Not-for-profit entrepreneurship: Towards an analytical framework', paper presented at the Babson College Entrepreneurship Research Conference, Seattle.

Chrisman, J.J., A. Bauerschmidt and C.W. Hofer (1998), 'The determinants of new venture performance: an extended model', *Entrepreneurship Theory and Practice*, **23**(1), 5–30.

Colbert, B.A. (2004), 'The complex resource-based view: implications for theory and practice in strategic human resources management', *Academy of Management Review*, **29**(3), 341–58.

Cooper, A.C. (1993), 'Predicting new firm performance', *Journal of Business Venturing*, **8**, 241–53.

Cooper, A.C., F.J. Gimeno-Gascon and C.Y. Woo (1994), 'Initial human and financial capital as predictors of new venture performance', *Journal of Business Venturing*, **9**, 371–95.

Davidsson, P. and B. Honig (2003), 'The role of human capital among nascent entrepreneurs', *Journal of Business Venturing*, **18**(3), 301–31.

Dees, J.G. (1998), 'The meaning of social entrepreneurship in non-profit and voluntary discussion groups', ARNOUVA-L@WUNUN.WUNET.EDU.

Delmar, F. and S. Shane (2004), 'Legitimating first: organizing activities and the survival of new ventures', *Journal of Business Venturing*, **19**, 385–410.

Dimaggio, W. and W. Powell (1983), 'The iron cage revisited: institutional isomorphism and collective rationality in organizational fields', *American Sociological Review*, **48** (April): 147–60.

Dollinger, M.J. (1995), Entrepreneurship – Strategies and Resources, Homewood, IL: Irwin.

Drucker, F.P. (1985), *Innovation and Entrepreneurship*, New York: Harper & Row.

Dubini, P. and H. Aldrich (1993), 'Personal and extended networks are central to the entrepreneurial process', *Journal of Business Venturing*, **6**: 305–13.

Duchesneau, D.A. and W.B. Gartner (1990), 'A profile of new venture success and failure in an emerging industry', *Journal of Business Venturing*, **5**(5), 297–312.

Eadie, D.C. (1997), *Changing by Design*, San Francisco, CA: Jossey-Bass.

Edward, B.K. (1995), 'Grass roots leadership: A qualitative study of social activism at the very source', unpublished doctoral dissertation, Los Angeles, CA: University of California, School of Education.

Eisenhardt, K.M. (1989), 'Building theories from case study research', *Academy of Management Review*, **14**(4), 532–50.

Emerson, J. (1998), 'The US non-profit capital market: An introductory overview of developmental stages, investors and funding instruments', *American Philanthropy Review*, accessed at www.redf.org.

Emerson, J. and F. Twersky (1996), *New Social Entrepreneurs: The Success Challenge and Lessons of Non-profit Enterprise Creation*, San Francisco, CA: The Roberts Foundation.

Gartner, W. (1985), 'A conceptual framework for describing the phenomenon of new venture creation', *Academy of Management Review*, **10**(4), 696–706.

Gimeno, J., T.B. Folta, A.C. Cooper and C. Woo (1997), 'Survival of the fittest? Entrepreneurial human capital and the persistence of underperforming firms', *Administrative Science Quarterly*, **42** (4), 750 –83.

Himmelman, A.T. (1996), 'On the theory and practice of transformational collaboration: From social service to social justice', in C. Huxham (ed.), *Creating Collaborative Advantage*, London: Sage.

Hisrich, R.D., E. Freeman, A.R. Standly, J.A. Yankey and D.R. Young (1997), 'Entrepreneurship in the not-for-profit sector', in D.L. Sexton and R.W. Smilor (eds), *Entrepreneurship 2000*, Chicago, IL: Upstart Publishing Co.

Hitt, M.A., L. Bierman, K. Shimizu and R. Kochhar (2001), 'Direct and moderating effects of human capital on strategy and performance in professional service firms: A resource-based perspective', *Academy of Management Journal*, **44**(1), 13–28.

Hrebiniak, L.G., and W.F. Joyce (1985), 'Organizational adaptation: Strategic choice and environmental determinism', *Administrative Science Quarterly*, **30**, 336–49.

Huxham, C. (1996), *Creating Collaborative Advantage*, London: Sage.

Ireland, R.D., M.A. Hitt and D.G. Sirmon (2003), 'A model of strategic entrepreneurship: the construct and its dimensions', *Journal of Management*, **29**(6), 963–89.

Jack, S.L. and A.R. Anderson (2002), 'The effects of embeddedness on the entrepreneurial process', *Journal of Business Venturing*, **17**, 467–87.

Jackson, S.E. and R.S. Schuler (2000), 'Understanding human resource management in the context of organizations and their environments', in R.S. Schuler and S.E. Jackson (eds), *Strategic Human Resource Management*, Boston, MA: Blackwell, pp. 4–28.

Johannisson, B. (1996), 'The dynamics of entrepreneurial networks', *Frontiers of Entrepreneurship Research*, Babson Park, MA: Babson College.

Johannisson, B. (1987), 'Beyond process and structure', *International Studies of Management & Organization*, **17**(1), 3–23.

Johnson, S. (2001), 'Social literature review', http//www.bus.ualberta.ca/ccse-whats_new/review.htm.

Kalleberg, A.L. and K.T Leicht (1991), 'Gender and organizational performance: Determinants of small business survival and success', *Academy of Management Journal*, **34** (1), 136–61.

Kirchhoff, B.A. (1997), 'Entrepreneurship economics', in W.D. Bygrave (ed.), *The Portable MBA in Entrepreneurship*, New York: John Wiley & Sons, Inc.

Light, P.C. (1998), *Sustaining Innovation: Creating Non-profit and Government Organizations that Innovate Naturally*, San Francisco, CA: Jossey-Bass.

Maidique, M.A. (1986), 'Key success factors in high-technology ventures', in D.L. Sexton and R.W. Smilor (eds), *The Art and Science of Entrepreneurship*, Cambridge, MA: Ballinger, pp. 169–80.

McGee, J.E., M.J. Dowling and W.L. Megginson (1995), 'Cooperative strategy and new venture performance: the role of business strategy and management experience', *Strategic Management Journal*, **16**: 565–80.

McLeod, H.R. (1997), The social entrepreneur, *INC Magazine*.

MacMillan, I.C., L. Zemann and P.N. Subbanarasimha (1987), 'Criteria distinguishing successful from unsuccessful ventures in the venture screening process', *Journal of Business Venturing*, **2**, 123–7.

Merz, G.R and M.H. Sauber (1995), 'Profiles of managerial activities in small firms', *Strategic Management Journal*, **16**, 551–64.

Nahapiet, J. and S. Ghoshal (1998), 'Social capital, intellectual capital and the organizational advantage', *Academy of Management Review*, **23**(2), 242–66.

Pfeffer, J. (1972), 'Merger as a response to organizational interdependence', *Administrative Science Quarterly*, **17**: 382–94.

Pfeffer, J. (1987), 'Bringing the environment back in: the social context of business strategy', in D.J. Teece (ed.), *The Competitive Challenge: Strategies of Industrial Innovation and Renewal*, Cambridge, MA: Ballinger, pp. 119–35.

Pfeffer, J. and G.R. Salancik (1978), *The External Control of Organizations: A Resource Dependence Perspective*, New York: Harper & Row.

Piltz, D.M. (1995), 'A study of the characteristics and start-up activities of entrepreneurs in non-profit (non-governmental) organizations', unpublished dissertation, Nova Southeastern University, School of Business and Entrepreneurship.

Porter, M.E. (1996), 'What is strategy?', *Harvard Business Review*, **74**(6), 61–78.

Roper, J. and G. Cheney (2005), 'Leadership, learning and human resource management: the meaning of social entrepreneurship today', *Corporate Government*, **5**(3), 95–104.

Roure, B.R. and R.H. Keeley (1990), 'Predictors of success in new technology based ventures', *Journal of Business Venturing*, **5**, 201–20.

Sarasvathy, S.D. (2001), 'Causation and effectuation: toward a theoretical shift from economic inevitability to entrepreneurial contingency', *Academy of Management Review*, **26**(2), 243–6.

Shane, S. (2003), *A General Theory of Entrepreneurship*, Cheltenham, UK and Northampton, MA, US: Edward Elgar.

Shane, S. and S. Venkataraman (2000), 'The promise of entrepreneurship as a field of research', *Academy of Management Review*, **25**, 217–26.

Sharir, M. and M. Lerner (2006), 'Gauging the success of social ventures initiated by individual social entrepreneurs', *Journal of World Business, Special Issue on Social Entrepreneurship*, **41**(1), 6–20.

Sink, D. (1996), 'Five obstacles to community-based collaboration and some thoughts on overcoming them', in C. Huxham (ed.), *Creating Collaborative Advantage*, London: Sage.

Skloot, E. (1988), *The Non-profit Entrepreneur*, New York: Foundation Center Press.

Stevenson, H and J.C. Jarilo (1991), 'A new entrepreneurial paradigm', in A. Etzioni and P.R. Lawrence (eds), *Socio Economics Towards a New Synthesis*, Armonk, NY: M.E. Sharp, Inc, pp. 185–208.

Stinchcombe, A.L. (1965), 'Organizations and social structure', in J.G. March (ed.), *Handbook of Organizations*, Chicago, IL: Rand-McNally, pp. 142–93.

Sullivan Mort G., J. Weerawardena and K. Carnegie (2003), 'Social entrepreneurship: toward conceptualization', *International Journal of Nonprofit and Voluntary Sector Marketing*, **8**(1), 76.

Thompson, J., G. Alvy and A. Lees (2000), 'Social entrepreneurship: a new look at the people and the potential', *Management Decision*, **38**(5), 328–38.

Tropman, J.E. (1989), 'Human service entrepreneurship: The four "c" approach', *Administration in Social Work*, **13**(3/4), 219–42.

Tuckman, H.P. (1998), 'Competition, commercialization, and the evolution of non-profit organizational structures', in B.A. Weisbrod (ed.), *To Profit or not to Profit: The Commercial Transformation of the Non-profit Sector*, Cambridge: Cambridge University Press.

Ulrich, D. (1998), 'A new mandate for human resource', *Harvard Business Review*, **76**(1),124–34.

Van de Ven, A.H. and W. Joyce (1981), *Perspectives on Organization Design and Behavior*, New York: John Wiley and Sons.

Van de Ven, A.H., R. Hudson and D.M. Schroeder (1984), 'Designing new business startups: entrepreneurial, organizational and ecological considerations', *Journal of Management*, **10**(1), 87–107.

Waddock, S.A. and J.M. Post (1991), 'Social entrepreneurship and analytic change', *Public Administration Review*, **51**(5), 393–401.

Westhead, P., M. Wright and D. Ucbasaran, (2001), 'The internationalization of new and small firms: a resource-based view', *Journal of Business Venturing*, **16**(4), 333–58.

Wickham, P.A. (1998), *Strategic Entrepreneurship: A Decision-making Approach to New Venture Creation and Management*, New York: Pitman Publishing.

Wisnieski, J.M. and M. Dowling (2000), 'Does alliance structure follow theory?', www.sbaer.uca.edu/Research/200/USABE-SBIDA/-Winsnieski.

Wright, P.M. and S.A Snell (1998), 'Toward a unifying framework for exploring fit and flexibility in strategic human resource management', *Academy of Management Review*, **23**, 756–72.

Young, D.L. (1986), 'Entrepreneurship and the behavior of non-profit organization: Elements of a theory', in S.R. Acerman (ed.), *The Economics of Nonprofit Institutions: Studies in Structure and Policy*, Oxford: Oxford University Press.

Index